WITHDRAWN

# HOME WORKSHOP
# TECHNIQUES

TIME
**LIFE**
BOOKS ®

*Other Publications:*

AMERICAN COUNTRY

VOYAGE THROUGH THE UNIVERSE

THE THIRD REICH

THE TIME-LIFE GARDENER'S GUIDE

MYSTERIES OF THE UNKNOWN

TIME FRAME

FIX IT YOURSELF

FITNESS, HEALTH & NUTRITION

SUCCESSFUL PARENTING

HEALTHY HOME COOKING

UNDERSTANDING COMPUTERS

LIBRARY OF NATIONS

THE ENCHANTED WORLD

THE KODAK LIBRARY OF CREATIVE PHOTOGRAPHY

GREAT MEALS IN MINUTES

THE CIVIL WAR

PLANET EARTH

COLLECTOR'S LIBRARY OF THE CIVIL WAR

THE EPIC OF FLIGHT

THE GOOD COOK

WORLD WAR II

HOME REPAIR AND IMPROVEMENT

THE OLD WEST

# HOME WORKSHOP TECHNIQUES

TIME-LIFE BOOKS
ALEXANDRIA, VIRGINIA

*Fix It Yourself* was produced by
## ST. REMY PRESS

| | |
|---|---|
| *MANAGING EDITOR* | Kenneth Winchester |
| *MANAGING ART DIRECTOR* | Pierre Léveillé |

**Staff for *Home Workshop Techniques***

| | |
|---|---|
| *Series Editor* | Brian Parsons |
| *Editor* | Kent J. Farrell |
| *Series Art Director* | Diane Denoncourt |
| *Art Director* | Francine Lemieux |
| *Research Editor* | Heather L. Mills |
| *Designer* | Luc Germain |
| *Editorial Assistant* | Bryan Zuraw |
| *Contributing Writers* | Iris Clendenning, Randy Lake, Grant Loewen, Anita Malhotra, Jo Serrentino, Frances Slingerland |
| *Electronic Designers* | Maryse Doray, Nicolas Moumouris, Robert Paquet, Jean-Luc Roy |
| *Contributing Illustrators* | Gérard Mariscalchi, Jacques Proulx |
| *Cover* | Robert Monté |
| *Index* | Christine M. Jacobs |
| *Administrator* | Denise Rainville |
| *Administrative Assistant* | Natalie Watanabe |
| *Coordinator* | Michelle Turbide |
| *Systems Manager* | Shirley Grynspan |
| *Systems Analyst* | Simon Lapierre |
| *Studio Director* | Maryo Proulx |

*Time-Life Books Inc. is a wholly owned subsidiary of*
## TIME INCORPORATED

| | |
|---|---|
| *Editor-in-Chief* | Jason McManus |
| *Chairman and Chief Executive Officer* | J. Richard Munro |
| *President and Chief Operating Officer* | N. J. Nicholas Jr. |
| *Editorial Director* | Richard B. Stolley |

## THE TIME INC. BOOK COMPANY

| | |
|---|---|
| *President and Chief Executive Officer* | Kelso F. Sutton |
| *President, Time Inc. Books Direct* | Christopher T. Linen |

## TIME-LIFE BOOKS INC.

| | |
|---|---|
| *EDITOR* | George Constable |
| *Executive Editor* | Ellen Phillips |
| *Director of Design* | Louis Klein |
| *Director of Editorial Resources* | Phyllis K. Wise |
| *Editorial Board* | Russell B. Adams Jr., Dale M. Brown, Roberta Conlan, Thomas H. Flaherty, Lee Hassig, Jim Hicks, Donia Ann Steele, Rosalind Stubenberg |
| *Director of Photography and Research* | John Conrad Weiser |
| *PRESIDENT* | John M. Fahey Jr. |
| *Senior Vice Presidents* | Robert M. DeSena, James L. Mercer, Paul R. Stewart, Joseph J. Ward |
| *Vice Presidents* | Stephen L. Bair, Stephen L. Goldstein, Juanita T. James, Andrew P. Kaplan, Carol Kaplan, Susan J. Maruyama, Robert H. Smith |
| *Supervisor of Quality Control* | James King |
| *Publisher* | Joseph J. Ward |

**Editorial Operations**

| | |
|---|---|
| *Copy Chief* | Diane Ullius |
| *Production* | Celia Beattie |
| *Library* | Louise D. Forstall |
| *Correspondents* | Elisabeth Kraemer-Singh (Bonn); Christina Lieberman (New York); Maria Vincenza Aloisi (Paris); Ann Natanson (Rome). |

## THE CONSULTANTS

Consulting Editor **David L. Harrison** served as an editor for several Time-Life Books do-it-yourself series, including *Home Repair and Improvement*, *The Encyclopedia of Gardening* and *The Art of Sewing*.

**Richard Day**, a do-it-yourself writer for nearly a quarter of a century, is a founder of the National Association of Home and Workshop Writers and is the author of several home repair books.

**Joseph Truini** is Senior Editor of Home Mechanix Magazine. He specializes in how-to articles for do-it-yourselfers and has worked as a cabinetmaker, home improvement contractor and carpenter.

**Karl Marcuse**, special consultant for Canada, is a self-employed carpenter and contractor. He has worked as a home renovator in many countries and is now completing restoration of his century-old home.

**Charles Self** has written numerous home-repair books in his 15 years as a do-it-yourself writer. He owns a fully-equipped home workshop and is a member of the National Association of Home and Workshop Writers.

**Library of Congress Cataloging-in-Publication Data**
Home workshop techniques.
     p. cm. – (Fix it yourself)
  Includes index.
  ISBN 0-8094-6276-1.
  ISBN 0-8094-6277-X (lib. bdg.)
1. Workshops.
2. Do-it-yourself work.
  I. Time-Life Books.  II. Series.
  TT153.H67   1989
  684—dc20          89-37451
                     CIP

For information about any Time-Life book, please write:
Reader Information
Time-Life Customer Service
P.O. Box C-32068
Richmond, Virginia
23261-2068

# CONTENTS

# HOW TO USE THIS BOOK

*Home Workshop Techniques* is divided into three sections. The Emergency Guide on pages 8 to 13 provides information that can be indispensable, even lifesaving, in the event of a workshop emergency. Take the time to study this section *before* you need the important advice it contains.

The Repair Techniques section—the heart of the book—is a comprehensive approach to choosing the tools and mastering the techniques necessary for measuring, cutting, trimming, smoothing, fastening and finishing your workpieces when you are making a repair. Shown below are four sample pages from

the chapter entitled Trimming And Smoothing, with captions describing the various features of the book and how they work. For example, if your problem is to trim the inaccurately-cut edge of a drywall panel, the Troubleshooting Guide on page 79 will tell you to use a surface-forming tool and refer you to page 87 for detailed instructions on how to get the tool ready for use and how to work with it to trim the edge. Or, if you need to trim a wood edge, you will be referred to procedures on page 86 if it is end grain, and directed to page 80 to prepare the block plane required for trimming it.

---

**Introductory text**
Describes how trimming and smoothing operations are used during repairs, and what basic tools and procedures are involved.

**Setting up to work**
General information on workshop procedures, including the use of benches, vises and clamps, is covered in the Setting Up To Work section *(page 14)*. When a specific set-up tool or method is required for a job, it is described within the step-by-step procedure.

**Troubleshooting Guide**
To use this chart, locate the problem in column 1 that most closely resembles the particular trimming or smoothing task you have to perform, then follow the recommended procedures in column 2. Simple procedures may be explained on the chart; in most cases you will be directed to an illustrated step-by-step procedure.

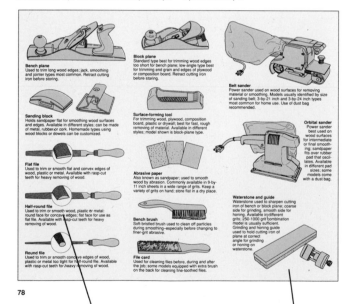

**Variations**
Differences in tools and materials are described throughout the book, particularly if a procedure varies from one type of tool or material to another.

**Tool box diagrams**
Show the basic tools required for trimming and smoothing jobs, and describe the specific uses of each tool.

Before deciding on a particular tool and technique, read all the instructions carefully, including any on inspecting the tool and preparing it for use. Then, consult the Setting Up To Work chapter *(page 14)* for details on choosing your work surface, setting up your workpiece, choosing any safety gear required for the job, and properly lighting and ventilating your work. Be guided by your own confidence and the tools and time available to you. When you use a tool for the first time or in a new way, practice on a scrap of your workpiece material until satisfied with the tool performance and your technique.

Most of the procedures in *Home Workshop Techniques* involve the basic hand and portable power tools for simple carpentry, metal work and masonry work that the average do-it-yourselfer already has on hand around the house. If you are a novice at home repair, consult the tool box diagrams at the beginning of each chapter for information on tools you may need and their uses. The Setting Up To Work chapter can provide you with valuable ideas for organizing a basic workshop, for storing your tools and supplies, and working safely and comfortably.

**Name of repair**
You will be referred by the Troubleshooting Guide to the first page of a specific tool-use procedure.

**Cross-references**
Direct you to important information elsewhere in the book, including alternative techniques and preparation steps.

**Step-by-step procedures**
Follow the numbered sequence of the procedure carefully. Depending on the result of each step, you may be directed to a later step, or to another part of the book, to complete the procedure.

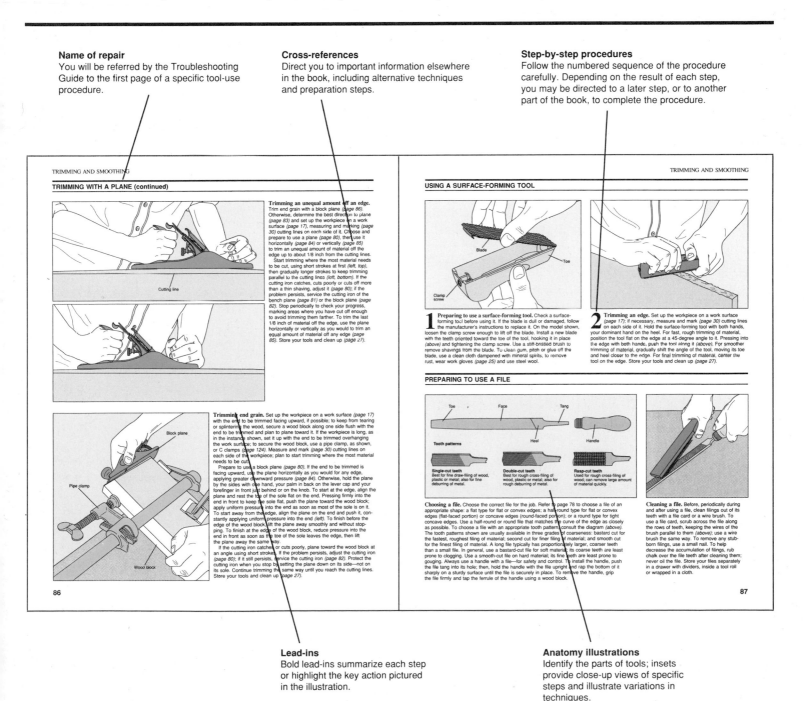

**Lead-ins**
Bold lead-ins summarize each step or highlight the key action pictured in the illustration.

**Anatomy illustrations**
Identify the parts of tools; insets provide close-up views of specific steps and illustrate variations in techniques.

# EMERGENCY GUIDE

**Preventing problems in the home workshop.** Most workshop mishaps can be prevented by exercising the commonsense precautions presented in this chapter; accidents, however, can befall even the most careful worker. Sharp tools can cut. Faulty power tools can shock or throw off particles that may injure an eye. Many solvents, adhesives and finishing products contain chemicals that can burn the skin or emit toxic fumes, causing dizziness, faintness or even loss of consciousness. A chemical spill can occur almost at any time. If you act quickly and properly, you can prevent serious harm or damage in an emergency.

The Troubleshooting Guide on page 9 puts emergency procedures at your fingertips; it lists quick-action steps to take and refers you to pages 10 to 13 for more detailed information. Read the instructions thoroughly in case you ever need to use them. Prevent emergencies by working safely at all times. Always wear the proper personal safety gear for a job *(page 25)*. Only use tools that are in good condition. Work with good lighting and ventilation. After a job, clean up the work area thoroughly. The list of safety tips at right covers basic guidelines for using the tools and performing the techniques described in this book. Refer to each chapter for more specific safety information; carefully review Setting Up To Work *(page 14)* for proper set-up and clean-up procedures.

Be prepared to act quickly in any emergency. Label the main circuit breaker, the main fuse block or the service disconnect breaker for your electrical system; also map the circuits of your home and label them at the service panel. In the event of a workshop electrical emergency, you will want anyone to be able to shut off power quickly *(page 10)*. Always be prepared for fire *(page 11)*. Install a smoke detector in the workshop and test it regularly. Keep a fire extinguisher rated ABC by the workshop exit and check its pressure gauge monthly. Store a well-stocked first-aid kit in a convenient, accessible location; in the event of a workshop medical emergency, you will want anyone to be able to find it and administer minor first aid *(page 12)*. Keep an adequate stock of clean-up supplies on hand—clay-based cat litter and absorbent cloths for mopping up spills of paints, adhesives or other chemicals and cleaning solvents for any product you use or store in the workshop. If you act quickly to clean up spills *(page 13)*, harm and damage can be prevented.

When in doubt about your ability to handle an emergency, call for help. Post numbers for the local fire department, hospital emergency room, poison control center and physician near the telephone. In most areas, dial 911 in the event of any life-threatening emergency. Even in non-emergency situations, qualified professionals can answer questions about the safety of your workshop. When you dispose of chemical containers and refuse, call the local department of environmental protection or public health for information about the proper procedures and any special regulations in effect in your community.

## SAFETY TIPS

**1.** Before using any tool or undertaking any technique described in this book, read through the entire procedure carefully. Familiarize yourself with the specific safety information presented in each chapter.

**2.** Always choose the right tool for the job and inspect it carefully; do not use a broken or worn tool.

**3.** Wear the proper safety gear for the job *(page 25)*: safety goggles with power tools or hammers; work gloves with sharp or rough objects; rubber gloves with chemicals; respiratory protection with tools that create dust or chemicals that emit hazardous vapors; hearing protection with noisy tools. Avoid wearing loose clothing, tie back long hair and remove jewelry.

**4.** Concentrate on the job; do not rush or take short cuts. Never work if you are tired, stressed or have been drinking alcohol or using medication that induces drowsiness.

**5.** Keep children out of the workshop or away from the job site. Store tools and chemicals well out of a child's reach.

**6.** Use power tools and extension cords that bear a recognized seal of approval; look for the UL (Underwriters Laboratories) or CSA (Canadian Standards Association) stamp. Carefully read the manuals for your power tools.

**7.** Never use an extension cord of a rating less than the amperage of a power tool; outdoors, use an extension cord rated for outdoor use *(page 23)*. Use an extension cord to supply electricity only temporarily—not as permanent wiring.

**8.** Never work with electricity in damp conditions. To guard against electrical shock, plug a tool only into a GFCI-protected outlet *(page 24)* and do not touch anything metal while using it.

**9.** Always use a power tool's guards and safety devices. Turn off and unplug the tool and let it cool before changing a part or adjusting it. Make sure the tool is turned off before plugging it in; keep it unplugged when it is not in use.

**10.** Never force a tool to work beyond its capability. Never leave a tool on the ground where it can be tripped over. When working with a cutting tool, stand to one side and never cut directly towards yourself.

**11.** Read and keep the labels of finishes, solvents, adhesives and other chemical products. Follow the manufacturer's instructions for the safe use of a product, paying close attention to information about hazards, antidotes, storage and disposal.

**12.** When working with flammable chemical products, keep away from sources of heat and work only in a well-ventilated area—outdoors, if possible, out of direct sunlight.

**13.** Store flammable chemical products in airtight containers away from sources of heat; never store oil with other flammables. Wash cloths soaked with chemicals for reuse or store them for disposal in airtight metal or glass jars—outdoors preferably, away from sunlight.

**14.** Bag chemical waste, including empty containers, separately from other household refuse and keep it outdoors until it can be disposed of. Ask the local department of environmental protection or public health about proper disposal procedures.

**15.** Post the telephone numbers of your local fire department, hospital emergency room, poison control center and physician near the telephone.

# TROUBLESHOOTING GUIDE

| SYMPTOM | PROCEDURE |
|---|---|
| **Electrical fire: flames or smoke from power tool, extension cord or outlet** | Have someone call fire department immediately |
| | If fire not small and contained or if flames or smoke come from wall or ceiling, evacuate house and call fire department from home of neighbor |
| | Control fire using ABC fire extinguisher (p. 11) |
| | Shut off electricity to circuit or system (p. 10) |
| | Have fire department inspect house—even if fire out |
| | Have electrical fault located and remedied as soon as possible |
| **Chemical fire: flames or smoke from paint, solvent or other chemical product** | Have someone call fire department immediately |
| | If fire not small and contained or if flames or smoke come from wall or ceiling, evacuate house and call fire department from home of neighbor |
| | Control fire using ABC fire extinguisher (p. 11) |
| | Have fire department inspect house—even if fire out |
| **Electrical shock** | If victim immobilized by live current, knock him free using wooden implement (p. 10) |
| | Have someone call for medical help immediately |
| | If victim not breathing, administer artificial respiration; if victim has no pulse, administer cardiopulmonary resuscitation (CPR) only if qualified |
| | If victim breathing and has pulse, and has no back or neck injury, place in recovery position (p. 10) |
| **Sparks, shocks or burning odor from power tool, extension cord or outlet** | Do not touch power tool, extension cord or outlet |
| | Shut off electricity to circuit or system (p. 10) |
| | If electricity cannot be shut off immediately, protect hand with thick, dry towel or heavy work glove and unplug power tool or extension cord from outlet |
| | Have electrical fault located and remedied as soon as possible |
| **Burn** | If burn severe, seek medical help immediately |
| | Treat burn (p. 12) |
| **Wound, cut or scratch** | Stop bleeding (p. 12) |
| | If bleeding persists or wound deep or gaping, seek medical help immediately |
| | If wound, cut or scratch caused by rusty or dirty object, see physician for tetanus treatment |
| **Object embedded in or under skin** | Do not attempt to remove object; seek medical help immediately |
| **Splinter** | Pull out splinter (p. 12) |
| **Particle in eye** | Do not attempt to remove particle if on cornea, embedded or adhered, or cannot be seen; seek medical help immediately |
| | Remove particle from eye (p. 12) |
| **Chemical product splashed in eye** | Flush chemical from eye (p. 12) |
| | Seek medical help immediately |
| **Faintness, dizziness, nausea or blurred vision when working with chemical product** | Move victim immediately to well-ventilated area—outdoors, if possible |
| | Have victim sit with head between knees; loosen clothing at neck, chest and waist |
| | If symptoms persist, seek medical help immediately |
| **Chemical product ingested** | Do not give victim anything to eat or drink or induce vomiting unless advised by professional |
| | Immediately call local poison control center, hospital emergency room or physician for instructions; provide information on victim's age and weight, and type and amount of poison ingested |
| | If professional medical treatment necessary, bring product container with you |
| **Chemical product spilled on skin** | Immediately brush off dry product or wipe off liquid product |
| | Wash thoroughly with soap and water |
| | Seek medical help if skin irritation develops |
| **Chemical product spilled in work area** | Immediately ventilate area, extinguish sources of heat or flame, and turn off electrical units nearby |
| | If spill of more than 1 quart of flammable product or more than 1 gallon of toxic product, evacuate and call fire department |
| | Clean up chemical spill (p. 13) |

## SHUTTING OFF ELECTRICITY

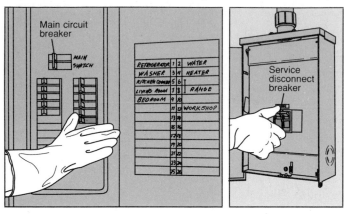

**Shutting off power at a circuit breaker panel.** If the floor is flooded, do not touch the panel; if it is damp, wear rubber boots. Locate the circuit breaker for the circuit to be shut off. Wearing heavy rubber gloves, keep one hand in a pocket or behind your back and use your other hand to flip the circuit breaker to OFF *(above, left)*; do not touch anything metal. If the circuit is not labeled, locate the main circuit breaker, a double breaker usually above the others and labeled MAIN; flip it to OFF the same way. If there is no main circuit breaker, locate the service disconnect breaker in a separate box nearby or outdoors by the electricity meter and flip it to OFF the same way *(above, right)*. To restore power, flip the circuit breaker fully to OFF, then to ON.

**Shutting off power at a fuse box.** If the floor is flooded, do not touch the box; if it is damp, wear rubber boots. Locate the plug fuse or fuse block for the circuit to be shut off. Wearing heavy rubber gloves, keep one hand in a pocket or behind your back and do not touch anything metal. Grasp a plug fuse by its insulated rim and unscrew it *(above)*; grip a fuse block by its handle and pull it straight out. If the circuit is not labeled, locate the main fuse block or blocks, usually at the top of the box; pull each block straight out *(inset)*. If there is no main fuse block, locate the main circuit breaker or service disconnect breaker *(step left)*, or the shutoff lever on the side of the box; pull down the lever. To restore power, screw in the plug fuse, push the fuse block until it snaps into place or push up the shutoff lever.

## RESCUING A VICTIM OF ELECTRICAL SHOCK

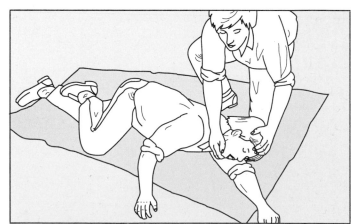

**1** **Freeing a victim of electrical shock.** A person who contacts live electrical current is usually thrown back from the source; sometimes, however, muscles contract involuntarily around the source. Do not touch the victim or the source. Immediately shut off power at the main circuit breaker, the service disconnect breaker or the main fuse block *(steps above)*. If power cannot be shut off immediately, unplug the source, if possible, or use a wooden broom handle or other implement to knock the victim free *(above)*.

**2** **Handling a victim of electrical shock.** Call for medical help immediately. Check the victim's breathing and pulse; if you are qualified, administer artificial respiration if there is no breathing and cardiopulmonary resuscitation (CPR) if there is no pulse. If the victim is breathing and has no back or neck injury, place him in the recovery position *(above)*, tilting the head back with the face to one side and the tongue forward to maintain an open airway. Keep the victim calm until medical help arrives.

## CONTROLLING A FIRE

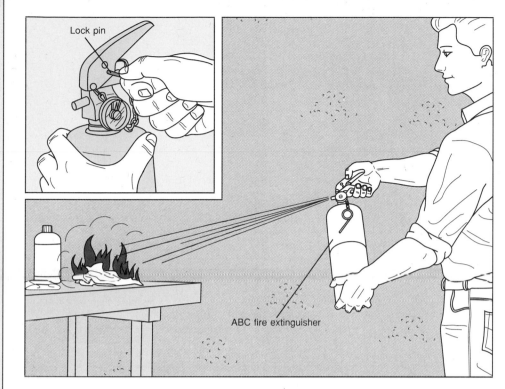

Lock pin

ABC fire extinguisher

**Extinguishing a fire.** Have someone call the fire department immediately; if the fire is not small and contained or flames or smoke come from the walls or ceilings, evacuate and call the fire department from a neighbor's home. To control a small, contained fire, use a fire extinguisher rated ABC. **Caution:** Never use water on an electrical or a chemical fire. Lift the extinguisher from its bracket, set it upright on the floor and pull the lock pin out of its handle *(inset)*. Keeping the extinguisher upright, lift it and aim its nozzle or hose at the base of the fire, positioning yourself 6 to 10 feet away with your back to an accessible exit. Squeeze the handle levers together *(left)* and spray in a quick side-to-side motion. Keep spraying until the fire is out. Watch for flashback—rekindling of the fire—and be ready to spray again. If the fire spreads or the extinguisher empties before the fire is out, evacuate. After an electrical fire, shut off power *(page 10)*. Have the fire department inspect the site of any fire—even if it is out. Replace the extinguisher or have it professionally recharged.

## INSTALLING FIRE EXTINGUISHERS AND SMOKE DETECTORS

CLASS ABC FIRE EXTINGUISHER

**Class ABC fire extingisher.** Install a multipurpose, dry-chemical fire extinguisher in the workshop; an ABC type *(left)* is effective against any small, contained fire involving an electrical unit, flammable liquid or ordinary combustible. Only buy an extinguisher that bears a recognized seal of approval; look for the UL (Underwriters Laboratories) or CSA (Canadian Standards Association) stamp. A typical household extinguisher holds a pressurized cargo of 2 1/2 to 7 pounds and lasts 8 to 20 seconds; in the workshop, install one of at least 5 pounds. Mount the extinguisher on the wall near an exit, away from potential fire hazards and no more than 5 feet above the floor. Check the pressure gauge of the extinguisher monthly; if the arrow points to RECHARGE or any time you discharge the extinguisher, have it professionally recharged or buy a new one.

IONIZATION SMOKE DETECTOR

Test button

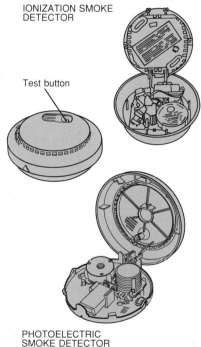

PHOTOELECTRIC SMOKE DETECTOR

**Smoke detectors.** Install at least one smoke detector on the workshop ceiling above potential fire hazards. An ionization smoke detector *(left, top)* senses atomic particles and responds quickly to hot fires with little smoke; however, it may set off annoying false alarms. The photoelectric cell of a photoelectric smoke detector *(left, bottom)* "sees" molecules; it responds well to a smoldering fire and is not prone to false alarms. Some smoke detectors have a built-in light to illuminate an escape route when the detector sounds. Test a smoke detector battery once a week by pressing its test button *(left, center)* and holding it for several seconds. Replace the battery if the smoke detector does not sound when it is tested or it emits a chirping sound, indicating a worn battery. Vacuum or wipe dust off the smoke detector vents regularly.

## PROVIDING MINOR FIRST AID

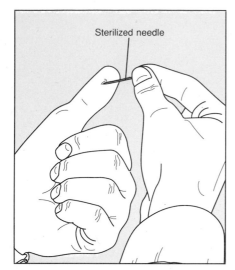

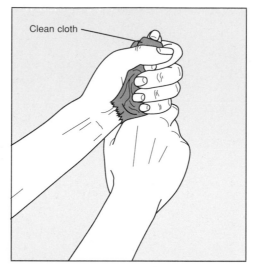

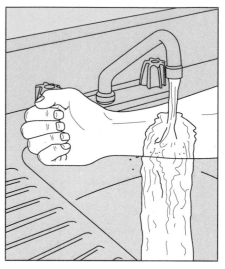

**Pulling out a splinter.** Wash the skin around the splinter with soap and water. A metal splinter may require treatment for tetanus; seek medical help. Otherwise, sterilize a needle and tweezers with rubbing alcohol or over a flame. Ease out the splinter from under the skin using the needle *(above)*, then pull it out with the tweezers. Wash the wound again with soap and water. If the splinter cannot be removed or the wound becomes infected, seek medical help.

**Treating a cut.** To stop a wound from bleeding, apply direct pressure with a clean cloth or gauze dressing and elevate the injury *(above)*. If the cloth or dressing becomes blood-soaked, add another one over the first; avoid lifting the cloth or dressing to inspect the wound. Contine applying direct pressure and elevating the injury until the bleeding stops. If the wound is minor, wash it with soap and water, then bandage it. If the bleeding persists or the wound is deep or gaping, seek medical help.

**Treating a burn.** Gently remove any clothing from the burn; do not remove any clothing adhered to it. If the burn is severe, gently cover it with a gauze dressing and seek medical help immediately. Otherwise, flush the burn in a gentle flow of cool water from a faucet *(above)* or cover it lightly with a clean cloth soaked in water. Flush or soak the burn for at least 5 minutes, then bandage it. Do not apply antiseptic spray or ointment, butter or oil, or baking soda or alcohol.

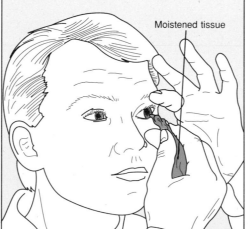

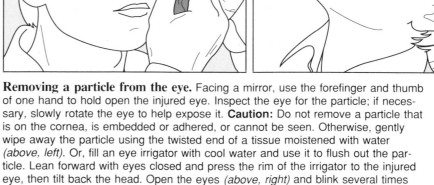

**Flushing a chemical from the eye.** Holding the eyelids of the injured eye apart with your fingers, position the injured eye under a gentle flow of cool water from a faucet *(above)* or pitcher; tilt the head to one side to prevent the chemical from washing into the uninjured eye. Flush the eye for 15 to 30 minutes, then, moving the eye as little as possible, seek medical help immediately.

**Removing a particle from the eye.** Facing a mirror, use the forefinger and thumb of one hand to hold open the injured eye. Inspect the eye for the particle; if necessary, slowly rotate the eye to help expose it. **Caution:** Do not remove a particle that is on the cornea, is embedded or adhered, or cannot be seen. Otherwise, gently wipe away the particle using the twisted end of a tissue moistened with water *(above, left)*. Or, fill an eye irrigator with cool water and use it to flush out the particle. Lean forward with eyes closed and press the rim of the irrigator to the injured eye, then tilt back the head. Open the eyes *(above, right)* and blink several times to flush out the particle. Lean forward again to remove the irrigator. If the particle cannot be removed, seek medical help immediately.

## CLEANING UP A CHEMICAL SPILL

**Cleaning up and disposing of spilled chemicals.** Immediately open nearby doors and windows, extinguish all sources of heat and turn off electrical units operating nearby. Keep people and pets away from the spill site. **Caution:** Check the label of the spilled product; if it is marked EXTREMELY FLAMMABLE and you have spilled more than 1 quart, or if it is marked with POISON vapor or ventilation warnings and you have spilled more than 1 gallon, leave the spill site and call the fire department.

Otherwise, clean up the spill quickly wearing rubber boots, heavy rubber gloves and safety goggles *(page 25)*; if the label of the spilled product is marked with POISON vapor or ventilation warnings, also wear a respirator *(page 26)*. If the spill is small, soak it up with cloths or paper towels; dispose of them in a metal container double-lined with heavy-duty plastic garbage bags. If the spill is large, spread an absorbent material such as clay-based cat litter on it; when the spill is soaked up, sweep up the absorbent material with a whisk broom and dustpan *(right)*, then dispose of it the same way.

To clean up any remaining residue, choose an appropriate solvent *(step below)*. Check the label of the solvent; if it is marked with POISON vapor or ventilation warnings, be sure to wear a respirator. Apply the solvent following its directions, using a scrub brush on a masonry surface *(inset)* or a soft, clean cloth on another surface. Clean up the solvent as you did the original spill. Close any reusable container and store it safely *(page 28)*. Seal the waste material, broken or empty containers, and any whisk broom or dustpan in the metal container and store them outdoors, away from heat and light. Call your local department of environmental protection or public health for recommended disposal procedures.

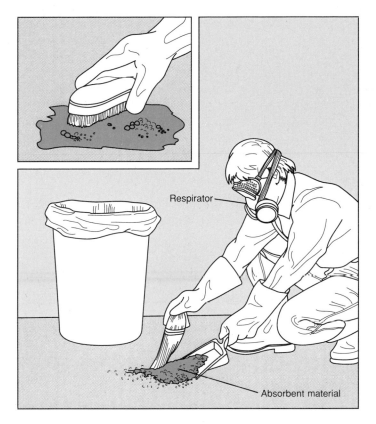

Respirator

Absorbent material

| PRODUCT SPILLED | SOLVENT REQUIRED |
|---|---|
| Mineral spirits | Household detergent and water |
| Paint thinner | Household detergent and water |
| Turpentine | Household detergent and water; or, mineral spirits or paint thinner, then household detergent and water |
| Paint remover | Mineral spirits or paint thinner, then household detergent and water |
| Muriatic acid | Water |
| Denatured alcohol | None |
| Methyl hydrate | None |
| 1,1,1 trichloroethane | None |
| Acetone | None |
| Lacquer thinner | None |
| Latex paint, water-based stain or preservative | Household detergent and water |
| Alkyd paint, oil-based paint, stain or preservative | Mineral spirits or paint thinner, then household detergent and water |
| Urethane or polyurethane | Mineral spirits or paint thinner, then household detergent and water |

| PRODUCT SPILLED | SOLVENT REQUIRED |
|---|---|
| Varnish | Mineral spirits or paint thinner, then household detergent and water |
| Lacquer | Lacquer thinner |
| Shellac | Denatured alcohol (ethyl alcohol) or methyl hydrate (alcohol stove fuel) |
| White glue | Water |
| Yellow glue | Water |
| Epoxy glue | Acetone |
| Contact cement (water-based) | Household detergent and water; or, contact cement cleaner or thinner |
| Contact cement (solvent-based, flammable) | Contact cement cleaner or thinner; or, acetone |
| Contact cement (solvent-based, non-flammable) | Contact cement cleaner or thinner; or, 1,1,1 trichloroethane |
| Linseed oil | Mineral spirits or paint thinner, then household detergent and water |
| Machine or motor oil | Household detergent and water; or, TSP (trisodium phosphate) and water; or, mineral spirits or paint thinner, then household detergent and water |

**Choosing a solvent.** Use the chart above to identify the solvent you need to clean up residue from a spilled product. **Caution:** Check the label of the spilled product for any special solvent required. Buy only as much solvent as you need for a job. Never mix solvents unless you are specifically instructed by the manufacturer; combinations of solvents can be lethal. Carefully read the safety instructions on the label of a solvent before opening and using it; note whether the solvent may damage the surface you are cleaning.

# SETTING UP TO WORK

The professional-caliber workshop, filled with stationary power tools and fine woodworking benches, is a dream for many do-it-yourselfers. However, most home repair tasks can be undertaken safely and effectively with a selection of good hand and portable power tools in a modest basement or garage workshop. The basic workshop at right illustrates the main features of any good shop: adequate lighting and ventilation, a safe, dependable supply of electrical power, sturdy and versatile work surfaces, well-organized storage units and essential safety devices; the inventory on page 16 shows some of the accessory tools and supplies needed. More important than the size or layout of your workshop is your ability to marshall its many resources when you set up for a repair project; you will need to choose not only the best tools, but the best work surface, lighting and ventilation. A safe, well-organized job setup is the key to good work; it ensures that you can handle your tools and materials comfortably and properly, and work with care and precision.

The first requirement for any job is to choose a work surface *(page 17)*. A stationary worktable, a utility vise, a portable workbench, a pair of sawhorses and an assortment of C clamps provide a good range of options for holding most workpieces. Choose the surface or combination of surfaces large and sturdy enough to hold your workpiece securely—that also permits you to work comfortably and safely. Ensure that the work area is well-lit. There should be bright overhead light; for precision tasks, also use direct, focused light on your workpiece and tools. To use a power tool far from an outlet, choose an extension cord that is properly rated for the job *(page 23)*. Before plugging in a power tool or extension cord, check that the outlet can provide sufficient power and has ground-fault protection *(page 24)*. Ensure that the workshop is adequately ventilated—for both your comfort and safety. If you are using a material or substance that is flammable or emits hazardous vapors, work outdoors, if possible. If you must work indoors, ensure a supply of fresh air by opening windows and doors to the outdoors and setting up a sturdy fan to direct vapors out of the workshop.

Always wear the appropriate safety gear for the job *(page 25)*. To handle sharp, rough, dirty or hazardous materials, wear gloves. For work that creates dust or flying debris or when there is a risk of a chemical splash, wear safety goggles; if necessary, also a face shield. For work with noisy power tools, use hearing protection. With dust-creating cutting, grinding, drilling or sanding tools or chemicals that emit hazardous vapors, use respiratory protection.

After completing a job, take the time to store all your tools and supplies properly, accessible and in good condition for the next job. Storage options are practically limitless; cabinets, shelves, boxes, bins and containers of every size, shape and description are sold at most hardware stores and building supply centers, and can be used in imaginative combinations to organize your materials *(page 27)*. Clean the workshop thoroughly, properly disposing of hazardous refuse *(page 29)*. Keep the workshop locked when it is not in use.

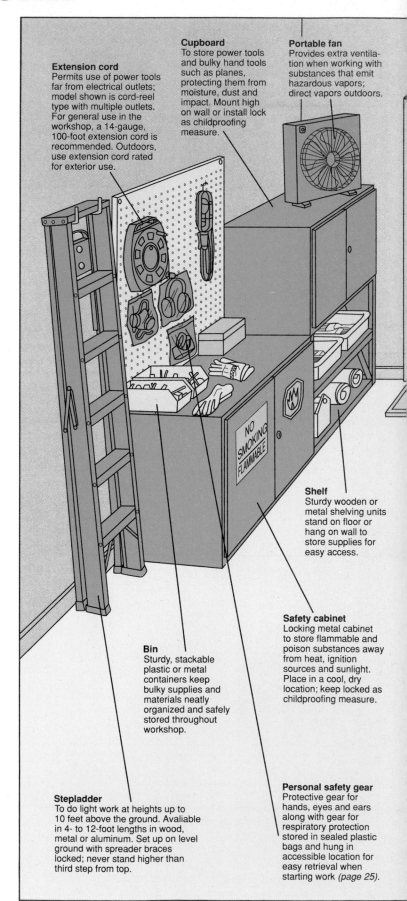

**Extension cord**
Permits use of power tools far from electrical outlets; model shown is cord-reel type with multiple outlets. For general use in the workshop, a 14-gauge, 100-foot extension cord is recommended. Outdoors, use extension cord rated for exterior use.

**Cupboard**
To store power tools and bulky hand tools such as planes, protecting them from moisture, dust and impact. Mount high on wall or install lock as childproofing measure.

**Portable fan**
Provides extra ventilation when working with substances that emit hazardous vapors; direct vapors outdoors.

**Shelf**
Sturdy wooden or metal shelving units stand on floor or hang on wall to store supplies for easy access.

**Safety cabinet**
Locking metal cabinet to store flammable and poison substances away from heat, ignition sources and sunlight. Place in a cool, dry location; keep locked as childproofing measure.

**Bin**
Sturdy, stackable plastic or metal containers keep bulky supplies and materials neatly organized and safely stored throughout workshop.

**Stepladder**
To do light work at heights up to 10 feet above the ground. Avaliable in 4- to 12-foot lengths in wood, metal or aluminum. Set up on level ground with spreader braces locked; never stand higher than third step from top.

**Personal safety gear**
Protective gear for hands, eyes and ears along with gear for respiratory protection stored in sealed plastic bags and hung in accessible location for easy retrieval when starting work *(page 25)*.

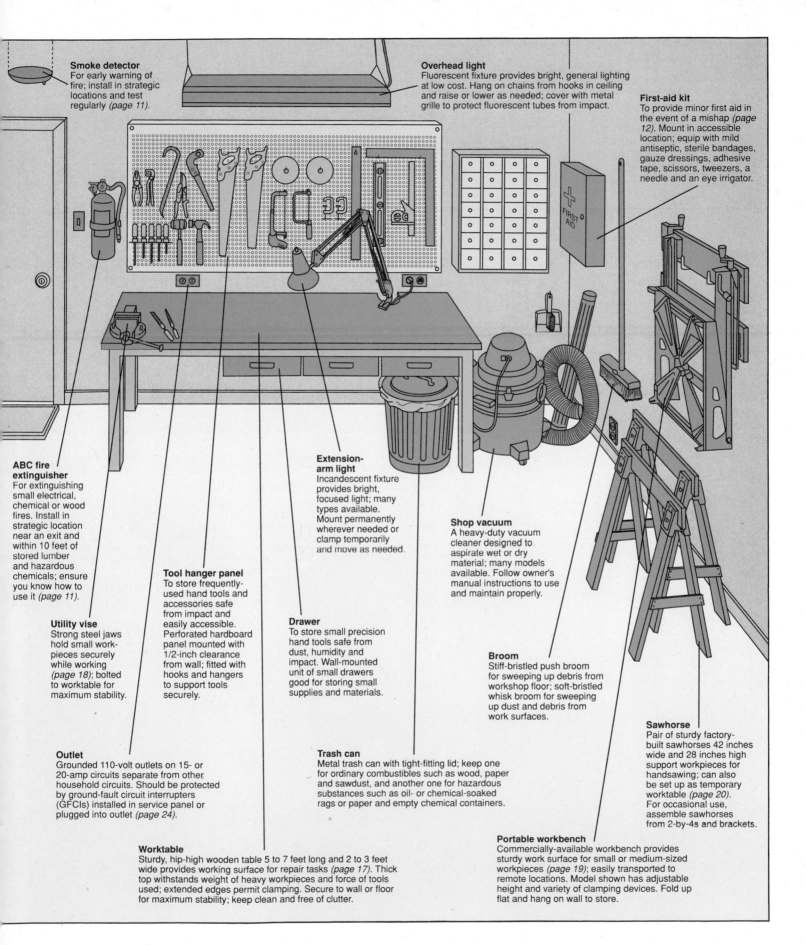

**Smoke detector**
For early warning of fire; install in strategic locations and test regularly *(page 11)*.

**Overhead light**
Fluorescent fixture provides bright, general lighting at low cost. Hang on chains from hooks in ceiling and raise or lower as needed; cover with metal grille to protect fluorescent tubes from impact.

**First-aid kit**
To provide minor first aid in the event of a mishap *(page 12)*. Mount in accessible location; equip with mild antiseptic, sterile bandages, gauze dressings, adhesive tape, scissors, tweezers, a needle and an eye irrigator.

**ABC fire extinguisher**
For extinguishing small electrical, chemical or wood fires. Install in strategic location near an exit and within 10 feet of stored lumber and hazardous chemicals; ensure you know how to use it *(page 11)*.

**Utility vise**
Strong steel jaws hold small workpieces securely while working *(page 18)*; bolted to worktable for maximum stability.

**Tool hanger panel**
To store frequently-used hand tools and accessories safe from impact and easily accessible. Perforated hardboard panel mounted with 1/2-inch clearance from wall; fitted with hooks and hangers to support tools securely.

**Extension-arm light**
Incandescent fixture provides bright, focused light; many types available. Mount permanently wherever needed or clamp temporarily and move as needed.

**Shop vacuum**
A heavy-duty vacuum cleaner designed to aspirate wet or dry material; many models available. Follow owner's manual instructions to use and maintain properly.

**Drawer**
To store small precision hand tools safe from dust, humidity and impact. Wall-mounted unit of small drawers good for storing small supplies and materials.

**Broom**
Stiff-bristled push broom for sweeping up debris from workshop floor; soft-bristled whisk broom for sweeping up dust and debris from work surfaces.

**Outlet**
Grounded 110-volt outlets on 15- or 20-amp circuits separate from other household circuits. Should be protected by ground-fault circuit interrupters (GFCIs) installed in service panel or plugged into outlet *(page 24)*.

**Trash can**
Metal trash can with tight-fitting lid; keep one for ordinary combustibles such as wood, paper and sawdust, and another one for hazardous substances such as oil- or chemical-soaked rags or paper and empty chemical containers.

**Sawhorse**
Pair of sturdy factory-built sawhorses 42 inches wide and 28 inches high support workpieces for handsawing; can also be set up as temporary worktable *(page 20)*. For occasional use, assemble sawhorses from 2-by-4s and brackets.

**Worktable**
Sturdy, hip-high wooden table 5 to 7 feet long and 2 to 3 feet wide provides working surface for repair tasks *(page 17)*. Thick top withstands weight of heavy workpieces and force of tools used; extended edges permit clamping. Secure to wall or floor for maximum stability; keep clean and free of clutter.

**Portable workbench**
Commercially-available workbench provides sturdy work surface for small or medium-sized workpieces *(page 19)*; easily transported to remote locations. Model shown has adjustable height and variety of clamping devices. Fold up flat and hang on wall to store.

# INVENTORY OF TOOLS AND SUPPLIES

**C clamp**
To temporarily hold wood or metal workpieces to work surfaces for cutting, trimming or smoothing, or to each other for fastening. Available with 1- to 12-inch openings and regular or deep throats. Stock a variety of sizes.

**Spring clamp**
To temporarily hold light workpieces to work surfaces while working, or to each other for fastening. Available with 1- to 3-inch jaw openings. Keep a few pairs in different sizes on hand.

**Scissors**
For cutting paper, cloth, string or cord.

**Lubricant**
Keep several types on hand: light machine oil for moving tool parts; penetrating oil for stuck or rusted metal pieces and fasteners; graphite for frozen locks; silicone for moving parts, especially wood.

**Compressed air**
Canned air used to blow dust and debris out of tool parts not accessible with brush or cloth; extension tube directs air stream where needed.

**Funnel**
To pour and transfer cleaners, solvents or finishing products.

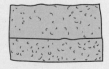

**Sponge**
For applying cleaners or solvents. Stock a variety of sizes.

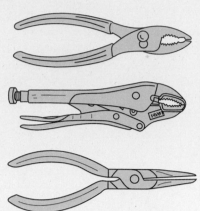

**Work knife**
All-purpose cutting and scraping tool for rough work.

**Pencil**
To mark workpieces for drilling, fastening, cutting or trimming. Keep several sharpened soft HB lead types on hand.

**Pail**
For mixing cleaning and finishing products as well as for hauling tools, supplies and materials. Keep several on hand.

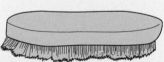

**Brush**
All-purpose cleaning tool for wet scrubbing or dry brushing. Keep both stiff- and soft-bristled types on hand.

**Steel wool**
For applying cleaners or solvents, especially to metal objects and tool parts. Keep a variety of grades on hand.

**Pliers**
All-purpose tool for gripping, bending and pulling. Slip-joint (utility) pliers *(top)* with two opening widths used for most purposes—except for gripping or turning fasteners; locking pliers *(center)* with strong snap-lock jaws used to grip and pull or turn objects such as rusted or stuck fasteners; long-nose pliers *(bottom)* with serrated, tapered jaws used to grip small objects in tight spaces. Store in accessible location.

**Masking tape**
Handy for temporary fastening, bunching and storing small objects, and labeling containers. Use duct tape similarly and for sealing joints.

**Tweezers**
For holding small delicate objects.

**Cord**
Stock a supply of rope, cord and string in different sizes to tie up and store, or hoist or haul supplies and materials.

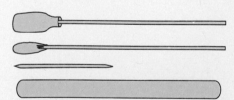

**Utility knife**
For scoring and cutting thin sheet materials such as cardboard, plastic or veneer. Keep a stock of replaceable blades on hand.

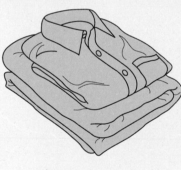

**Clothing and protective coverings**
Stock a supply of old clothes for messy work. Stock old sheets, newspapers, rolls of plastic sheeting and drop cloths to protect surfaces when applying finishing products or cutting, sanding, grinding or drilling.

**Swabs and sticks**
For applying cleaners, solvents and adhesives. Many sizes, shapes and types, including foam swabs, cotton swabs, toothpicks and wooden sticks.

**Cloths**
Keep a large stock on hand for applying cleaners, solvents, lubricants and finishing products, and for cleaning up.

## CHOOSING A WORK SURFACE

**Preparing to set up.** The typical home repairs workshop *(page 14)* contains a number of work surfaces on which basic measuring, cutting, trimming, fastening and finishing tasks can be performed. One of the first requirements when setting up for any job in the workshop is to choose the best work surface: the one that ensures a safe, quality job with a minimum of frustration.

• **The worktable.** For precision work on small or medium-sized workpieces, the worktable is the best general choice *(step below)*. A good, sturdy worktable is the right height for most chiseling, filing, routing, sanding, drilling or fastening, and making fine cuts with backsaws or coping saws. The worktable offers the possibility of setting up workpieces on it, above it, or overhanging the edge of it.

• **The utility vise.** For work on small workpieces, especially when filing, drilling, sanding or using small handsaws, a utility vise is ideal *(page 18)*. The utility vise can hold a workpiece at a height suitable for doing precise work and is strong enough to withstand considerable force on the workpiece from any tool used.

• **The portable workbench.** For forceful work on small or medium-sized workpieces, such as when planing or cutting with large handsaws or power saws, a portable workbench is a good

A good work surface is one large and strong enough to support the workpiece or pieces you are handling. The right surface should also enable you to hold the workpiece in a position and at a height suitable for properly operating the tools for the job. When a task requires the application of strong pressure or force, a work surface must be sturdy and stable enough to withstand it.

choice *(page 19)*. The portable workbench is also the surface of choice when doing work outside the workshop. The bench on some models can be adjusted in height and a workpiece of any shape can be clamped to it securely using its vise jaws or swivel pegs.

• **The sawhorse.** For work on long workpieces, especially when sawing, sanding or finishing, a pair of sawhorses provides the best surface *(page 20)*. Sawhorses can be assembled quickly and easily. When set up as a temporary worktable, a pair of sawhorses can also be used for many other jobs on large workpieces.

• **The floor.** For work on very large workpieces such as panels, especially when doing forceful jobs such as routing, power sanding or cutting with power saws, the floor is a viable work surface option *(page 22)*. A workpiece can be securely set up on spacers to work on the floor.

## SETTING UP ON A WORKTABLE

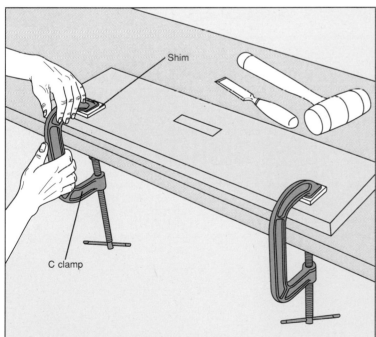

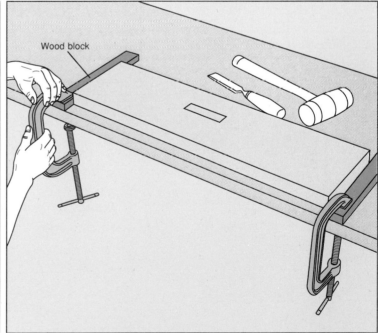

**Securing a workpiece on the worktable surface.** For access to opposite surfaces of the workpiece, secure it above the worktable surface; for access to an entire edge of it, secure it overhanging the worktable edge *(page 18)*. For access to one surface of the workpiece, secure it completely supported on the worktable. Position the workpiece flat on the worktable, as close to an edge as possible.

To secure the workpiece on the worktable, use as many C clamps as necessary *(page 22)*. To install a C clamp, fit it over the edge of the workpiece and under the edge of the worktable; positioning any shim to protect the workpiece surface or wood block to distribute pressure along

it, ensure the C clamp is straight and tighten the screw by turning the T handle. Install as many C clamps as necessary the same way *(above, left)*.

For unobstructed access to the entire surface of the workpiece, secure it between wood blocks clamped to the worktable. Position wood blocks slightly less thick than the workpiece along opposite edges of it. Butting each wood block in turn against the edge of the workpiece, use the same procedure to install as many C clamps as necessary to secure it in place *(above, right)*. Or, if C clamps obstruct access to the entire surface of the workpiece, secure each wood block by driving a nail through it and partway into the worktable.

## SETTING UP ON A WORKTABLE (continued)

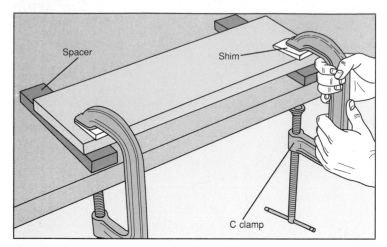

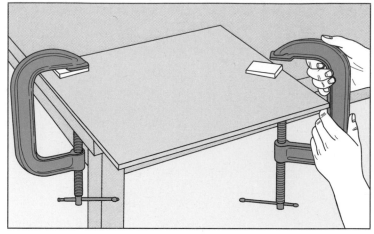

**Securing a workpiece above the worktable surface.** For access to one surface of the workpiece, secure it on the worktable surface *(page 17)*; for access to an entire edge of it, secure it overhanging the worktable edge *(step right)*. For access to opposite surfaces of the workpiece, secure it on spacers above the worktable surface. For spacers, use as many wood blocks as necessary of dimensions appropriate for the workpiece; ensure each spacer is the same thickness to keep the workpiece flat. Position the spacers flat on the worktable, then position the workpiece flat on them; if you are cutting the workpiece, position a spacer under it on each side of the cutting line. To secure the workpiece on the spacers, use as many C clamps as necessary *(page 22)*; fit each C clamp over the edge of the workpiece at a spacer and under the edge of the worktable *(above)*, then tighten the screw.

**Securing a workpiece overhanging the worktable edge.** For access to one surface of the workpiece, secure it on the worktable surface *(page 17)*; for access to opposite surfaces of it, secure it above the workpiece surface *(step left)*. For access to an entire edge of the workpiece, secure it overhanging the worktable edge. Position the workpiece flat on the worktable, overhanging it only as much as necessary; if you are cutting the workpiece, position the cutting line parallel to the edge of the worktable, overhanging it enough to keep from cutting it. To secure the workpiece on the worktable, use as many C clamps as necessary *(page 22)*; fit each C clamp over an edge of the workpiece adjacent to the edge you are working on and under the edge of the worktable *(above)*, then tighten the screw.

## SETTING UP IN A UTILITY VISE

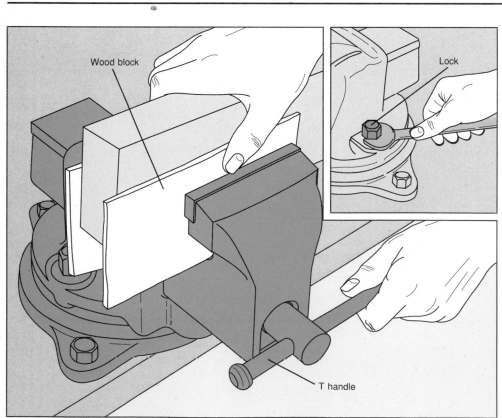

**Securing a workpiece in a utility vise.** Inspect a utility vise before using it, ensuring it is bolted securely to the worktable. Tighten any loose bolts. To check the jaws of the utility vise, open them by turning the T handle. If the jaw inserts are chipped, worn or otherwise damaged, do not use the utility vise; buy replacement jaw inserts and install them following the manufacturer's instructions. If the utility vise is in good condition, set up the workpiece.

To set up the workpiece in the utility vise, turn the T handle to open the jaws enough to position it between them; position a wood block on each surface of the workpiece to protect it, if necessary. Holding the workpiece and any wood blocks in the utility vise and butted against the stationary jaw, turn the T handle to close the movable jaw *(left)*, stopping when the workpiece is held securely in place; avoid overtightening the jaws against it. If necessary, swivel the utility vise to position the workpiece at the best angle for the task; on the model shown, loosen each lock on the base using a wrench *(inset)*, then swivel the utility vise and tighten each lock. Provide support under each end of a long workpiece to avoid straining the jaws of the utility vise.

## SETTING UP ON A PORTABLE WORKBENCH

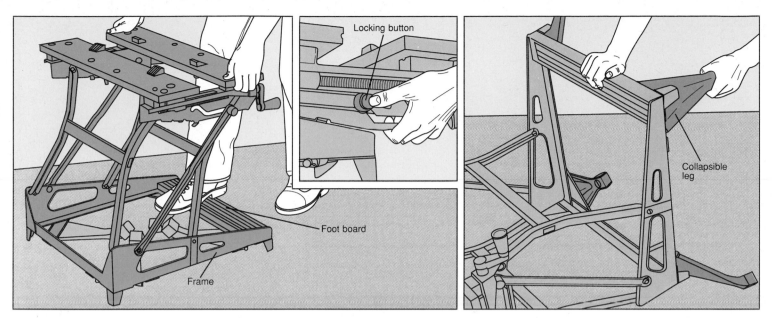

Locking button

Collapsible leg

Foot board

Frame

**Unfolding a portable workbench.** To set up a portable workbench, follow the owner's manual instructions. With the model shown, place the workbench frame-down on the floor. Stand facing the front of the workbench, then reach under each side to grip the frame behind the adjusting handle. Use your thumbs to depress the locking buttons *(inset)*, lifting slightly to release the frame. Reposition your hands to grip the front vise jaw and rest a foot on the foot board, then pull up *(above, left)* to lock the frame into place. For most cutting using a saw, leave the workbench at this height. To raise the height of the workbench for tasks such as planing, filing or drilling, set the workbench onto its back and unfold the collapsible legs *(above, right)*; then, stand it upright.

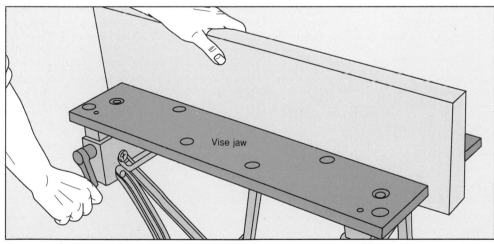

Vise jaw

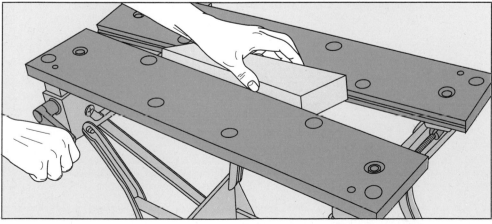

**Securing a workpiece between the vise jaws.**
Unfold the workbench *(step above)*. If the workpiece is too wide or thin to be secured between the vise jaws of the workbench, secure it between swivel pegs *(page 20)*. To secure the workpiece between the vise jaws of the workbench, turn each adjusting handle to open the jaws enough to position it between them. Holding the workpiece centred between the jaws and butted against the stationary jaw, turn each adjusting handle in turn to close the movable jaw, stopping when the workpiece is held securely in place *(left, top)*; avoid overtightening the jaws against it. If the workpiece is irregularly shaped, secure it between the jaws of the workbench using the same procedure, turning each adjusting handle in turn to close the movable jaw at an angle against it *(left, bottom)*. Provide support under each end of a long workpiece to keep the workbench from tipping over.

## SETTING UP ON A PORTABLE WORKBENCH (continued)

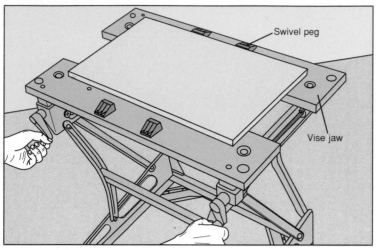
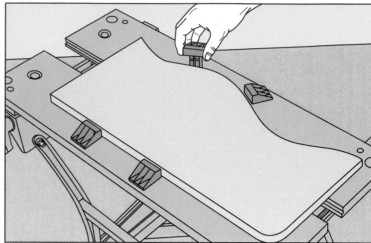

**Securing a workpiece between swivel pegs.** Unfold the workbench *(page 19)*. If the workpiece is too wide or thin to be secured between the vise jaws *(page 19)*, secure it between swivel pegs. To secure the workpiece between swivel pegs, turn each adjusting handle to open the jaws enough to position opposite edges of it completely flat on them. Centering the workpiece, fit swivel pegs along the opposite edges of it into the nearest holes in the jaws; install an equal number of swivel pegs along each edge, one directly opposite another. Then, turn the adjusting handles to close the jaws *(above, left)*, stopping when the workpiece is held securely in place between the swivel pegs; avoid overtightening the swivel pegs against it. If the workpiece is irregularly shaped, secure it using the same procedure, fitting swivel pegs into place along opposite edges of it *(above, right)*, then turning the adjusting handles to close the jaws. Provide support under each end of a long workpiece to keep the workbench from tipping over.

## SETTING UP ON SAWHORSES

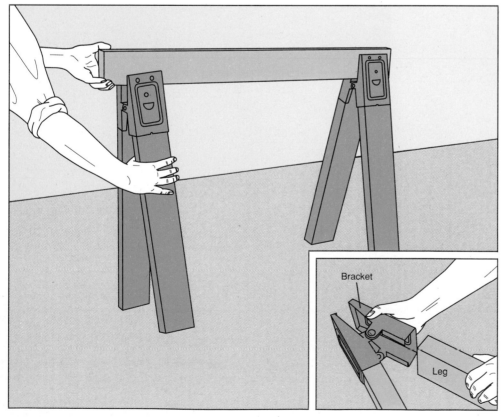

**Assembling a sawhorse.** Use sawhorses to support a workpiece or as a temporary worktable. In general, buy and keep two sturdy factory-built sawhorses for the workshop—each with a saddle about 42 inches long for supporting 4-by-8 sheets and an overall height of about 28 inches for comfort when sawing.

For occasional use, assemble sawhorses of the same or other dimensions using commercially-available sawhorse brackets and 2-by-4s, following the manufacturer's instructions. For the model shown, first assemble a pair of legs, fitting two 2-by-4s of the same length into the base of each bracket *(inset)*. Then, assemble the saddle, fitting one end of a 2-by-4 into the top of the bracket on one pair of legs, then the other end of it into the top of the bracket on the other pair of legs *(left)*. To fasten the sawhorse assembly, drive screws through the bracket holes into the legs and the saddle; for added stability, install a brace midway down the outside edge on each pair of legs. Use the same procedure to assemble a second sawhorse.

## SETTING UP ON SAWHORSES (continued)

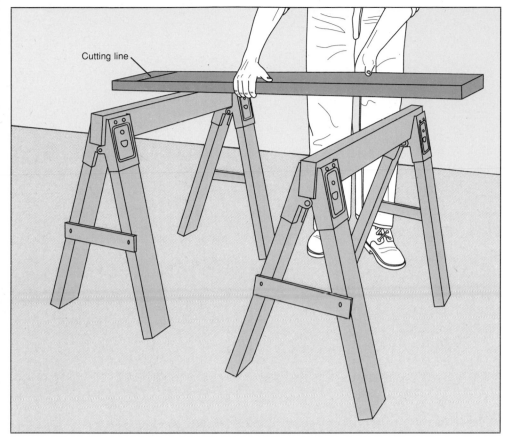

Cutting line

**Securing a workpiece on sawhorses.** Assemble sawhorses, if necessary *(page 20)*. Stand the sawhorses on a solid, flat surface, positioning them parallel to each other at a distance slightly less than the length of the workpiece from each other. Set the workpiece flat on the sawhorses *(left)*, ensuring it overhangs them by about the same amount at each end; if it is wider than the sawhorses, also ensure it is centered on them. Position the workpiece so that any cutting line on it overhangs the outside edge of a sawhorse—a distance of 6 inches is usually enough to avoid cutting the sawhorse. Adjust the position of the sawhorses as necessary until they are stable and the workpiece is well-balanced on them. If the workpiece sags in the center, move the sawhorses closer together under it; if the workpiece sags at the ends, move the sawhorses farther apart.

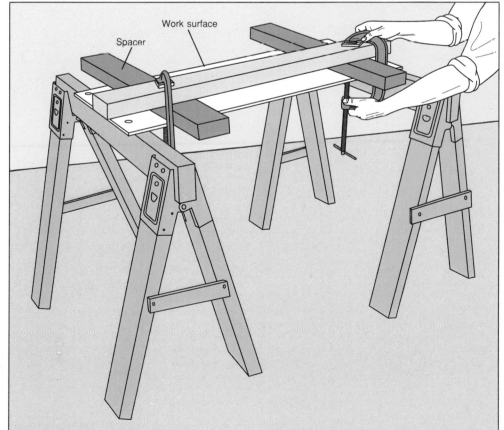

Work surface

Spacer

**Using sawhorses as a temporary worktable.** Assemble sawhorses, if necessary *(page 20)*. Stand the sawhorses on a solid, flat surface, positioning them parallel to each other; for a work surface, use plywood strong enough to support the workpiece. Set the plywood flat on the sawhorses, ensuring it is centered and overhanging them by about the same amount of each end. Adjust the position of the sawhorses as necessary until they are stable and the plywood is well-balanced on them. If the plywood sags in the center, move the sawhorses closer together under it; if the plywood sags at the ends, move the sawhorses farther apart. When the sawhorses are stable and the plywood is well-balanced, drive screws through the plywood into the saddle of each sawhorse; or, use C clamps *(page 22)* to secure the plywood on the sawhorses.

When the temporary worktable is assembled, secure the workpiece as you would on any other worktable *(page 17)*. In the instance shown, secure the workpiece on spacers above the worktable surface. For spacers, use as many wood blocks as necessary of dimensions appropriate for the workpiece; ensure each spacer is of the same thickness to keep the workpiece flat. Position the spacers flat on the worktable, then position the workpiece flat on them and use as many C clamps as necessary to secure it *(left)*.

## SETTING UP ON THE FLOOR

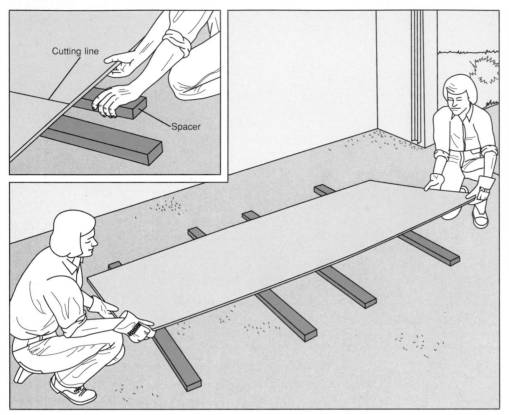

**Setting a workpiece onto spacers on the floor.** For work on large panels or very large boards, the floor is often a convenient work surface. Choose a flat area of the floor that is clean and dry for setting the workpiece onto spacers on it. For spacers, use as many wood blocks as necessary of dimensions appropriate for the workpiece; ensure each spacer is of the same thickness to keep the workpiece flat—2-by-4s longer than the width of the workpiece set down on their widest surface are usually sufficient. Position the spacers flat on the floor parallel to each other, then position the workpiece flat on them, working with a helper, if necessary *(left)*; if you are cutting the workpiece, position a spacer under it on each side of the cutting line *(inset)*. Adjust the position of the spacers as necessary until the workpiece is stable and well-balanced on them; if necessary, add spacers under the workpiece.

## USING C CLAMPS

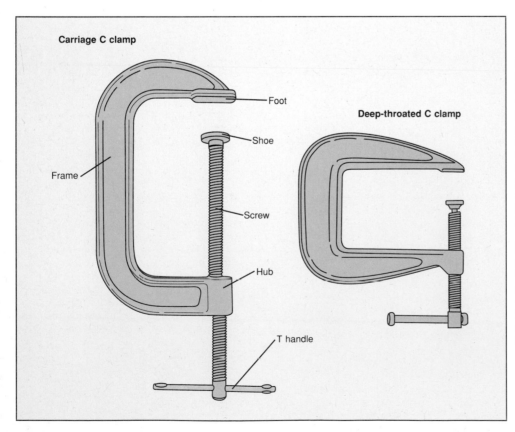

**1 Choosing a C clamp.** To hold a workpiece securely in position, hold together pieces for drilling or installing fasteners, or hold tool accessories such as cutting guides or miter boxes, use a C clamp for any span up to 12 inches. Choose the right size and type of C clamp for the job. C clamps are available in different sizes with reaches from 1 to 12 inches; choose a type with a reach slightly greater than the combined thickness of the materials to be clamped—a 6-inch carriage type is usually sufficient. For extended clamping reach away from the edge of the materials, use deep-throated C clamps. Use C clamps of the right material for the job: malleable iron or drop-forged steel for most jobs; aluminum for very light jobs.

Inspect a C clamp carefully *(left)* before using it. If the frame is bent or cracked or the shoe does not swivel freely in its socket, discard the C clamp. Turn the T handle of the C clamp in each direction; the screw should turn smoothly with it, moving the shoe toward or away from the foot. To lubricate the screw, apply a few drops of light machine oil, then wipe off any excess using a clean cloth.

## USING C CLAMPS (continued)

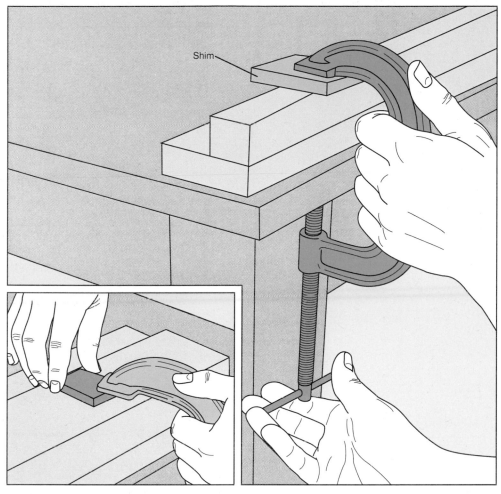

Shim

**2** **Installing a C clamp.** To install a C clamp, ensure that the materials to be clamped are in position and aligned with each other, then turn the T handle enough to fit the jaws loosely across them. If one of the materials is less than 1 inch thick, use a thick, flat block of hardwood equal in length to the material to distribute the pressure of the C clamp evenly along it. Otherwise, use a thin, flat block of wood as a shim to keep the foot *(inset)* or shoe of the C clamp from marking the materials. Holding the frame of the C clamp straight, turn the T handle to thread the screw through the hub until the shoe is securely in place *(left)*. Install any other C clamps you need the same way, then tighten each one in turn a little at a time by hand; do not overtighten a C clamp or use a tool to apply turning force to it.

## USING AN EXTENSION CORD

| NAMEPLATE AMPS | 2.0 - 6.0 | 6.1 - 10.0 | 10.1 - 12.0 | 12.1 - 15.0 |
|---|---|---|---|---|
| EXTENSION CORD LENGTH | RECOMMENDED WIRE GAUGE (AWG) | | | |
| 25 ft. | 18 | 18 | 16 | 14 |
| 50 ft. | 16 | 16 | 16 | 12 |
| 100 ft. | 16 | 14 | 14 | Not recommended |
| 150 ft. | 14 | 12 | 12 | Not recommended |

**1** **Choosing an extension cord.** Always use an extension cord of the correct wire gauge for the power tool; never use a standard household extension cord. To determine the gauge, or size, of extension cord needed, find the amperage rating of the power tool on its nameplate *(page 24)*; then, estimate the length of extension cord you need. With this information, consult the chart *(above)* to determine which gauge of extension cord is appropriate. Never use an extension cord that is undersized, having a higher gauge number than recommended, and avoid working with a series of extension cords; the resulting voltage reduction can cause the power tool to overheat and eventually burn out. For a tool with a three-prong plug, use only a similar extension cord; never bend or remove the third, or grounding, prong of any plug. If you are working outdoors, choose an extension cord rated for outdoor use; if the electrical circuit you are using is not protected by a ground-fault circuit interrupter (GFCI), choose an extension cord with a built-in GFCI. Ensure that any extension cord you use is approved; check for the UL (Underwriters Laboratories) or CSA (Canadian Standards Association) label on it.

## USING AN EXTENSION CORD (continued)

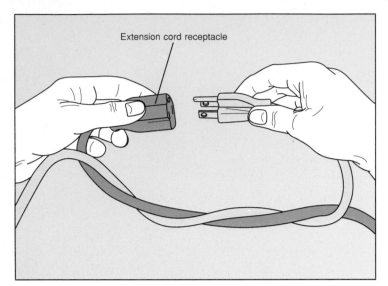

Extension cord receptacle

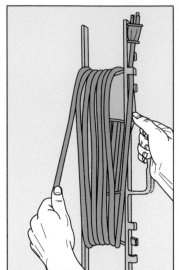

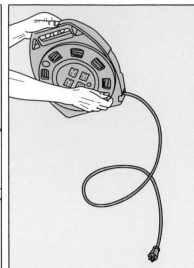

**2** **Setting up an extension cord.** Inspect an extension cord before using it. If the extension cord is worn or damaged, replace it; never splice an extension cord. If the extension cord is in good condition, check that the power tool is turned off, then plug it into the extension cord; if necessary, loop the power cord and the extension cord together loosely before plugging it in *(above)* to prevent it from disconnecting. Run the extension cord to the nearest wall outlet, keeping it away from areas of heavy foot traffic and clear of obstructions, water and heat. Plug in the extension cord safely *(steps below)*.

**3** **Putting away an extension cord.** Before unplugging an extension cord, ensure the power tool is turned off. Unplug the extension cord from the wall outlet, then unplug the power tool from it. Do not twist an extension cord into a figure-8; it will eventually break. To put away an extension cord, use an extension cord hanger, snapping its plug into a slot, then winding it snugly around the frame *(above, left)* and snapping its receptacle into another slot. To put away an extension cord reel, turn the handle on the case to retract the extension cord *(above, right)*, then hang the reel in a dry, cool place.

## PLUGGING IN SAFELY

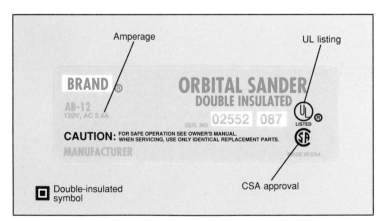

Amperage

UL listing

**BRAND** ®

**ORBITAL SANDER**
DOUBLE INSULATED

AB-12
120V, AC 2.4A

SER. NO **02552 087**

**CAUTION:** FOR SAFE OPERATION SEE OWNER'S MANUAL. WHEN SERVICING, USE ONLY IDENTICAL REPLACEMENT PARTS.

MANUFACTURER

Double-insulated symbol

CSA approval

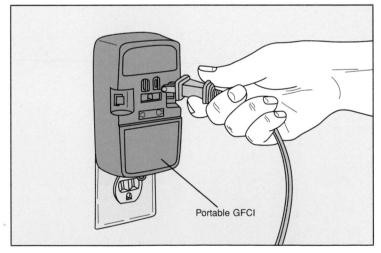

Portable GFCI

**Checking grounding and load requirements.** Ensure a power tool is rated electrically safe, checking its nameplate *(above)*; it should be UL (Underwriters Laboratories) listed or CSA (Canadian Standards Association) approved. Also ensure the power tool is grounded or double-insulated. A grounded tool has a three-prong plug and may be marked "grounding required"; a double-insulated tool is marked "double insulated" and may bear the symbol shown. For a power tool or extension cord with a three-prong plug, use only a similar outlet; never bend or remove the third, or grounding, prong of a plug. Ensure that the outlet, usually on a 15- or 20-ampere electrical circuit, can provide sufficient current for the power tool. Check the amperage rating of the power tool on its nameplate; if it is rated at 10 or more amperes, turn off any high current-drawing appliances operating on the electrical circuit. After ensuring that the electrical circuit is GFCI-protected *(step right)*, plug in the power tool or extension cord.

**Using a portable ground-fault circuit interrupter (GFCI).** A GFCI provides protection against electrical shock by monitoring the flow of current in an electrical circuit; the moment an irregularity in the current is detected, the GFCI automatically shuts off the electrical circuit. A home built or wired before 1975 is unlikely to have GFCIs permanently installed. If you do not have GFCIs permanently installed, use a portable GFCI as a safety precaution at any outlet outdoors or in the workshop, basement, utility room, kitchen, bathroom or garage. Plug the GFCI into the outlet following the manufacturer's instructions; after checking the grounding and load requirements of the power tool *(step left)*, then plug the power tool or extension cord into the GFCI *(above)*.

## USING PERSONAL SAFETY GEAR

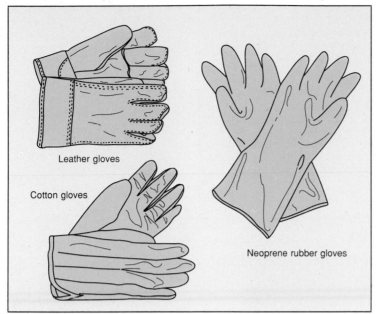

Leather gloves

Cotton gloves

Neoprene rubber gloves

**Using hand protection.** To prevent burns, cuts and allergic reactions when handling sharp, rough or toxic materials, choose the correct type of gloves *(left)*. Use household rubber gloves or disposable vinyl gloves only for light cleaning with household detergents; for other tasks, use stronger gloves. For light-duty handling of workshop tools and materials, use cotton gloves. For heavy-duty handling of rough or sharp pieces of wood, metal or masonry or when handling pressure-treated wood, use leather work gloves. When handling or applying finishes, solvents, adhesives or paint strippers, use neoprene rubber gloves; however, since no rubber can withstand all chemicals, always check with the retailer or manufacturer to be sure that the gloves can be used for protection against a particular chemical. To apply a chemical with an abrasive such as steel wool, wear cotton gloves on top of neoprene rubber gloves. Choose a glove that fits snugly, permitting a good grip without restricting hand movement; as a general rule, do not wear gloves to operate a power tool. Ensure that the gloves extend beyond your wrists; for extra protection when working with chemicals, choose gloves with elasticized cuffs or gauntlets with extended cuffs. Inspect the gloves before using them; if they are worn or torn, replace them.

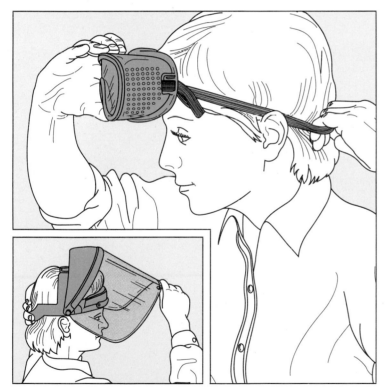

**Using eye and face protection.** To prevent an eye injury from flying dust or debris or a chemical splash, wear safety goggles; if the risk of injury is great, also wear a face shield. Ensure that any safety goggles or face shield you use is approved by the American National Standards Institute (ANSI) or Canadian Standards Association (CSA) and is recommended for the particular hazard. In general, use safety goggles with perforated vent holes for protection from impact injury; with baffled vents for protection from chemical injury; with no vents for extremely dusty work or work using a chemical that emits irritating fumes. Before starting to work, put on the safety goggles to test their fit *(above)*; adjust the headstrap, if necessary. If the safety goggles are scratched, cracked, pitted or clouded, replace them. Check a face shield the same way, putting it on to test its fit *(inset)*.

**Using hearing protection.** To prevent hearing damage from the high-intensity noise of a router, a circular or saber saw, or a belt sander, wear ear muffs or ear plugs—whichever device is most comfortable and convenient. Use only a device with a noise reduction rating (NRR) listed on its package; recommended is a NRR of at least 25, reducing noise entering the ears by at least 25 decibels. Before starting to work, put on the ear muffs to test their fit *(above)*; adjust the headstrap, if necessary. If ear muffs interfere with your movement or with any eye or head protection, use foam ear plugs—unless you have chronic ear problems. Ensuring your hands and the ear plugs are clean, roll each ear plug in turn between your fingers to compress it, then gently insert it into the ear canal *(inset);* hold it in place until it expands to fit the shape of the ear canal.

## USING PERSONAL SAFETY GEAR (continued)

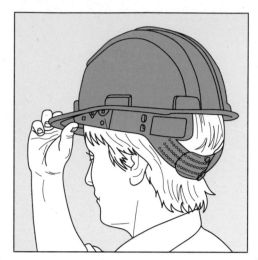

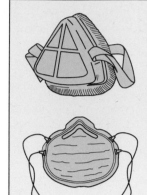

**Reusable dust mask**
Replaceable cotton fiber or gauze filters permit repeated-use protection against nuisance dust and mist. Choose a model of neoprene rubber or soft plastic with an adjustable headstrap.

**Disposable dust mask**
For single-use protection against nuisance dust and mist. Choose a model with sturdy headstraps, a foam seal inside the top and a metal nose clip on the outside that conforms to the shape of your nose.

**Dual-cartridge respirator**
For protection against toxic dust, mist and vapor. Fitted with interchangeable filters or cartridges for protection against specific hazards. Contaminated air purified as inhaled through filters or cartridges, then expelled through exhalation valve.

**Using head protection.** To prevent impact injury to your head when working above your head or in a tight space with little headroom, wear a safety helmet. Choose a safety helmet with the correct American National Standards Institute (ANSI) or Canadian Standards Association (CSA) rating for the job: a type rated A or B if there is any electrical hazard. Before starting to work, put on the safety helmet to test its fit *(above)*; adjust the suspension harness to ensure it fits snugly, if necessary.

**Using respiratory protection.** For dusty work or work using chemicals that emit hazardous vapors, work outdoors, if possible. If you must work indoors, ensure the work area is provided with a constant supply of fresh air and plan to clean up periodically during the job. For the job, choose the best respiratory-protection device *(above)*; ensure it is approved by the National Institute of Occupational Safety and Health (NIOSH) or the Mine Safety and Health Administration (MSHA). For protection against the hazardous dust and mist of materials such as asbestos, fiberglass or pressure-treated wood or the hazardous vapors of chemicals marked with POISON vapor and ventilation warnings, wear a dual-cartridge respirator fitted with the appropriate filters or cartridges *(step below)*. For protection against the nuisance dust and mist of wood, metal, plastic, drywall or masonry, wear the appropriate type of dust mask. For single-use protection, choose a disposable dust mask and throw it away. For repeated-use protection, choose a reusable dust mask with replaceable filters; change the filter after each use of the dust mask.

## USING A RESPIRATOR

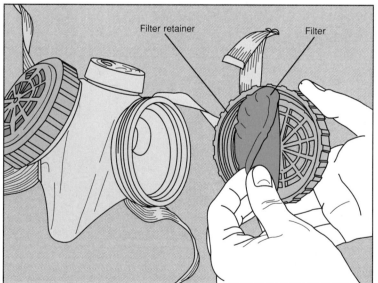

Filter retainer

Filter

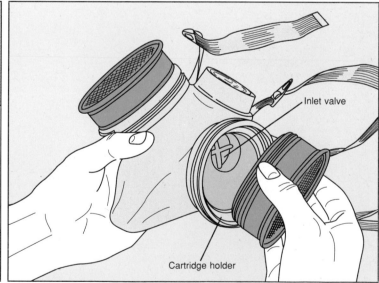

Inlet valve

Cartridge holder

**1** **Installing respirator filters or cartridges.** Before putting on a respirator, fit it with filters or cartridges of the type designed for protection against the particular dust, mist or vapor hazard: filters for dust or mist; cartridges for vapor; or, filters and cartridges for dust or mist and vapor. Consult the owner's manual for the respirator or a safety-equipment supply company that sells respirator accessories for recommendations on specific filters and cartridges; use only types designed for your model of respirator. Remember to buy pairs of filters or cartridges at a time, one for each inlet valve on the respirator; check

the date on each filter or cartridge to ensure it has not expired. To install filters or cartridges in a respirator, follow the owner's manual instructions. On the model shown, unscrew each filter retainer and take it off the cartridge holder. To install filters, fit each one in turn flat into the inside of the filter retainer *(above, left)*, then screw the filter retainer back onto the cartridge holder. To install cartridges, screw each one into the cartridge holder *(above, right)*, then, screw the filter retainers back onto the cartridge holders. To install filters and cartridges, use the same procedure to install first each cartridge and then each filter.

## USING A RESPIRATOR (continued)

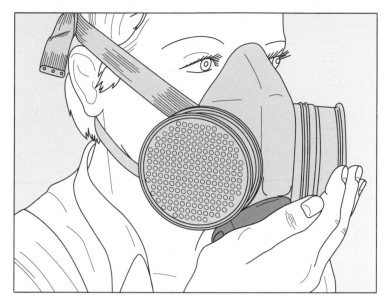

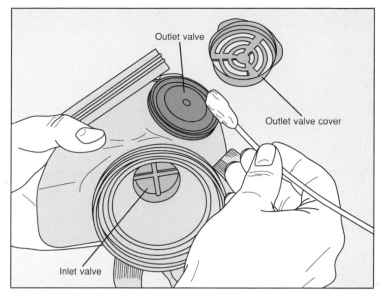

Outlet valve

Outlet valve cover

Inlet valve

**2** **Testing the respirator.** To put on the respirator, hold it cupped under your chin with the facepiece low on your nose, then pull the headstrap back over your head; adjust the headstrap to ensure the respirator fits snugly, if necessary. Then, perform a positive pressure-fit test. Pressing the palm of your hand over the outlet valve cover to block it *(above)*, exhale gently; there should be no air leakage around the edges. If there is air leakage around the edges, adjust the respirator and repeat the test. If you cannot get the respirator to fit snugly, replace it. When you are using the respirator, pay attention to air quality. If you smell or taste a contaminant, any irritation occurs or breathing is difficult, replace the filters or cartridges *(step 1)*.

**3** **Cleaning and storing the respirator.** After using the respirator, remove the filters or cartridges, reversing the procedure used to install them *(step 1)*. If the filters or cartridges can still be used, store them in sealed plastic bags; otherwise, discard them. To clean the respirator, follow the owner's manual instructions; for many models, special cleaning solutions are available. With the model shown, use a soft cloth to wipe the inside and outside surfaces of the respirator. Remove the outlet valve cover and use a foam swab to clean the outlet valve *(above)*; then, clean the inlet valve the same way. If the outlet or inlet valve is damaged, replace it with an exact duplicate. Store the respirator in a sealed plastic bag.

## STORING TOOLS AND CLEANING UP

**Putting away tools and supplies.** After completing a workshop project, take time to carefully put away all tools and supplies used. Proper storage and cleanup keeps a workshop with limited space well-organized for the next project—ensuring that tools remain in good working order and safety hazards to you and your family members are minimized. When you store your tools and supplies, keep in mind a few simple rules. Sort out and store the smallest items first *(step right)*. If a tool or supply needs special protection from light, heat, moisture, dust or impact, store it in the way that best protects it *(page 28)*. Store tools and supplies so you can find them easily; keep like tools and supplies together in designated spots or in clearly-labeled containers or drawers close to where you use them. Store hazardous cutting and power tools as well as chemical products out of the reach of children, hanging them up *(page 28)* or locking them away *(page 29)*. After storing your tools and supplies, clean the workshop thoroughly *(page 29)*. Always lock the workshop when it is not in use.

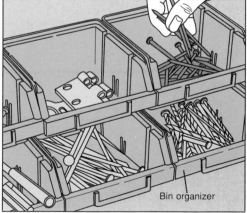

Bin organizer

**Sorting out small tools and supplies.** To avoid loosing small tools and supplies, begin a cleanup by collecting them first. Gather up small tools and tool attachments such as router, drill and screwdriver bits, saber saw and reciprocating saw blades, nail sets and punches; many have their own storage cases. Sort out sandpaper and steel wool, as well as fasteners and hardware. Pick up scissors and work knives, pencils, tape, swabs and toothpicks. To store small items so you can find them easily, use drawer organizers *(above, left)* and bin organizers *(above, right)*; glass jars with tight-fitting lids also make good storage containers. Use masking tape to clearly label the contents of each drawer, bin or jar. Keep organizer units and containers together, handy and neat: on the worktable; on shelves or in cupboards above or below the worktable; or mounted and hung from shelf bottoms or perforated hardboard wall panels.

## STORING TOOLS AND CLEANING UP (continued)

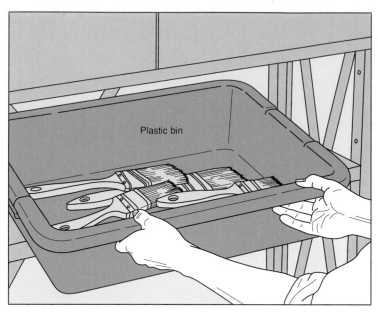

**Safeguarding precision tools.** To avoid damaging delicate hand tools such as screwdriver or wrench sets, files, chisels or planes, store them in a safe place, shielded from dust and humidity, and protected from impact damage. Hang hand tools you use frequently *(step below)* or keep them in their original boxes or in special storage cases. For example, use a canvas tool roll *(above)* to keep sets of precision tools together in one place and ensure they remain clean, dry and protected. Store tools placed in boxes, cases or tool rolls in drawers, then label the drawers so the tools can be easily found.

**Shelving bulky supplies.** To maximize order and minimize clutter in the workshop, batch and store together tools and supplies used for cleaning or finishing jobs. Also collect up similar types of fasteners, hardware and construction materials, setting them aside together where they will not get in the way. For example, use plastic bins *(above)* to keep together finishing supplies such as paintbrushes and rollers, along with cloths, sponges and drop cloths. Store the bins on shelves; or, use stackable bins, which can be assembled and set neatly on the floor against a wall, stacked as high as necessary.

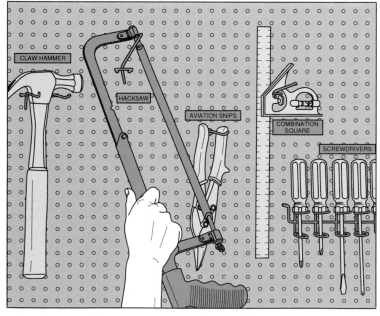

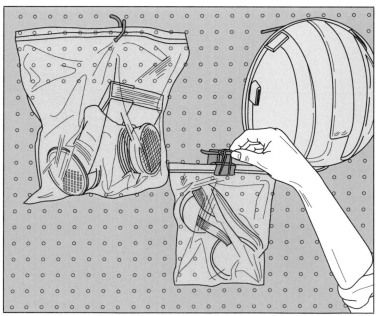

**Hanging up hand tools and safety gear.** Hang up heavy or bulky hand tools and safety gear used frequently in the workshop, providing a safe, accessible storage site for them and minimizing clutter. Clamps, handsaws and other cutting tools, hammers, measuring tools, scrapers, putty knives, screwdrivers and wrenches can all be hung where they are visible and easy to find. Install perforated hardboard panels on the workshop walls and fit them with hooks for tools; U hooks, looped hooks, racks, clamps and other devices to hold individual or sets of tools are available at hardware stores and building supply centers.

Arrange hanging tools to maximize space *(above, left)*, positioning similar tools and attachments near each other, far enough apart that they do not bang one another; hang heavy or sharp tools low down in case they fall. Label the position of each tool with masking tape so you can remember where it goes. If you hang up saw blades, label them by type; apply a thin coat of light machine oil to each blade to protect it from rust and hang it by itself to protect the teeth. With safety gear such as a respirator, ear muffs, ear plugs or safety goggles, place each item in a sealed plastic bag to protect it, then hang up the bag *(above, right)*.

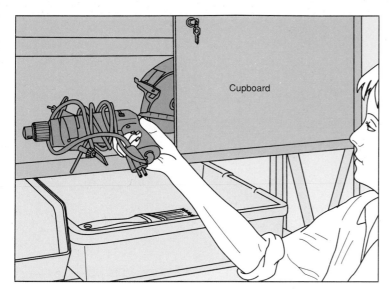

**Closing away power tools.** To prevent damage to power tools and keep them away from children, store them closed up in a cupboard *(above)* in their own special storage cases, if possible. After using any power tool, turn it off and unplug it, then remove any accessory such as a bit, a blade or a guide from it. Store the accessory in the case with the power tool; or, store a small accessory separately *(page 27)*. Consult your owner's manual for the power tool and follow any special pre-storage maintenance procedures and storage instructions. To store a power tool without a case, wind its power cord loosely around it, then stand or lie the tool in a secure spot, clear of other tools and supplies.

**Locking away hazardous chemicals.** Store hazardous finishing and cleaning products, lubricants, solvents, adhesives and paint strippers locked up in a metal safety cabinet *(above)*, keeping them safely away from children and preventing spills or fires. Place the cabinet in a cool, dry spot away from heat or ignition sources and as far as possible from any exit. Post a NO SMOKING sign on the cabinet and install a smoke detector on the ceiling above it as well as a fire extinguisher rated ABC on a wall within 10 feet of it *(page 11)*. Before storing a hazardous chemical, read the label for any special storage instructions and ensure the container is well-marked, undamaged and tightly closed.

**Disposing of waste and debris.** Clean the workshop thoroughly after a job to ready it for the next project. Assemble the necessary cleaning supplies; if necessary, wear work gloves or rubber gloves *(page 25)* and respiratory protection *(page 26)*. Clean up any chemical refuse first, throwing empty containers and applicators into a metal container double-lined with plastic garbage bags *(inset)*; do not dispose of chemicals or containers marked FLAMMABLE or POISON with other household or workshop refuse. Seal the container and place it outdoors, away from heat and light; call your local department of environmental protection or public health for recommended disposal procedures in your community.

To clean up other debris and refuse, work methodically from the highest to the lowest surfaces and finish by cleaning the floor. Collect by hand and store any reusable pieces of scrap material. Using a whisk broom and dust pan for any small surface or a push broom for the floor, sweep up large disposable pieces of scrap material and throw them into a trash can lined with a plastic garbage bag. Seal the bag and dispose of it with your other household refuse. Then, use a shop vacuum to remove remaining debris, particles and dust *(left)*. Store your cleaning tools and supplies, then lock the workshop when you leave it.

# MEASURING AND MARKING

A vital part of many home workshop jobs is the preliminary reading and transferring of measurements. Workpieces must be measured and marked before they can be cut or trimmed, and surfaces need to be measured and marked before fasteners are installed. The measuring and marking tools presented in this chapter are used to perform all the basic functions typically required for home repairs; refer to the inventory on page 31. Included are techniques for measuring and marking distances using a tape measure *(page 32)*; measuring and marking angles using a try square *(page 35)*, a carpenter's square, a combination square *(page 36)* or a sliding bevel *(page 37)*; and checking horizontal orientations using a carpenter's level *(page 39)*, a line level or a water level *(page 40)*, and checking vertical orientations using a carpenter's level *(page 39)* or a plumb bob *(page 41)*. To choose the correct tool for the problem or task at hand, consult the Troubleshooting Guide *(below)*.

Measuring and marking can be a precise science, often resembling a geometry exercise. Home repair projects, however, rarely require complex measuring or marking; deviations of 1/16 inch are usually acceptable. Avoid errors by using the same tool for all measuring and marking done on a job. When possible, avoid measuring; for instance, if marking a piece to be cut to the shape of another, use the original as a template instead of measuring and transferring its dimensions. Care and accuracy pays off when a piece fits as planned—with no waste. Check that corners are square using a try square *(page 35)* or a combination square *(page 36)*; check that surfaces are flat using a straightedge *(page 33)*. To correct irregularities, see Trimming And Smoothing *(page 78)*. Measuring tools are precision instruments. Inspect a measuring tool closely before using it and handle it carefully while using it; after using it, wipe off dirt and moisture with a soft cloth, then store it safely away.

## TROUBLESHOOTING GUIDE

| PROBLEM | PROCEDURE |
| --- | --- |
| Measuring an outside or inside distance | Use tape measure to measure outside or inside distance *(p. 32)* |
| Measuring a diameter | Use tape measure to measure diameter *(p. 33)* |
| Measuring a circumference | Use tape measure to measure circumference *(p. 33)* |
| Measuring an angle | Use sliding bevel to measure angle *(p. 37)* |
| Marking a measured distance | Use tape measure to mark measured distance *(p. 32)* |
| Marking a point level with another point | For points close together, use carpenter's level *(p. 39)*; for points far apart, use line level *(p. 40)*; for points on different surfaces, use water level *(p. 40)* |
| Marking a point directly below another point | Use plumb bob to mark point *(p. 41)* |
| Marking a line between points | For short line, use straightedge *(p. 33)*; for long line, use chalk line *(p. 34)* |
| Marking a line at 90 degrees to edge | Use try square *(p. 35)*, carpenter's square or combination square *(p. 36)* to mark line |
| Marking a line at 90 degrees to another line | Use carpenter's square to mark line *(p. 36)* |
| Marking a line at 45 degrees to edge | Use carpenter's square or combination square to mark line *(p. 36)* |
| Marking a line at angle other than 90 or 45 degrees to edge | Use sliding bevel to mark line *(p. 37)* |
| Marking a line parallel to edge | Use combination square to mark line *(p. 37)* |
| Copying a line from curved or irregular edge | Use compass or dividers to copy edge *(p. 38)* |
| Marking a line level (perfectly horizontal) | For short line, use carpenter's level *(p. 39)*; for long line, use line level or water level *(p. 40)* |
| Marking a line plumb (perfectly vertical) | For short line, use carpenter's level *(p. 39)*; for long line, use plumb bob *(p. 41)* |
| Marking a circle | For small circle, use compass or dividers *(p. 38)*; for large circle, use trammel heads *(p. 38)* |
| Checking an angle is 90 degrees | Use try square *(p. 35)* or combination square *(p. 36)* to check angle |
| Checking an angle is 45 degrees | Use combination square to check angle *(p. 36)* |
| Checking a line is level (perfectly horizontal) | For short line, use carpenter's level *(p. 39)*; for long line, use line level or water level *(p. 40)* |
| Checking a line is plumb (perfectly vertical) | For short line, use carpenter's level *(p. 39)*; for long line, use plumb bob *(p. 41)* |
| Checking a surface is flat | Use straightedge to check surface *(p. 33)* |
| Checking a surface is level (perfectly horizontal) | For small surface, use carpenter's level *(p. 39)*; for large surface, use water level *(p. 40)* |
| Checking a surface is plumb (perfectly vertical) | For small surface, use carpenter's level *(p. 39)*; for large surface, use plumb bob *(p. 41)* |

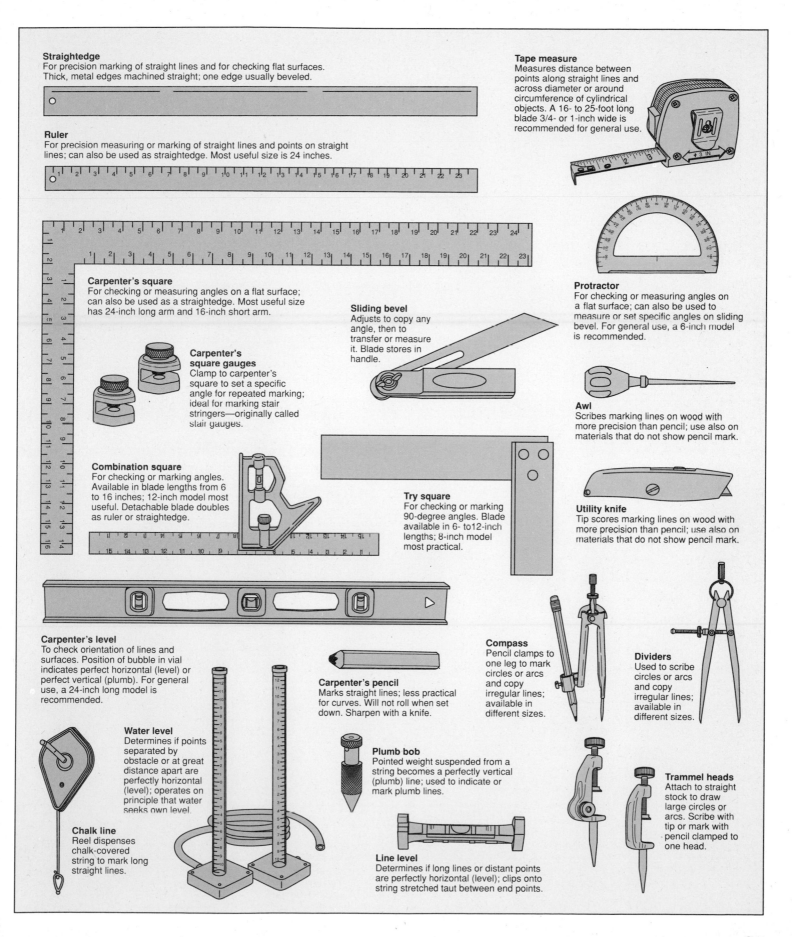

**Straightedge**
For precision marking of straight lines and for checking flat surfaces. Thick, metal edges machined straight; one edge usually beveled.

**Ruler**
For precision measuring or marking of straight lines and points on straight lines; can also be used as straightedge. Most useful size is 24 inches.

**Tape measure**
Measures distance between points along straight lines and across diameter or around circumference of cylindrical objects. A 16- to 25-foot long blade 3/4- or 1-inch wide is recommended for general use.

**Carpenter's square**
For checking or measuring angles on a flat surface; can also be used as a straightedge. Most useful size has 24-inch long arm and 16-inch short arm.

**Carpenter's square gauges**
Clamp to carpenter's square to set a specific angle for repeated marking; ideal for marking stair stringers—originally called stair gauges.

**Combination square**
For checking or marking angles. Available in blade lengths from 6 to 16 inches; 12-inch model most useful. Detachable blade doubles as ruler or straightedge.

**Sliding bevel**
Adjusts to copy any angle, then to transfer or measure it. Blade stores in handle.

**Try square**
For checking or marking 90-degree angles. Blade available in 6- to 12-inch lengths; 8-inch model most practical.

**Protractor**
For checking or measuring angles on a flat surface; can also be used to measure or set specific angles on sliding bevel. For general use, a 6-inch model is recommended.

**Awl**
Scribes marking lines on wood with more precision than pencil; use also on materials that do not show pencil mark.

**Utility knife**
Tip scores marking lines on wood with more precision than pencil; use also on materials that do not show pencil mark.

**Carpenter's level**
To check orientation of lines and surfaces. Position of bubble in vial indicates perfect horizontal (level) or perfect vertical (plumb). For general use, a 24-inch long model is recommended.

**Water level**
Determines if points separated by obstacle or at great distance apart are perfectly horizontal (level); operates on principle that water seeks own level.

**Chalk line**
Reel dispenses chalk-covered string to mark long straight lines.

**Carpenter's pencil**
Marks straight lines; less practical for curves. Will not roll when set down. Sharpen with a knife.

**Plumb bob**
Pointed weight suspended from a string becomes a perfectly vertical (plumb) line; used to indicate or mark plumb lines.

**Line level**
Determines if long lines or distant points are perfectly horizontal (level); clips onto string stretched taut between end points.

**Compass**
Pencil clamps to one leg to mark circles or arcs and copy irregular lines; available in different sizes.

**Dividers**
Used to scribe circles or arcs and copy irregular lines; available in different sizes.

**Trammel heads**
Attach to straight stock to draw large circles or arcs. Scribe with tip or mark with pencil clamped to one head.

## PREPARING TO USE A TAPE MEASURE

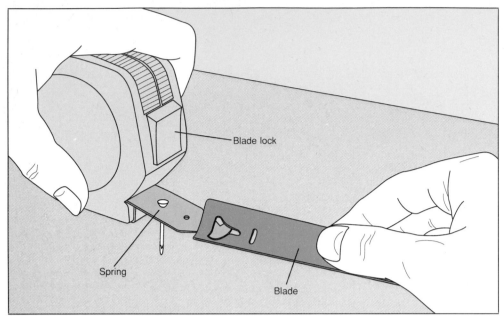

**Inspecting and servicing a tape measure.**
To inspect a tape measure, pull out the blade and depress the blade lock; then, release the blade lock. If the blade does not lock or rewind, replace the tape measure. If the blade is worn or damaged, replace it with an exact duplicate. To remove the old blade, pull it out all the way, exposing the spring at the end. Depress the blade lock and insert a nail in the spring hole to keep the spring from rewinding. Twisting the end of the blade slightly, detach it from the hooked end of the spring *(left)*. To install the new blade, hold it firmly, still coiled and with its markings facing up. Slip the slotted end of the blade over the hooked end of the spring, then pull straight back to lock it to the spring. Holding the blade steady with one hand, remove the nail from the spring hole and release the blade lock. Ease the end of the blade into the case, then release it; as the blade rewinds, slow it to keep its hook from hitting the case.

## USING A TAPE MEASURE

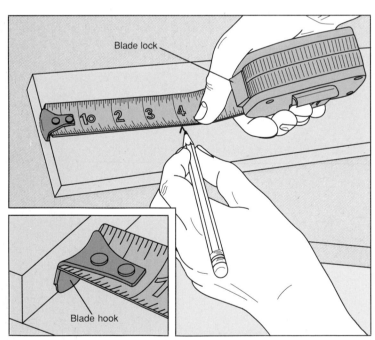

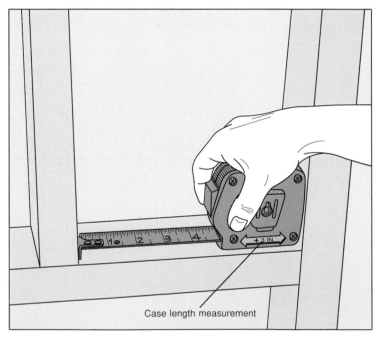

Case length measurement

**Measuring and marking an outside distance.** Prepare to use your tape measure *(step above)*. Place the blade hook at the starting point for the measurement, butting it against an inside edge *(inset)* or hanging it over an outside edge; if the starting point is not at an edge, measure as you would a diameter *(page 33)*. Pull the case to extend the blade, stopping just past the point to which you are measuring, then depress the blade lock; if you are measuring from an inside edge, hold the blade with your finger as you pull the case. Tilt the case so the blade edge is flush against the surface. To take a measurement, read the appropriate blade marking; to mark a measurement, use a sharp pencil to mark a crow's foot at the appropriate blade marking *(above)*. Release the blade lock to rewind the blade.

**Measuring an inside distance.** Prepare to use your tape measure *(step above)*. Place the blade hook at the starting point for the measurement, butting it against an inside edge. Holding the blade steady with your finger, pull the case to extend the blade, stopping when the case is flush against the opposite inside edge; depress the blade lock *(above)*. To calculate the distance of the enclosed space, read the blade marking just where the blade exits the case, then add to it the case length measurement—usually marked on the side or bottom of the case. On some tape measures, the back of the blade is specially marked for inside measurements; read the marking on the back of the blade just where it exits the case. Release the blade lock to rewind the blade.

## USING A TAPE MEASURE (continued)

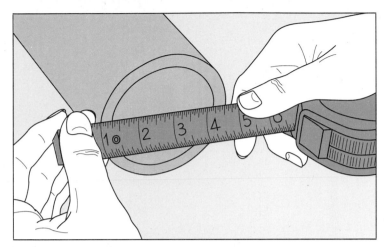

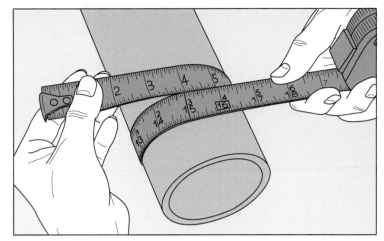

**Measuring a diameter.** Prepare to use your tape measure *(page 32)*. To measure a diameter or from a starting point with no well-defined edge, use a blade marking rather than the blade hook as a starting reference point. Holding the blade hook, place the 1-inch blade marking, for example, at the starting point for the measurement. Pull the case to extend the blade just past the point to which you are measuring, then depress the blade lock. To measure a diameter, move the blade along the edge of the curve opposite the starting point to find the point at which the distance is greatest *(above)*. To calculate the distance in inches, subtract the number at the starting point from the number of inches at the end point; in the instance shown, subtract 1 from 4 1/2 to find a diameter of 3 1/2 inches. Release the blade lock to rewind the blade.

**Measuring a circumference.** Prepare to use your tape measure *(page 32)*. To measure a circumference, use a blade marking rather than the blade hook as a starting reference point. Holding the blade hook, pull the case to extend the blade, then depress the blade lock. Wrap the blade around the circumference, holding the blade hook away from the surface to prevent interference; then, pull gently until the blade lies flat against the surface, with two edges touching *(above)*. To calculate the distance in inches, take any two perfectly aligned blade markings and subtract the lesser number from the greater number; in the instance shown, subtract 4 from 15 to find a circumference of 11 inches. Release the blade lock to rewind the blade. An alternate method for finding a circumference is to measure the diameter *(step left)*, then multiply it by 3.1416.

## USING A STRAIGHTEDGE

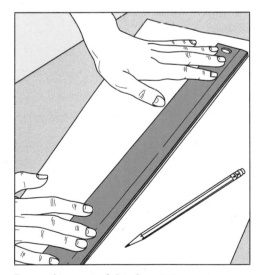

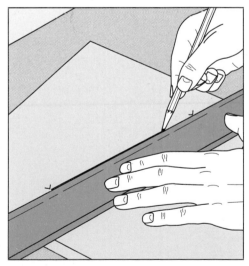

**Inspecting a straightedge.** Before using a straightedge, check it for warpage. Lay the straightedge flat on a piece of paper and mark a line along one edge, then turn the straightedge around and align the same edge on the opposite side of the marked line. If the edge deviates from the line *(above)*, the straightedge is warped and should not be used. Check the other edge the same way.

**Checking a surface for flatness.** Inspect your straightedge *(step left)*, then place it flat- or beveled-edge down across the surface; repeat the test at several places along the surface at different angles across it. If there are gaps or light is visible between the surface and the straightedge *(above)*, the surface is not perfectly flat. If necessary, trim or smooth the surface *(page 78)*.

**Marking a straight line.** If necessary, use a tape measure to mark any end point for the line *(page 32)*. Inspect your straightedge *(step far left)*, then lay it flat on the surface, aligning its beveled edge with any marked end point. Holding a sharp pencil firmly against the beveled edge, draw lightly along it *(above)*; for greatest precision and neatness, use a utility knife or a scratch awl the same way.

## USING A CHALK LINE

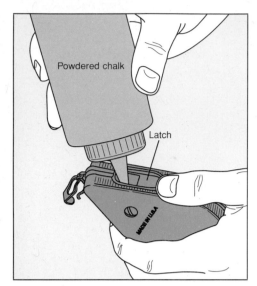

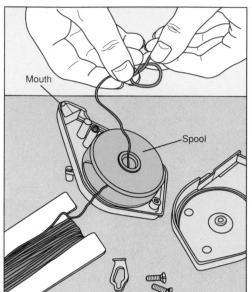

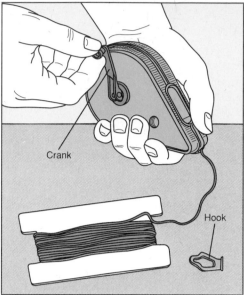

**1** **Inspecting and servicing a chalk line.** Inspect a chalk line before using it. If the string is frayed or broken, replace it *(step 2)*. Check the chalk level in the case; on most models, slide open the latch or unscrew the cap. If the chalk does not cover the coiled string, buy powdered chalk at a hardware store and refill the case *(above)*, gently squeezing in enough to just cover the coiled string. When the chalk just covers the coiled string, close the case and use the chalk line to mark a straight line *(step 3)*.

**2** **Replacing the string.** If the string is frayed or broken near the hook, cut off the damaged section and retie the hook. If a large section of the string is frayed or broken, buy an identical string at a hardware store. Open the case latch or cap and empty out the chalk. Unlock the crank and pull out the old string, then cut off the hook and set it aside. Unscrew and separate the sections of the case; note the arrangement of internal components for reassembly. Cut the string off the spool. To fasten the new string on the model shown, thread one end through the hole in the spool and knot it *(above, left)*. Pulling the string taut, wind it onto the spool several turns. Position the string at the mouth of the case and reassemble it. Turn the crank to reel in the string *(above, right)*, stopping near the end to tie on the hook. Reel in the rest of the string and fill the case with chalk *(step 1)*.

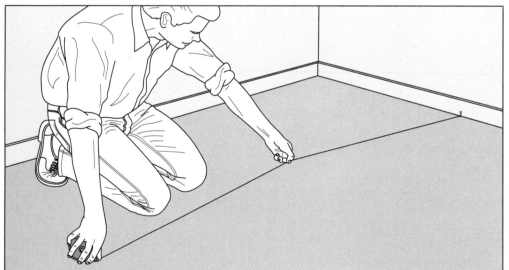

**3** **Marking a straight line.** Use a chalk line to mark a straight line longer than a few feet. If necessary, use a tape measure to mark any end point for the line *(page 32)*. To check that marked end points on a vertical surface are perfectly horizontal, use a line level or water level *(page 40)*; to check that marked end points on a vertical surface are perfectly vertical, hang the chalk line as you would a plumb bob *(page 41)*. Drive a nail partway into the surface at one end point; on a vertical surface, at the top. Hook the chalk line over the nail and unreel it to the other end point, keeping it off the surface. Pull the string taut and press it against the end point with the thumb of one hand. If the line is less than 12 feet in length, use the other hand to lift the string near the center and snap it once only against the horizontal *(above)* or vertical *(right)* surface. If the line is 12 feet or more in length, have a helper press the string at the center, then snap it twice the same way, once only on each side of the center. Unhook the chalk line and reel it in.

## PREPARING TO USE A SQUARE

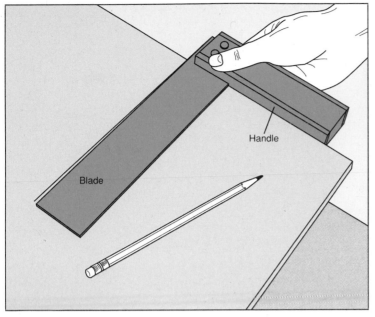

**Choosing and inspecting a square.** Choose the square best suited to the measuring or marking job. Any square can be used along an edge to check angles or mark lines at angles; as a rule, a try square is the best size for short lines, a combination square for medium-length lines and a carpenter's square for long lines. To check angles or mark lines at angles when there is no edge for a reference, use a carpenter's square—the only square that can be used away from an edge. If you must measure lines you are marking with a square, use a combination square or a carpenter's square; both have numbered rules. If the blade or arm of a square is not long enough for a job, extend its reach using a straightedge, placing the beveled edge along it.

Before using a square, check that its angle is perfectly square. To check a try square, press the handle flush against a straight edge so the blade rests flat on the surface. Use a sharp pencil to mark a line along the outer edge of the blade, then flip the square over and align the same edge on the opposite side of the line; if it deviates from the line *(left)*, the square should not be used. To check a combination square or a carpenter's square, use the same procedure; with the carpenter's square, press the long arm flush against a straight edge and mark a line along the short arm.

## USING A TRY SQUARE

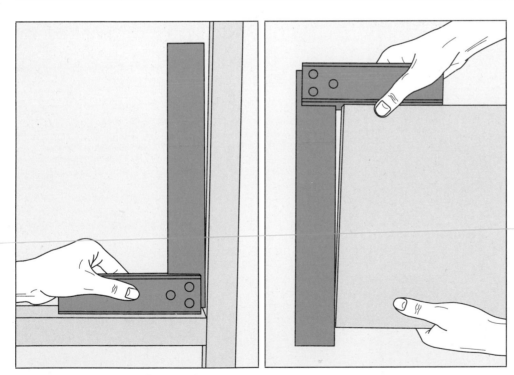

**Checking for a 90-degree angle.** Prepare to use your try square *(step above)*. To check that an angle formed by two surfaces is 90 degrees, choose one surface as a reference—generally, the surface to which the other surface will be adjusted. Holding the handle of the square flush against the reference surface, butt the blade against the other surface; use the outer edges of the square to check an inside angle *(above, left)* and the inner edges of the square to check an outside angle *(above, right)*. If the blade and the handle fit flush against the surfaces, the angle is 90 degrees. If there is a gap or light is visible between the blade and the surface, as shown, the angle is not 90 degrees.

**Marking a line at 90 degrees to an edge.** If necessary, use a tape measure to mark any end point for the line *(page 32)*. Prepare to use your try square *(step above)*, then press the handle flush against the edge with the blade flat on the surface, its outer edge aligned with any marked end point. Holding a sharp pencil firmly against the outer edge, draw lightly along it *(above)*; for greatest precision and neatness, use a utility knife or a scratch awl the same way.

## USING A CARPENTER'S SQUARE

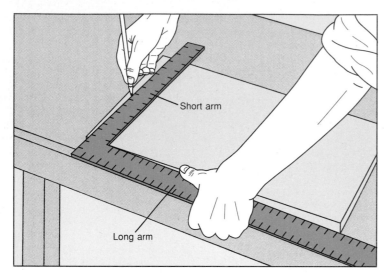

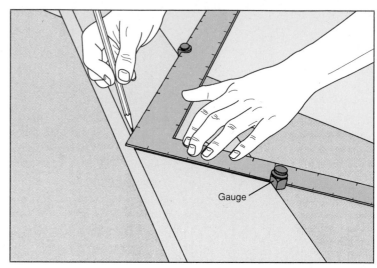

**Marking a line at a 90-degree angle.** If necessary, use a tape measure to mark any end point for the line *(page 32)*. Prepare to use your carpenter's square *(page 35)*. To mark a line at 90 degrees to an edge, press the inner edge of the long arm flush against the edge with the short arm flat on the surface, its outer edge aligned with any marked end point. Holding a sharp pencil firmly against the outer edge, draw lightly along it *(above)*; for greatest precision and neatness, use a utility knife or a scratch awl the same way. To mark a line at 90 degrees to another line, follow the same procedure, laying the square flat and aligning the inner edge of the long arm with the line.

**Marking a line at a 45-degree angle.** If necessary, use a tape measure to mark any end point for the line *(page 32)*. Prepare to use your carpenter's square *(page 35)*. To mark a line or repeated lines at 45 degrees to an edge, attach gauges to the carpenter's square, screwing one to the outer edge of each arm at the same distance from the corner. Hold the carpenter's square so the gauges are flush against the edge with the arms flat on the surface, the outer edge of the appropriate arm aligned with any marked end point. Holding a sharp pencil firmly against the outer edge, draw lightly along it *(above)*; for greatest precision and neatness, use a utility knife or a scratch awl the same way.

## USING A COMBINATION SQUARE

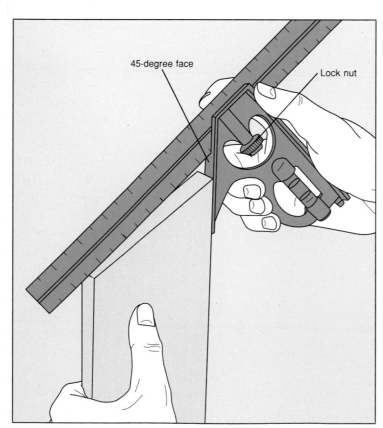

**Checking for a 45- or 90-degree angle.** Prepare to use your combination square *(page 35)*. To check that an outside angle formed by two surfaces is 45 degrees, use the 45-degree face of the handle and the inner blade edge; if necessary, loosen the lock nut and adjust the blade position, sliding it in either direction, then tighten the lock nut. Choose one surface as a reference—generally, the surface to which the other surface will be adjusted. Holding the 45-degree face of the handle flush against the reference surface, butt the blade against the other surface *(left)*. If the blade and the handle fit flush against the surfaces, the angle is 45 degrees. If there is a gap or light is visible between the blade and the surface, as in the instance shown, the angle is not 45 degrees.

To check for other angles with the combination square, determine the face of the handle and any blade edge to be used, then adjust and use the square following the same procedure. For an outside 90-degree angle, use the 90-degree face of the handle and the inner blade edge. For an inside 90-degree angle, use the 90-degree face of the handle and the outer blade edge. For an inside 45-degree angle, remove the blade, then use the 45-degree face and the 90-degree face of the handle.

## USING A COMBINATION SQUARE (continued)

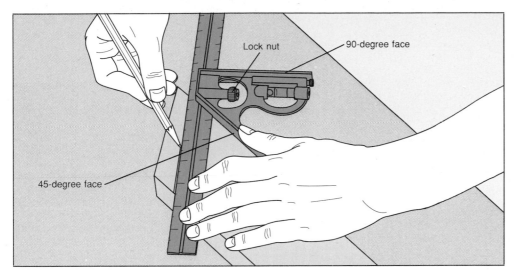

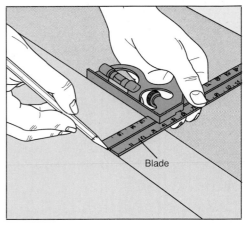

**Marking a line at 45 or 90 degrees to an edge.** If necessary, use a tape measure to mark any end point for the line *(page 32)*. Prepare to use your combination square *(page 35)*. To mark a line at 45 degrees to an edge, use the 45-degree face of the handle and the outer blade edge; if necessary, loosen the lock nut and adjust the blade position, then tighten the lock nut. Press the handle flush against the edge with the blade flat on the surface, its outer edge aligned with any marked end point. Holding a sharp pencil firmly against the outer edge, draw lightly along it *(above)*; for greatest precision and neatness, use a utility knife or a scratch awl the same way. To mark a line at 90 degrees to an edge, follow the same procedure, using the 90-degree face of the handle and the outer blade edge.

**Marking a line parallel to an edge.** If necessary, use a tape measure to mark any end point for the line *(page 32)*. Prepare to use your combination square *(page 35)*, then press the 90-degree face of the handle flush against the edge and loosen the lock nut; adjust the blade position, aligning its end with any marked end point or to the set distance from the edge, then tighten the lock nut. Holding a sharp pencil firmly against or in the notch at the end of the blade, slide the handle along the edge *(above)*; for greatest precision and neatness, use a utility knife or a scratch awl the same way.

## USING A SLIDING BEVEL

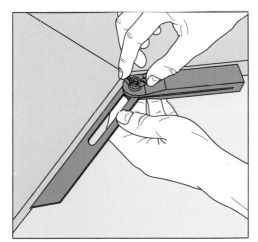

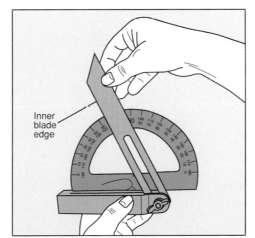

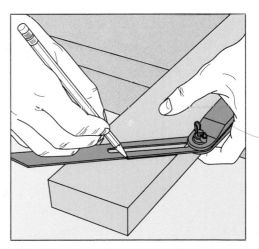

**1 Copying an angle.** Use a sliding bevel to set *(step 2)* or copy an angle. To copy an angle, loosen the blade—usually by unscrewing a wing nut. For an inside angle, hold the outer edge of the handle against one surface, then swing the blade so its outer edge lies flush against the other surface. Set the bevel by tightening the wing nut *(above)*. For an outside angle, follow the same procedure, using the inner edges of the handle and the blade. Measure the angle, if necessary *(step 2)*, then mark it *(step 3)*.

**2 Setting or measuring an angle.** To set or measure an angle, hold the inner edge of the handle against the base of a protractor, aligning the inner edge of the blade with its center point. To set an angle, loosen the blade—usually by unscrewing a wing nut; then, swing it until its inner edge intersects the desired numerical point on the protractor scale *(above)* and tighten the wing nut. To measure an angle, read the numerical point on the protractor scale intersected by the inner edge of the blade.

**3 Marking a line at an angle to an edge.** If necessary, use a tape measure to mark any end point for the line *(page 32)*. To mark the line at the angle of the sliding bevel, press the inner edge of the handle flush against the edge with the blade flat on the surface, its outer edge aligned with any marked end point. Holding a sharp pencil firmly against the outer edge, draw lightly along it *(above)*; for greatest precision and neatness, use a utility knife or a scratch awl the same way.

## USING A COMPASS OR DIVIDERS

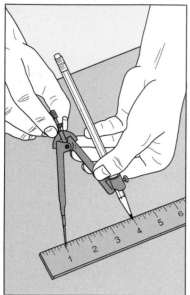
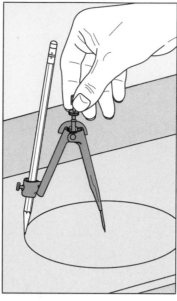
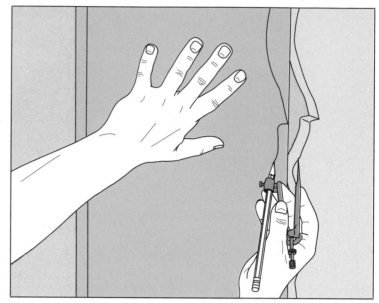

**Marking a circle.** If necessary, use a tape measure to mark a center point for the circle *(page 32)*. To mark a large circle, set up trammel heads *(step 1, below)*. Otherwise, use a compass or dividers. To set up a compass, close its legs, then loosen the thumbscrew and insert a sharp pencil into the holder. Align the end of the pencil with the tip of the other leg, then tighten the thumbscrew. Using a ruler as a guide, turn the lock nut to open the legs to the radius of the circle *(above, left)*. Holding the compass by its handle, position the tip on the marked center point. Turn the handle to rotate the compass on the tip, drawing the pencil along the surface in a smooth curve around it *(above, right)*. Set up and use dividers the same way.

**Copying a line from a curved or irregular edge.** To copy a curved or irregular edge, use a compass or dividers. To set up a compass, close its legs, then loosen the thumbscrew and insert a sharp pencil into the holder. Align the end of the pencil with the tip of the other leg, then tighten the thumbscrew. Butt the surface to be marked against the edge to be copied, as shown, and find the point where the gap is largest; turn the lock nut to open the legs to the distance. Holding the compass with the tip on the edge to be copied and the pencil on the surface to be marked, draw the tip along the edge, marking an identical line on the surface with the pencil *(above)*. Set up and use dividers the same way.

## USING TRAMMEL HEADS

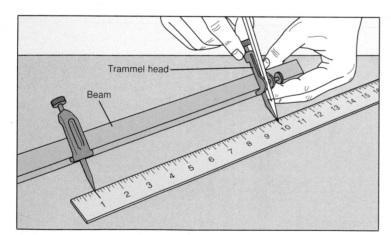
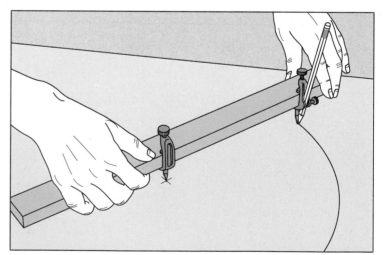

**1** **Setting up trammel heads.** To mark a small circle, set up and use a compass or dividers *(step above, left)*. Otherwise, set up a beam-type compass using trammel heads and a straight, rigid piece of wood or metal slightly longer than the circle radius and no wider than the trammel head clamps. If one trammel head holds a pencil, loosen its thumbscrew and align the end of a sharp pencil with its tip, then tighten the thumbscrew. Attach a trammel head near one end of the beam, turning its thumbscrew to clamp it. Using a ruler as a guide, position the other trammel head on the beam so the distance between the trammel head tips is equal to the radius of the circle; then, tighten its thumbscrew to clamp it *(above)*.

**2** **Marking the circle.** If necessary, use a tape measure to mark a center point for the circle *(page 32)*. Holding the beam steady by its ends, position the trammel head without a pencil on the tip of the marked center point for the circle. Support the beam firmly near the trammel head at the center point for the circle and slowly move the end of the beam at the other trammel head, rotating it on the tip of the trammel head and drawing the pencil along the surface in a smooth curve around it *(above)*.

## USING A CARPENTER'S LEVEL

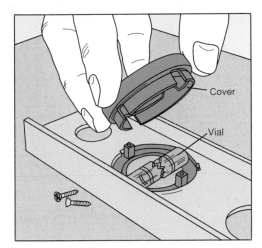

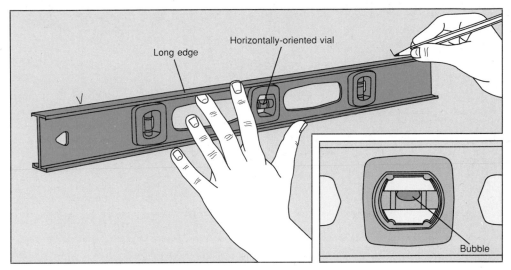

**Inspecting and servicing a carpenter's level.** Inspect a carpenter's level before using it. If a vial is broken, try to replace it. If the vial is molded to a casing, pry it out and snap in a replacement. On other models, unscrew the vial cover *(above)*, then replace the vial and put back the cover. To check the level, stand it level on one of its long edges; note the bubble position in the horizontal vial. Turn the level 180 degrees and stand it on the same edge at the same spot; the bubble position should be the same. Check the other long edge the same way. If the bubble position is not the same for each reading, the level should not be used.

**Marking and checking for level or plumb lines and points.** If necessary, use a tape measure to mark an end point for any line *(page 32)*. Prepare to use your carpenter's level *(step left)*. To mark a level (perfectly horizontal) line on a vertical surface, hold the level flat against it and align one end of a long edge with any marked end point or reference point; then, move the other end slightly up or down, examining the bubble in the horizontally-oriented vial. When the bubble is exactly centered in the vial *(inset)*, use a sharp pencil to mark points along the long edge *(above)*, then use a straightedge to mark a line between the points *(page 33)*.

To mark a plumb (perfectly vertical) line on a vertical surface, use the same procedure, holding the level vertical and examining the bubble in the horizontally-oriented vial. Mark a point that is level or plumb with another point on the same surface the same way. To check that a marked line is level, hold the level flat, aligning one long edge with the line. Examine the bubble in the horizontally-oriented vial; if it is exactly centered, the line is level. To check that a line is plumb, use the same procedure, holding the level vertical and examining the bubble in the horizontally-oriented vial.

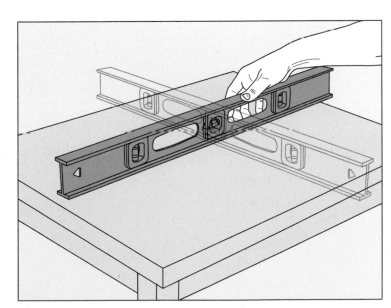

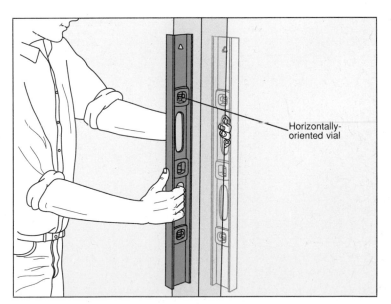

**Checking for a level surface.** Before checking that a horizontal surface is level (perfectly horizontal), check that it is flat *(page 33)*; if necessary, trim or smooth it *(page 78)*. To check that a flat surface is level, prepare to use your carpenter's level *(step above, left)*, then stand one long edge across the center of the surface and examine the bubble in the horizontally-oriented vial. Turn the level 90 degrees and stand it on the same edge across the same spot *(above)*; examine the bubble in the horizontally-oriented vial again. If the bubble is exactly centered for both readings, the surface is level.

**Checking for a plumb surface.** Before checking that a vertical surface is plumb (perfectly vertical), check that it is flat *(page 33)*; if necessary, trim or smooth it *(page 78)*. To check that a flat surface is plumb, prepare to use your carpenter's level *(step above, left)*, then hold one long edge against the surface and examine the bubble in the horizontally-oriented vial. If the bubble is exactly centered, the surface is plumb. To check that a vertical object is plumb, check two adjacent surfaces the same way *(above)*; if each surface is plumb, the object is plumb.

## USING A LINE LEVEL

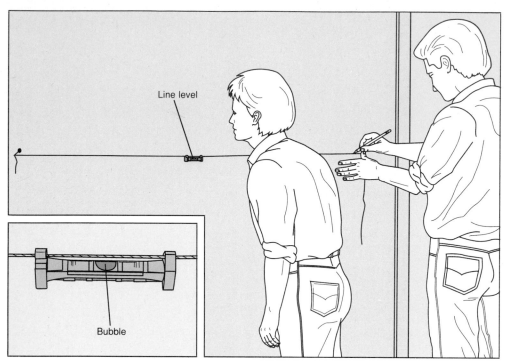

**Marking and checking for level.** If necessary, use a tape measure to mark an end point for any line *(page 32)*. To mark a point level (perfectly horizontal) with another point, use a line level and a strong string long enough to reach from the marked end point or reference point. Attach the string at the marked end point or reference point, then pull it taut to the surface to be marked and have a helper hang a line level on it at the midpoint. With your helper examining the bubble in the vial, hold the string against the surface and move it slightly up or down. When the bubble is exactly centered *(inset)*, steady the string and use a sharp pencil to mark a level point along it *(left)*.

To check that two points are level, use the line level and the string the same way, attaching the string at one point and pulling it taut to the other point; if the bubble is exactly centered, the points are level. To mark a level line between level points on the same surface, use a chalk line *(page 34)*. To check that a line is level, follow the same procedure with the line level and the string, attaching the string at one end point and pulling it taut to the other end point; if the bubble is exactly centered, the line is level.

## USING A WATER LEVEL

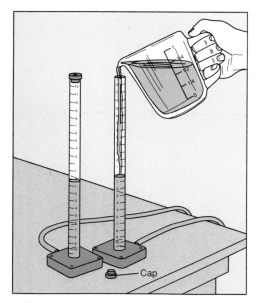

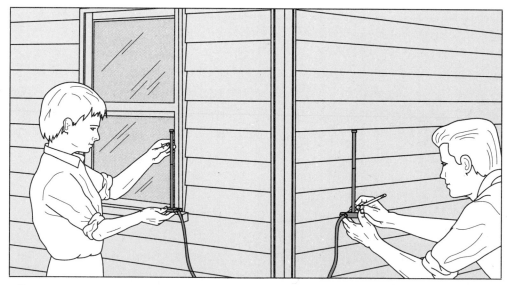

**1** **Setting up a water level.** Set up a water level with a hose long enough to reach between points being marked or checked. Attach the hose to each cylinder base; on the model shown, fit it onto the spigot. Stand the cylinders on a level surface and uncap one. Mix a little food coloring with water, then pour it into the uncapped cylinder *(above)* until it reaches the zero mark on each cylinder scale; tap the hose and the cylinders to release trapped air. Then, recap the cylinder. Hold a thumb over each cap hole to carry the cylinders.

**2** **Marking and checking for level.** If necessary, use a tape measure to mark an end point for any line *(page 32)*. To mark a point level (perfectly horizontal) with another point, have a helper align an edge of one cylinder base with the marked end point or reference point. Hold the other cylinder against the surface and move it slightly up or down. When the water level is at the zero mark on each cylinder scale, the cylinder bases are level; use a sharp pencil to mark a level point along the edge of the cylinder base corresponding to the one aligned by your helper *(above)*.

To check that two points are level, use the water level the same way, aligning a cylinder base at each point; if the water level is at the zero mark on each cylinder scale, the points are level. To mark a level line between level points on the same surface, use a chalk line *(page 34)*. To check that a line is level, follow the same procedure with the water level, aligning a cylinder base at each end point; if the water level is at the zero mark on each cylinder scale, the line is level. To check that a surface is level, stand each cylinder at opposite ends, then at opposite sides; if the water level is at the zero mark on each cylinder scale for both readings, the surface is level.

## USING A PLUMB BOB

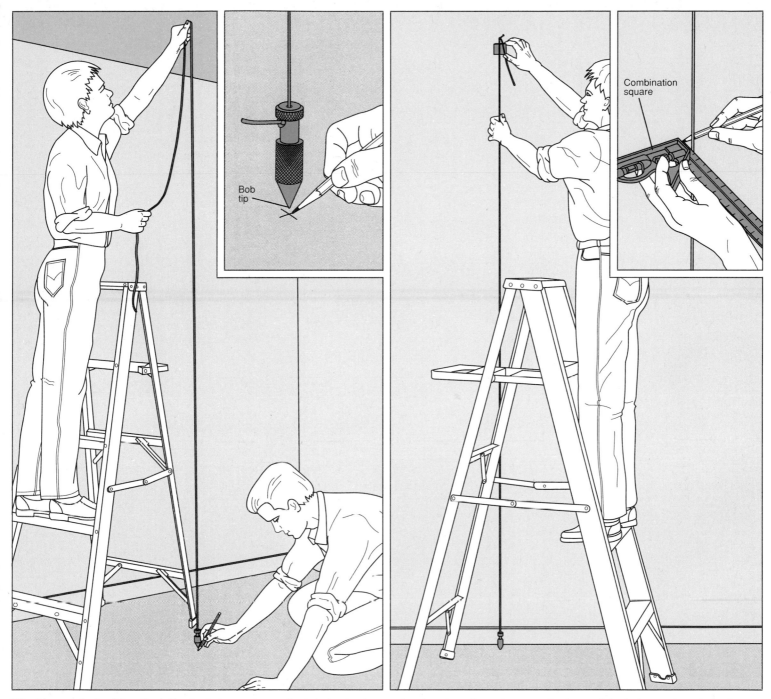

Bob
tip

Combination
square

**Marking and checking for plumb.** Before using a plumb bob, check the string; on the model shown, it should pass through the top and out the side of the bob, then be knotted. If necessary, use a tape measure to mark an end point for any line *(page 32)*. To hang a plumb bob, work with a helper and use a ladder, if necessary. To mark a point plumb (perfectly vertical) with another point on another surface, hold the string near the base of the bob at the marked end point or reference point. Slowly release the string, letting it slide through your fingers; stop when the bob tip is about 1/8 inch from the surface to be marked. If the bob swings, slow it. When the bob is still, have a helper use a sharp pencil to mark the point directly below its tip *(above, left)*, making an X *(inset, left)*. To check the mark, lower the bob so its tip just touches the surface; if it rests at the X center, the mark is plumb.

.To mark a point plumb with another point on the same surface, drive a nail partway into the surface at the marked end point or reference

point, then loop the string near the base of the bob over it and slowly release it until the bob tip is low enough for the surface to be marked. Tie the string to the nail; to keep it off the surface, wedge a 1-inch wood block behind it just below the nail *(above, right)*. Prepare to use your combination square *(page 35)*, then hold the 90-degree face of the handle against the surface with the blade just touching the string—but not deflecting it. Using a sharp pencil, mark a point along the edge of the handle directly behind the string *(inset, right)*.

To check that two points are plumb, use the plumb bob the same way. To mark a plumb line between plumb points on the same surface, use a chalk line *(page 34)*. To check that a line is plumb, follow the same procedure with the plumb bob and the combination square. To check that a surface is plumb, use the plumb bob and the combination square, measuring the distance between the surface and the string at a number of points; if each measurement is the same, the surface is plumb.

# CUTTING

Cutting tools are among the most frequently used in the home workshop; for almost every repair project, a piece needs cutting—to take it out of its position, or to fit it into place as a patch or a replacement. Cutting tasks fall into categories: sawing, routing, chiseling, snipping and scoring—and the first step in every job is choosing the right tool and technique. While some cutting tools like routers, chisels, tin snips and glass cutters are designed for specific cuts in specific materials, other cutting tools like power saws and handsaws can be used to make different cuts in different materials.

To choose the cutting tool best suited to your cutting task, refer to the inventory presented below and on page 44, and consult the Troubleshooting Guide *(page 45)*; check the section on the type of material you are cutting and refer to the inventory column for help in identifying types of cuts. In many instances, you may be given a choice of tools. For example, to make a wide groove cut in wood, you can use a router *(page 67)* or a wood chisel *(page 71)*. To help you choose the most appropriate cutting tool in these instances, refer to the specific repair acts included in the chapter.

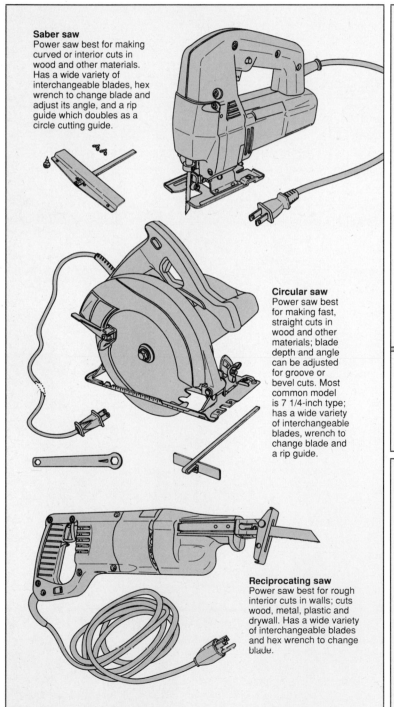

**Saber saw**
Power saw best for making curved or interior cuts in wood and other materials. Has a wide variety of interchangeable blades, hex wrench to change blade and adjust its angle, and a rip guide which doubles as a circle cutting guide.

**Circular saw**
Power saw best for making fast, straight cuts in wood and other materials; blade depth and angle can be adjusted for groove or bevel cuts. Most common model is 7 1/4-inch type; has a wide variety of interchangeable blades, wrench to change blade and a rip guide.

**Reciprocating saw**
Power saw best for rough interior cuts in walls; cuts wood, metal, plastic and drywall. Has a wide variety of interchangeable blades and hex wrench to change blade.

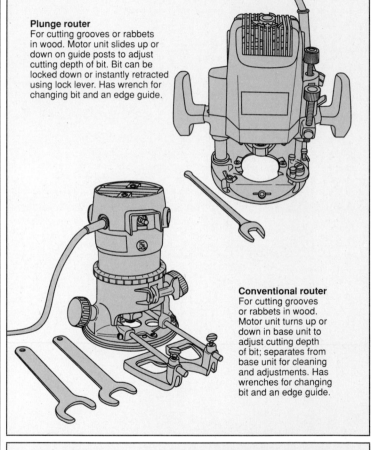

**Plunge router**
For cutting grooves or rabbets in wood. Motor unit slides up or down on guide posts to adjust cutting depth of bit. Bit can be locked down or instantly retracted using lock lever. Has wrench for changing bit and an edge guide.

**Conventional router**
For cutting grooves or rabbets in wood. Motor unit turns up or down in base unit to adjust cutting depth of bit; separates from base unit for cleaning and adjustments. Has wrenches for changing bit and an edge guide.

**Hole saw and electric drill**
Use a hole saw on a drill with a handle to cut holes 1 to 2-1/2 inches in diameter in wood; types for cutting metal or plastic also available. Install hole saw into chuck of drill and tighten with chuck key.

Safety and accuracy are essential for each cutting operation with any cutting tool; take the time to prepare properly. Read the chapter on Setting Up To Work *(page 14)* to determine the best, most secure setup for your job. As a general rule when you have a choice of cutting tools, use the one you are most comfortable handling—that is appropriate for the scale of the cutting task. For instance, the use of a power tool can require setup time that may not be worth taking for a small job; that may be worth taking for a small job if the alternative is a tool or technique unfamiliar to you.

Consult Measuring And Marking *(page 30)* to measure and mark accurately. Before using a cutting tool, carefully inspect it; repair it, if necessary. If you are working with a power tool, consult your owner's manual for instructions on its safe use; choose only the blades, bits or accessories recommended and ensure they are in good condition. When you use a cutting tool for the first time or in a new way and when you cut with a router, make test cuts in a scrap piece of your workpiece material; make a final cut only when you are satisfied with the tool performance and your technique.

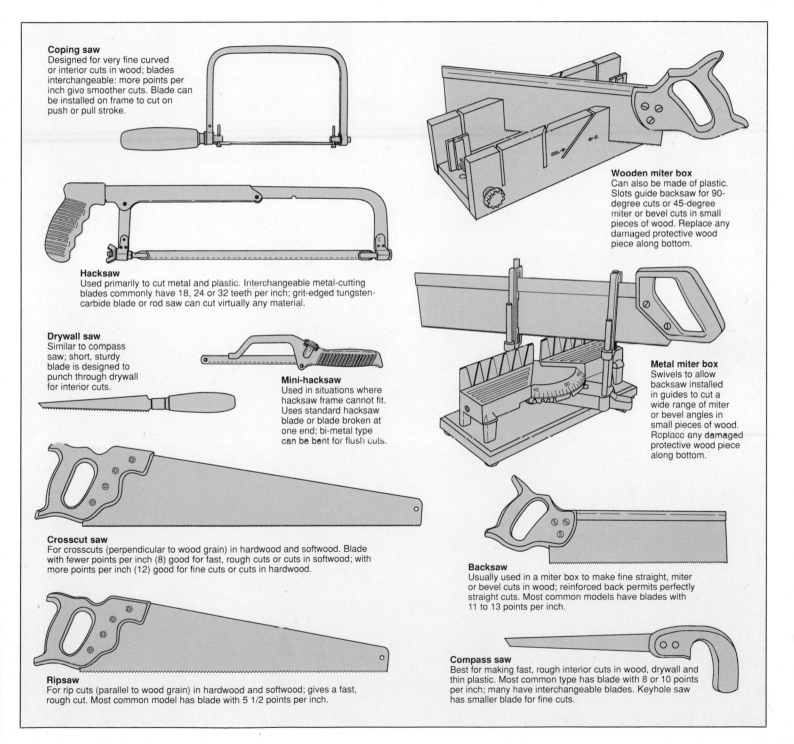

**Coping saw**
Designed for very fine curved or interior cuts in wood; blades interchangeable: more points per inch give smoother cuts. Blade can be installed on frame to cut on push or pull stroke.

**Hacksaw**
Used primarily to cut metal and plastic. Interchangeable metal-cutting blades commonly have 18, 24 or 32 teeth per inch; grit-edged tungsten-carbide blade or rod saw can cut virtually any material.

**Drywall saw**
Similar to compass saw; short, sturdy blade is designed to punch through drywall for interior cuts.

**Mini-hacksaw**
Used in situations where hacksaw frame cannot fit. Uses standard hacksaw blade or blade broken at one end; bi-metal type can be bent for flush cuts.

**Crosscut saw**
For crosscuts (perpendicular to wood grain) in hardwood and softwood. Blade with fewer points per inch (8) good for fast, rough cuts or cuts in softwood; with more points per inch (12) good for fine cuts or cuts in hardwood.

**Ripsaw**
For rip cuts (parallel to wood grain) in hardwood and softwood; gives a fast, rough cut. Most common model has blade with 5 1/2 points per inch.

**Wooden miter box**
Can also be made of plastic. Slots guide backsaw for 90-degree cuts or 45-degree miter or bevel cuts in small pieces of wood. Replace any damaged protective wood piece along bottom.

**Metal miter box**
Swivels to allow backsaw installed in guides to cut a wide range of miter or bevel angles in small pieces of wood. Replace any damaged protective wood piece along bottom.

**Backsaw**
Usually used in a miter box to make fine straight, miter or bevel cuts in wood; reinforced back permits perfectly straight cuts. Most common models have blades with 11 to 13 points per inch.

**Compass saw**
Best for making fast, rough interior cuts in wood, drywall and thin plastic. Most common type has blade with 8 or 10 points per inch; many have interchangeable blades. Keyhole saw has smaller blade for fine cuts.

Always wear the safety gear *(page 25)* recommended for the use of a cutting tool: safety goggles to protect your eyes from flying particles; respiratory protection to prevent the inhalation of harmful particles, dusts and mists; and hearing protection with a noisy power tool such as a circular saw or a router. Some types of materials that can be sharp when cut or that may be treated with chemicals—such as wood that is pressure-treated with preservatives—require skin protection when you handle them; as a rule, wear work gloves if you have any safety concerns about the material you are using.

Work slowly and carefully while using any cutting tool, standing with solid footing in a well-balanced position. Keep your fingers, hands and legs out of the cutting path. Never overreach during a cutting operation; stop and reposition your workpiece or yourself. If you are cutting with a power tool for an extended time, stop periodically and check that its blade or bit and adjustable parts are secure. Take care of your cutting tools; they are delicate instruments. Set a cutting tool down carefully to avoid damaging it; clean it properly after using it, then store it safely out of reach in a dry area.

**Wooden mallet**
Used to strike a wood chisel without damaging its handle; large face less likely to slip off chisel handle. May be used to strike a chisel with any type of handle.

**Hand drilling hammer**
Small sledgehammer used for striking a masonry chisel to cut brick or concrete block.

**Ball-peen hammer**
Used to strike wood chisel for heavy work; use only to strike chisel with plastic handle or wooden handle with ferrule at its end. May be used to strike masonry chisel when cutting brick or concrete block.

**Waterstone**
Used to sharpen chisels; coarse side for grinding, smooth side for honing. Available in different grits; 250-1000 grit model usually sufficient.

**Masonry chisels**
For scoring or cutting brick and concrete block; brick chisel has wide blade. Strike chisel with hand drilling hammer.

**Wood chisels**
Sharp beveled edge cuts and shapes wood; available in 1/4- to 2-inch widths and with wooden or plastic handles. For light work, use heel of hand to drive chisel; for heavy work, use wooden mallet or ball-peen hammer.

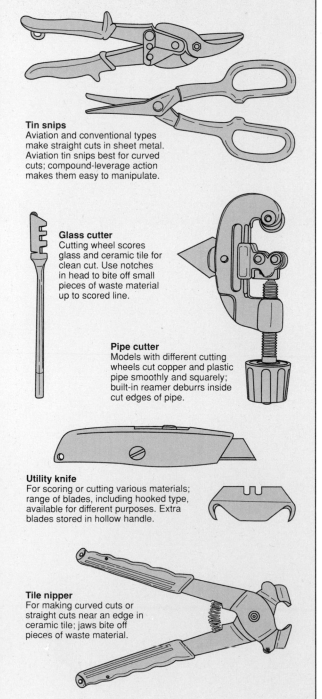

**Tin snips**
Aviation and conventional types make straight cuts in sheet metal. Aviation tin snips best for curved cuts; compound-leverage action makes them easy to manipulate.

**Glass cutter**
Cutting wheel scores glass and ceramic tile for clean cut. Use notches in head to bite off small pieces of waste material up to scored line.

**Pipe cutter**
Models with different cutting wheels cut copper and plastic pipe smoothly and squarely; built-in reamer deburrs inside cut edges of pipe.

**Utility knife**
For scoring or cutting various materials; range of blades, including hooked type, available for different purposes. Extra blades stored in hollow handle.

**Tile nipper**
For making curved cuts or straight cuts near an edge in ceramic tile; jaws bite off pieces of waste material.

# TROUBLESHOOTING GUIDE continued ►

| | PROBLEM | PROCEDURE |
|---|---|---|
| 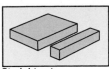 **Straight cut** | **WOOD** | |
| | **Making a cross cut (straight cut perpendicular to wood grain) in hardwood or softwood** | For a long cut, use a circular saw *(p. 50)* or a crosscut saw *(p. 59)* |
| | | For a short cut, use a saber saw *(p. 55)* or a backsaw *(p. 60)* |
| | | For a cut where no other saw can fit, use a compass saw or keyhole saw *(p. 61)* |
| 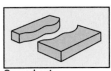 **Curved cut** | **Making a rip cut (straight cut parallel to wood grain) in hardwood or softwood** | For a long cut, use a circular saw *(p. 50)* or a rip saw *(p. 59)* |
| | | For a short cut, use a saber saw *(p. 55)* |
| | | For a cut where no other saw can fit, use a compass saw or keyhole saw *(p. 61)* |
| 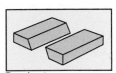 **Bevel cut** | **Making a straight cut in plywood or composition board** | For a long cut, use a circular saw *(p. 50)* or a crosscut saw *(p. 59)* |
| | | For a short cut, use a saber saw *(p. 55)* or a backsaw *(p. 60)* |
| | | For a cut where no other saw can fit, use a compass saw or keyhole saw *(p. 61)* |
| 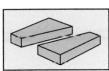 **Miter cut** | **Making a straight cut in veneer** | Use a circular saw *(p. 50)* or a utility knife *(p. 76)* |
| | **Making a curved cut** | Use a saber saw *(p. 55)* or a coping saw *(p. 62)* |
| | | For a cut where no other saw can fit, use a compass saw or keyhole saw *(p. 61)* |
| | | For a cut in veneer, use a utility knife *(p. 76)* |
| 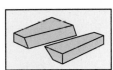 **Compound-angled cut** | **Making a miter cut** | For a long cut, use a circular saw *(p. 50)* or a crosscut saw *(p. 59)* |
| | | For a short cut, use a saber saw *(p. 55)* or a backsaw *(p. 60)* |
| | **Making a bevel cut** | For a long cut, use a circular saw *(p. 50)* |
| | | For a short cut, use a saber saw *(p. 55)* or a backsaw *(p. 60)* |
| 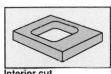 **Interior cut** | **Making a compound-angled (bevel/miter) cut** | For a long cut, use a circular saw *(p. 50)* |
| | | For a short cut, use a saber saw *(p. 55)* |
| | **Making an interior cut** | For a large square cutout, use a circular saw *(p. 52)* or a reciprocating saw *(p. 53)* |
| | | For a small square cutout, use a saber saw *(p. 56)* or a compass saw or keyhole saw *(p. 61)* |
| 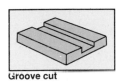 **Groove cut** | | For a large irregular or circular cutout, use a saber saw *(p. 56)* or a reciprocating saw *(p. 53)* |
| | | For a small irregular or circular cutout, use a saber saw *(p. 56)* or a coping saw *(p. 62)* |
| | | For a cut where no other saw can fit, use a compass saw or keyhole saw *(p. 61)* |
|  **Stopped groove cut** | **Making a hole** | Use a drill with a bit *(p. 100)*, a drill with a hole saw *(p. 58)* or a keyhole saw *(p. 61)* |
| | **Making a groove cut** | For a long, wide cut, use a router *(p. 67)* |
| | | For a long, narrow cut, use a circular saw *(p. 50)* |
| | | For a short, wide cut, use a wood chisel *(p. 71)* |
| | | For a short, narrow cut, use a backsaw *(p. 60)* |
| 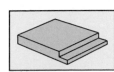 **Rabbet cut** | **Making a stopped groove cut** | Use a router *(p. 68)* |
| | **Making a rabbet cut** | For a long cut, use a router *(p. 69)* |
| | | For a short cut, use a backsaw *(p. 60)* |
| 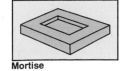 **Mortise** | **Making a mortise** | Use a wood chisel *(p. 72)* |

## TROUBLESHOOTING GUIDE (continued)

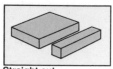

**Straight cut**

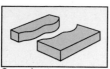

**Curved cut**

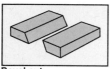

**Bevel cut**

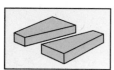

**Miter cut**

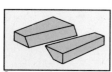

**Compound-angled cut**

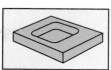

**Interior cut**

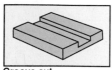

**Groove cut**

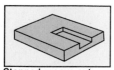

**Stopped groove cut**

**Rabbet cut**

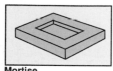

**Mortise**

| PROBLEM | PROCEDURE |
| --- | --- |
| **METAL** | |
| **Making a straight cut** | For a cut in sheet metal, use a hacksaw *(p. 63)*, tin snips *(p. 75)*, a circular saw *(p. 50)*, a saber saw *(p. 55)* or a utility knife *(p. 76)* |
| | For a cut in metal pipe, use a pipe or tubing cutter *(p. 76)*, a hacksaw *(p. 63)* or a circular saw *(p. 50)* |
| | For a cut in an extruded metal object, use a hacksaw *(p. 63)* or a circular saw *(p. 50)* |
| | For a cut in metal plate, use a hacksaw *(p. 63)* |
| | For a cut where no other saw can fit, use a mini-hacksaw *(p. 63)* |
| **Making a curved cut** | For a cut in sheet metal, use a hacksaw *(p. 63)*, tin snips *(p. 75)*, a saber saw *(p. 55)* or a utility knife *(p. 76)* |
| **Making an interior cut** | For a cut in sheet metal, use a hacksaw *(p. 63)*, tin snips *(p. 75)*, a saber saw *(p. 55)* or a utility knife *(p. 76)* |
| **Making a hole** | Use a drill with a bit *(p. 100)* or a hacksaw *(p. 63)* |
| **PLASTIC** | |
| **Making a straight cut** | For a cut in sheet plastic, use a circular saw *(p. 50)*, a saber saw *(p. 55)* or a utility knife *(p. 76)* |
| | For a cut in plastic pipe or tubing, use a pipe or tubing cutter *(p. 76)* or a hacksaw *(p. 63)* |
| | For a cut in plastic rod, use a hacksaw *(p. 63)* |
| | For a cut where no other saw can fit, use a mini-hacksaw *(p. 63)* |
| **Making a curved cut** | For a cut in sheet plastic, use a saber saw *(p. 55)*, a coping saw *(p. 62)*, a hacksaw *(p. 63)* or a utility knife *(p. 76)* |
| **Making an interior cut** | For a cut in sheet plastic, use a saber saw *(p. 56)*, a coping saw *(p. 62)*, a hacksaw *(p. 63)* or a utility knife *(p. 76)* |
| **Making a hole** | Use a drill with a bit *(p. 100)*, a coping saw *(p. 62)* or a hacksaw *(p. 63)* |
| **MASONRY** | |
| **Making a straight cut** | Use a masonry chisel *(p. 74)* or a circular saw *(p. 50)* |
| **CERAMIC TILE** | |
| **Making a straight cut** | Use a glass cutter *(p. 77)* or a hacksaw *(p. 63)* |
| | For a cut near an edge, use tile nippers *(p. 77)* |
| **Making a curved cut** | Use a coping saw *(p. 62)* or a hacksaw *(p. 63)* |
| | For a cut near an edge, use tile nippers *(p. 77)* |
| **Making a hole** | Use a drill with a bit *(p. 100)*, a coping saw *(p. 62)* or a hacksaw *(p. 63)* |
| **GLASS** | |
| **Making a straight cut** | Use a glass cutter *(p. 77)* |
| **DRYWALL** | |
| **Making a straight cut** | Use a saber saw *(p. 55)*, a compass saw, keyhole saw or drywall saw *(p. 61)* or a utility knife *(p. 76)* |
| **Making a curved cut** | Use a saber saw *(p. 55)* or a compass saw, keyhole saw or drywall saw *(p. 61)* |
| **Making an interior cut** | Use a reciprocating saw *(p. 53)*, a saber saw *(p. 56)* or a compass saw, keyhole saw or drywall saw *(p. 61)* |
| **Making a hole** | Use a drill with a bit *(p. 100)*, a drill with a hole saw *(p. 58)* or a keyhole saw or drywall saw *(p. 61)* |
| **PLASTER** | |
| **Making an interior cut** | Use a reciprocating saw *(p. 53)*, a saber saw *(p. 56)* or a compass saw or keyhole saw *(p. 61)* |

## SETTING UP A CUTTING GUIDE

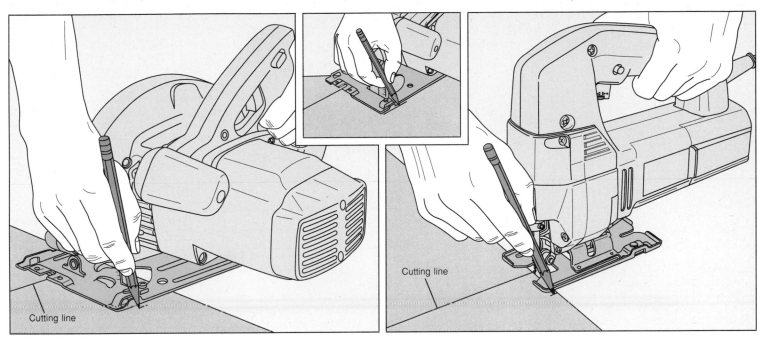

Cutting line

Cutting line

**1 Marking a position point.** If you are using a handsaw, choose and install a cutting guide *(step 3)*. If you are using a circular saw, unplug it and mark a position point for a cutting guide. If the cutting line is at 90 degrees to the edge of the workpiece, butt the saw blade against the end of it just to the waste side and rest the baseplate on the surface; orient the motor toward a supported end of the workpiece. Adjust the position of the saw until the line guide is aligned with the cutting line just to the waste side. Then, use a sharp pencil to mark a position point parallel to the cutting line along the baseplate on a supported end of the workpiece *(above, left)*. If the cutting line is at an angle other than 90 degrees to the edge of the workpiece, use the same procedure *(inset)*. If you are using a saber saw, unplug it and mark a position point for a cutting guide the same way, butting the saw blade against the end of the cutting line just to the waste side and marking a position point parallel to it along the baseplate *(above, right)*.

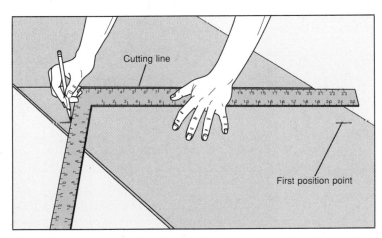

Cutting line

First position point

**2 Marking a second position point.** To measure the distance from the cutting line to the marked position point, use a carpenter's square *(page 36)*. If the cutting line is at 90 degrees to the edge of the workpiece, measure the distance from it to the marked position point along the edge. If the cutting line is at an angle other than 90 degrees to the edge of the workpiece, align the outer edge of the long arm with the cutting line and measure the distance from it to the marked position point along the outer edge of the short arm. To mark a second position point equal in distance from the cutting line on the same side at the other end of it, reposition the carpenter's square; then, align the outer edge of the long arm with the cutting line and mark the distance along the outer edge of the short arm using a sharp pencil *(above)*.

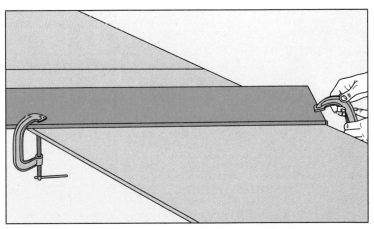

**3 Choosing and installing a cutting or routing guide.** If desired, buy a cutting guide and follow the manufacturer's instructions to set it up. To make a cutting or routing guide, use a straight-edged length of wood; the factory-cut edge of thick hardboard or plywood is ideal. Make sure the guide is of a width and height that can be clamped securely without it or the clamps obstructing your work. If you are using a circular saw, a saber saw or a router, use a guide that extends a few inches beyond each end of the cutting line. To install the guide, align its straight edge along the marked position points, then secure it with C clamps *(page 22)* along the edge farthest from the cutting line *(above)*; if necessary, use protective shims. If you are using a handsaw, use a guide at least as long as the cutting line; install it the same way, aligning its straight edge along the cutting line.

## PREPARING TO USE A CIRCULAR SAW

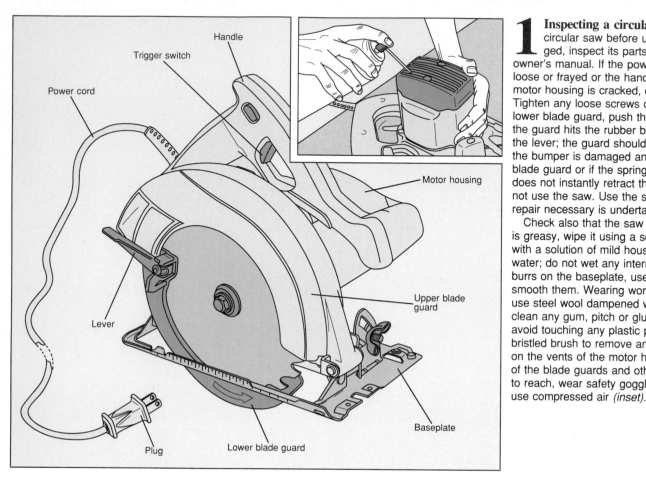

Power cord

Handle

Trigger switch

Lever

Plug

Lower blade guard

Motor housing

Upper blade guard

Baseplate

**1** **Inspecting a circular saw.** Check a circular saw before using it; with it unplugged, inspect its parts *(left)*, consulting your owner's manual. If the power cord or plug is loose or frayed or the handle, trigger switch or motor housing is cracked, do not use the saw. Tighten any loose screws or bolts. To check the lower blade guard, push the lever forward until the guard hits the rubber bumper, then release the lever; the guard should instantly retract. If the bumper is damaged and does not stop the blade guard or if the spring is damaged and does not instantly retract the blade guard, do not use the saw. Use the saw only after any repair necessary is undertaken.

Check also that the saw is clean. If the handle is greasy, wipe it using a soft cloth dampened with a solution of mild household detergent and water; do not wet any internal parts. If there are burrs on the baseplate, use a file *(page 88)* to smooth them. Wearing work gloves *(page 25)*, use steel wool dampened with mineral spirits to clean any gum, pitch or glue off the baseplate; avoid touching any plastic parts. Use a stiff-bristled brush to remove any caked sawdust; on the vents of the motor housing, the interior of the blade guards and other surfaces difficult to reach, wear safety goggles *(page 25)* and use compressed air *(inset)*.

**Standard combination blade**
All-purpose blade for wood, plywood or composition board; best for rough crosscuts (across grain) and rip cuts (along grain).

**Master combination (planer) blade**
All-purpose blade for wood, plywood or composition board; best for smooth crosscuts (across grain) and rip cuts (along grain).

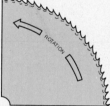

**Crosscut (cutoff) blade**
For crosscuts (across grain); leaves smoother cut edge than combination blade.

**Rip blade**
For rip cuts (along grain); provides greater cutting efficiency than a combination blade.

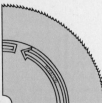

**Plywood (paneling) blade**
For splinter-free cuts in plywood, composition board or veneer; also good for cuts in thin plastic.

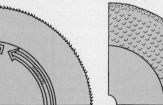

**Masonry abrasive blade**
Smooth-edged wheel for cutting concrete block, brick, slate or ceramic tile.

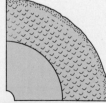

**Metal abrasive blade**
Smooth-edged wheel for cutting metal such as iron, steel, copper or aluminum.

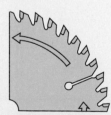

**Carbide-tipped blade**
Blade types with tungsten-carbide teeth more expensive but stay sharp longer; good for cutting most materials.

**2** **Choosing a circular saw blade.** Before using the circular saw, check that the blade is the right one for the job; consult the chart *(left)* to determine the blade best suited to the type of material and type of cut. A combination blade, for example, can cut wood, plywood or composition board, but if you need to make a large number of cuts or very fine cuts, use a specialty blade. For metal or masonry, use the appropriate wheel-type blade.

When buying a blade for your saw, read the label carefully. Check that the blade can be used on the material you are cutting and that its diameter matches the size of the saw (usually 7 1/4 inches). Also ensure that the arbor hole of the blade matches the arbor size of the saw (usually 5/8 inch). As well, check that the RPM rating of the blade is equal to or higher than the RPM rating of the saw—usually marked on its nameplate. In general, choose a blade marked hollow-ground or with a high number of teeth per inch for a smooth cut; one with a low number of teeth per inch for a rough cut.

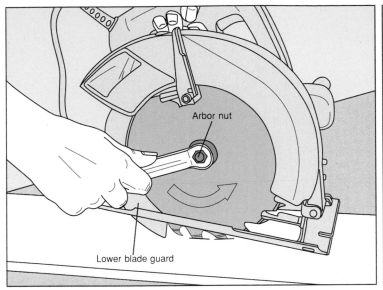

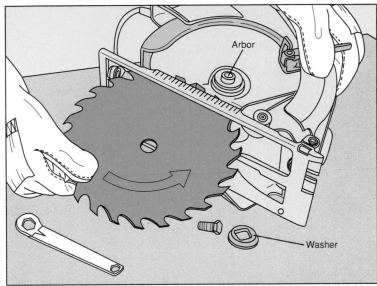

**3** **Inspecting, servicing and changing a blade.** To inspect, service or change a blade, ensure the circular saw is unplugged, then remove the blade. If the saw is equipped with an arbor lock, follow the owner's manual instructions to lock it; otherwise, as on the model shown, retract the lower blade guard enough to press the teeth of the blade into a scrap of soft wood. Holding the saw steady, loosen the arbor nut using the wrench supplied with the saw *(above, left)*. Remove the nut and any washers behind it, noting their positions for reassembly. Wearing work gloves *(page 25)*, retract the lower blade guard completely, then lift the blade off the arbor and slide it out. Use a small, stiff-bristled brush to clean any caked sawdust off the arbor. If the blade is bent or cracked or any teeth are chipped or missing, discard it.

If the blade is not damaged, use a soft cloth dampened with mineral spirits to wipe any gum, pitch or glue off it; dry it using a clean cloth. If you are changing the blade, apply a little light machine oil to it before storing it. Before installing a blade you have stored, wipe it with a soft cloth. Follow the owner's manual instructions to install the blade; it may require a special washer. On the model shown, retract the lower blade guard and slide in the blade *(above, right)*; ensure the rotational arrows on the blade face outward and in the same direction as any rotational arrow on the blade guard, and that the teeth of the blade point upward at the front of the saw. Fit the blade onto the arbor and install any washers necessary. Screw on and tighten the arbor nut by hand, then use the wrench to tighten it 1/8 of a turn.

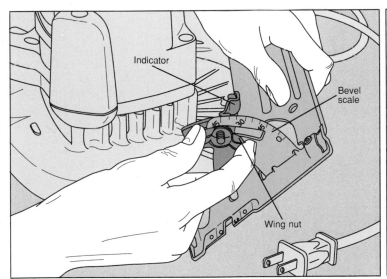

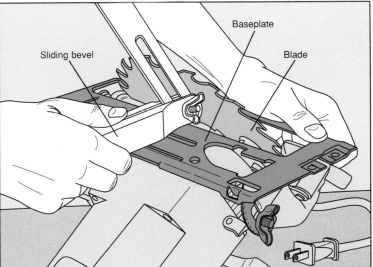

**4** **Adjusting the cutting angle of the blade.** Ensuring the circular saw is unplugged, follow the owner's manual instructions to set the cutting angle of the blade. For a straight, miter or groove cut, set the blade at an angle of 90 degrees; for a bevel or compound cut, set the blade at the angle desired. On the model shown, loosen the wing nut and carriage bolt on the bevel scale at the front of the saw, then pivot the baseplate until the indicator is aligned with the desired numerical point on the bevel scale *(above, left)*. Tighten the wing nut to set the baseplate position. If you are making a precision cut, check that the blade is set at the exact angle necessary; first, adjust the blade to its maximum cutting depth *(step 5)*.

To check a saw blade set at an angle other than 90 degrees, use a sliding bevel set to the angle desired *(page 37)*. Turn the saw upside down with its baseplate facing upward and retract the lower blade guard. Holding the outer edge of the bevel handle against the baseplate, butt its blade against the saw blade in the gullet between two teeth *(above, right)*. If the bevel blade and handle fit flush against the surfaces, the saw blade is set at the angle desired; otherwise, readjust its angle by resetting the baseplate position. If you cannot get the bevel blade and handle to fit flush against the surfaces, the saw may be out of alignment; have it professionally inspected. To check a saw blade set at an angle of 90 degrees, follow the same procedure using a try square *(page 35)*.

## PREPARING TO USE A CIRCULAR SAW (continued)

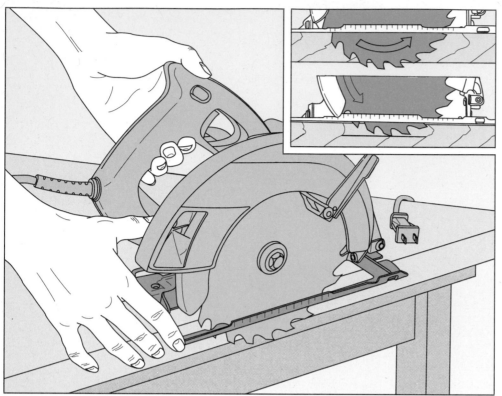

**5** **Adjusting the cutting depth of the blade.** Ensuring the circular saw is unplugged, follow the owner's manual instructions to set the cutting depth of the blade. If you are not cutting masonry or making a groove cut, set the blade to clear the workpiece. Holding the saw at the edge of the workpiece with the baseplate resting on the surface, retract the lower blade guard and press the blade against the edge, then release the guard. On the model shown, flip up the depth adjustment lever. Keeping the baseplate flat, pivot the saw by lifting the top handle until the lowest point of the blade is below the bottom edge of the workpiece: 1/8 inch if it is of metal; 1/4 inch if it is of another material *(inset, top)*. If the blade does not clear the workpiece at its maximum cutting depth, use a saber saw *(page 54)* or a handsaw *(page 58)*. Otherwise, lock the depth adjustment lever *(left)*.

If you are cutting masonry or making a groove cut, measure and mark *(page 30)* the cutting depth on the edge of the workpiece; with masonry, cut no deeper than 1/4 inch at one time. Then, set the cutting depth of the blade using the same procedure, locking the depth adjustment lever when the lowest point of the blade is aligned with the marked depth line *(inset, bottom)*.

## USING A CIRCULAR SAW (STRAIGHT AND GROOVE CUTS)

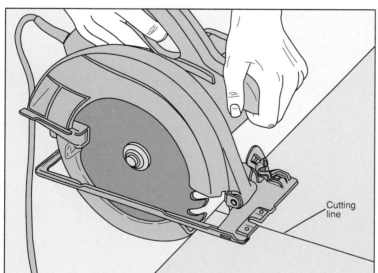

Cutting line

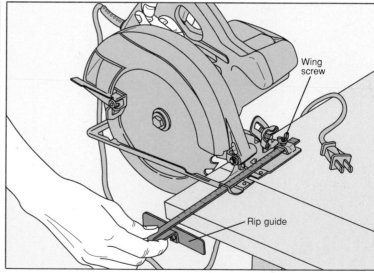

Wing screw

Rip guide

**Preparing to make a cut.** Set up the workpiece on a work surface *(page 17)* with its finished side facing down; measure and mark *(page 30)* a cutting line on it. Prepare to use a circular saw *(page 48)*; if you are cutting metal or masonry, ensure the work area is free of flammable materials. For a long or precision cut, set up a cutting guide *(page 47)*. For a long cut parallel to and less than 5 inches from a straight edge, buy a rip guide for your saw model and follow the manufacturer's instructions to install it; on the model shown, slide its arm into the baseplate slots. To position the saw, wear safety goggles, hearing protection *(page 25)* and respiratory protection *(page 26)*; if you are cutting metal or masonry, also wear work gloves *(page 25)*.

If you are not using a rip guide, plug in the saw *(page 24)* using an extension cord, if necessary *(page 23)*. Standing to one side of the cutting line, hold the saw by its top handle and auxiliary handle or knob; orient the motor toward a supported end of the workpiece. If you have not installed a cutting guide, butt the blade against the cutting line just to the waste side and rest the baseplate on the surface; if you installed a cutting guide, butt the side of the baseplate against it. Then, pull the saw back slightly so the blade is not touching the workpiece *(above, left)*. If you are using a rip guide, first slide it snug against the workpiece *(above, right)* and tighten its wing screw, then plug in the saw and position it. Ensure the power cord is clear of the blade.

## USING A CIRCULAR SAW (STRAIGHT AND GROOVE CUTS) (continued)

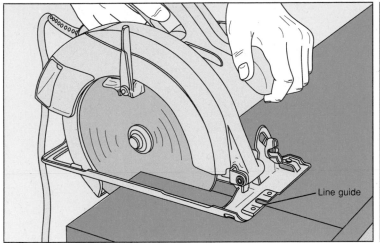

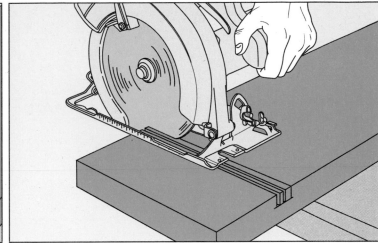

**Making a cut in wood or plastic.** Standing to one side of the saw and gripping it firmly, depress any trigger release button, then depress and hold the trigger switch. When the blade is turning at full speed, guide the saw into the workpiece at the cutting line; move it slowly if you are cutting plywood, composition board or plastic, or making a groove or bevel cut. The lower blade guard should retract as it hits the workpiece; if it catches, let go of the auxiliary handle or knob to retract it manually. **Caution:** Keep your hand clear of the blade. Watching the line guide position, continue along the cutting line *(above, left)*, letting the blade cut at its own speed. If the line guide veers from the cutting line, gently guide the saw forward to it. If you are using a cutting guide, keep the baseplate pressed firmly against it; if you are using a rip guide, keep it pulled snug against the workpiece.

If the blade slows while cutting, continue but do not force the saw; it may kick back. If the blade binds, immediately release the trigger switch and let the blade stop; to continue, fit a small wedge in the cut behind the saw, back up the saw slightly and position the blade, then start again. If the blade smokes, immediately release the trigger switch and let the blade stop; inspect the blade *(page 49)* before starting again. If the saw screeches or vibrates, immediately release the trigger switch; have the saw professionally inspected. To finish the cut, keep the trigger switch depressed and guide the saw out of the workpiece. When the saw is clear, release the trigger switch and allow the lower blade guard to retract, then let the blade stop and set the saw down. To make a series of parallel groove cuts, repeat the procedure at 1/8- to 1/4-inch intervals *(above, right)*, then clear the waste material using a chisel *(page 71)*. Store your tools and clean up *(page 27)*.

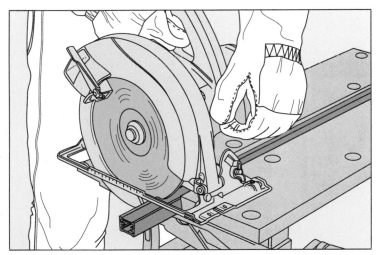

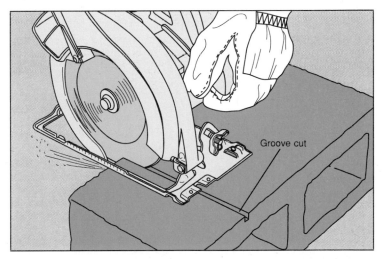

**Making a straight cut in metal.** Standing to one side of the saw and gripping it firmly, depress any trigger release button, then depress and hold the trigger switch. When the blade is turning at full speed, guide the saw slowly into the workpiece at the cutting line. The lower blade guard should retract as it hits the workpiece; if it catches, let go of the auxiliary handle or knob to retract it manually. **Caution:** Keep your hand clear of the blade. Watching the blade or line guide position, continue along the cutting line *(above)*, letting the blade cut at its own speed; it may shatter if forced or twisted. If the saw screeches or vibrates, immediately release the trigger switch; have the saw professionally inspected. To finish the cut, guide the saw out of the workpiece, then release the trigger switch and allow the lower blade guard to retract. Let the blade stop and set the saw down. To deburr any cut edge, use a file *(page 87)*. Store your tools and clean up *(page 27)*.

**Making a straight cut in masonry.** Standing to one side of the saw and gripping it firmly, depress any trigger release button, then depress and hold the trigger switch. When the blade is turning at full speed, guide the saw slowly into the workpiece at the cutting line. The lower blade guard should retract as it hits the workpiece; if it catches, let go of the auxiliary handle or knob to retract it manually. **Caution:** Keep your hand clear of the blade. Watching the line guide position, continue along the cutting line, letting the blade cut at its own speed. If the saw screeches or vibrates, immediately release the trigger switch; have the saw professionally inspected. To finish the cut, guide the saw out of the workpiece, then release the trigger switch and allow the lower blade guard to retract. Let the blade stop and set the saw down. Adjust the cutting depth *(page 50)* to repeat the procedure *(above)*, making successively deeper groove cuts. Store your tools and clean up *(page 27)*.

## USING A CIRCULAR SAW (INTERIOR CUTS)

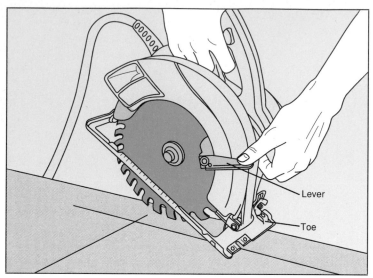

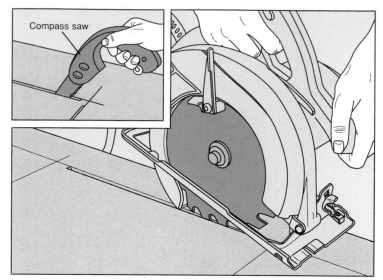

**1** **Preparing to make an interior cut.** Set up the workpiece on a work surface *(page 17)* with its finished side facing down; measure and mark *(page 30)* cutting lines on it. Prepare to use a circular saw *(page 48)*; wear safety goggles, hearing protection *(page 25)* and respiratory protection *(page 26)*. Plug in the saw *(page 24)* using an extension cord, if necessary *(page 23)*. Holding the saw by its top handle and retracting the lower blade guard manually, stand to the side at one end of a cutting line; orient the motor toward the supported side of the cutting line. Resting the toe of the baseplate on the surface, align the blade and the line guide with the cutting line near the end of it just to the waste side. Then, pivot the saw forward on the toe of the baseplate, raising the blade off the surface *(above)*; ensure the power cord is clear of the blade.

**2** **Making an interior cut.** Standing to one side of the saw and gripping it firmly, depress any trigger release button, then depress and hold the trigger switch. When the blade is turning at full speed, carefully lower it straight into the workpiece at the cutting line; when the baseplate rests flat on the surface, release the lower blade guard. Watching the line guide position, guide the saw along the cutting line, letting the blade cut at its own speed. If the line guide veers from the cutting line, gently guide the saw forward to it. When the blade reaches the end of the cutting line, release the trigger switch and let it stop. Pivot the saw forward on the toe of the baseplate to raise the blade and let the lower blade guide retract *(above)*, then lift the saw. Use the same procedure along each cutting line, then use a compass saw *(page 58)* to finish the cuts *(inset)*. Store your tools and clean up *(page 27)*.

## PREPARING TO USE A RECIPROCATING SAW

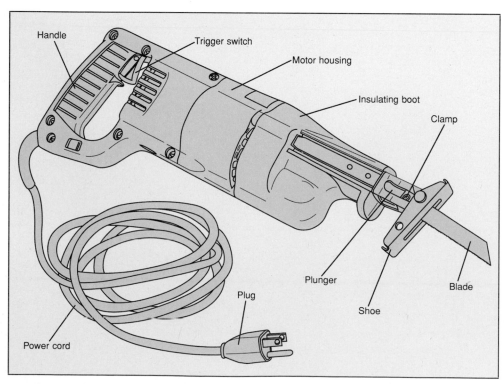

**1** **Inspecting a reciprocating saw.** Check a reciprocating saw before using it; with it unplugged, inspect its parts *(left)*, consulting your owner's manual. If the power cord or plug is loose or frayed, the handle, trigger switch, motor housing or insulating boot is cracked or the shoe is broken, do not use the saw. Tighten any loose screws. If the saw is equipped with a pivoting shoe, check that it pivots freely. Use the saw only after any repair necessary is undertaken.

Check also that the saw is clean. If the handle or insulating boot is greasy, wipe it using a soft cloth dampened with a solution of mild household detergent and water; do not wet any internal parts. If there are burrs on the shoe, use a file *(page 88)* to smooth them. Wearing work gloves *(page 25)*, use steel wool dampened with mineral spirits to clean any gum, pitch or glue off the shoe; avoid touching any plastic parts. Use a stiff-bristled brush to remove any caked sawdust from the shoe, clamp and plunger; on the vents of the motor housing and other surfaces difficult to reach, wear safety goggles *(page 25)* and use compressed air.

## PREPARING TO USE A RECIPROCATING SAW (continued)

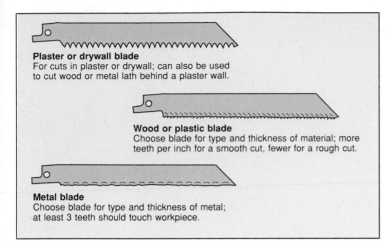

**Plaster or drywall blade**
For cuts in plaster or drywall; can also be used to cut wood or metal lath behind a plaster wall.

**Wood or plastic blade**
Choose blade for type and thickness of material; more teeth per inch for a smooth cut, fewer for a rough cut.

**Metal blade**
Choose blade for type and thickness of metal; at least 3 teeth should touch workpiece.

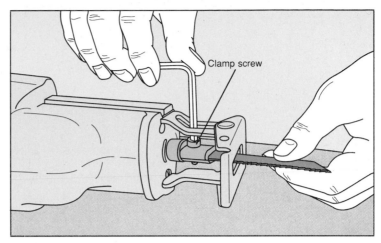

Clamp screw

**2** **Choosing a reciprocating saw blade.** Before using the reciprocating saw, check that the blade is the right one for the job. Consult the chart *(above)* to determine the blade best suited to the type of material and type of cut; many specialty blades are also available. In general, use a blade just long enough to pass through the workpiece; for a curved cut, use the narrowest blade possible. Choose a blade with a high number of teeth per inch for a smooth cut; one with a low number of teeth per inch for a rough cut. When buying a blade for your saw, read the label carefully. Check that the blade can be used on the material you are cutting and that it fits your saw. Buy several blades to keep on hand in the event one breaks; choose a type made of sturdy bi-metal rather than of steel.

**3** **Inspecting, servicing and changing a blade.** Ensure the reciprocating saw is unplugged, then remove the blade following the owner's manual instructions. On the model shown, loosen the clamp screw using the wrench supplied with the saw, then lift the clamp and pull out the blade. If the blade is bent or cracked or any teeth are chipped or missing, discard it. If the blade is not damaged, use a soft cloth dampened with mineral spirits to wipe any gum, pitch or glue off it; dry it using a clean cloth. To install a blade, refer to the owner's manual for its orientation; on the model shown, the teeth face the bottom of the saw. Lift the clamp and slide in the blade, positioning its hole under the clamp pin. Push the clamp down and use the wrench to tighten the clamp screw *(above)*.

## USING A RECIPROCATING SAW (INTERIOR CUTS)

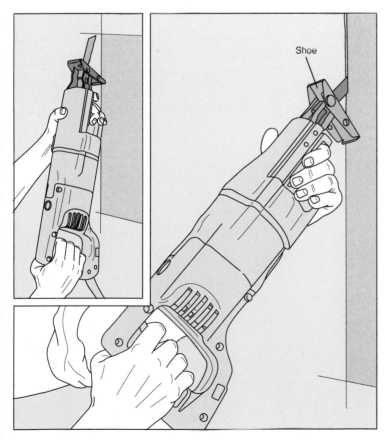

Shoe

**Making an interior cut.** Set up the workpiece on a work surface *(page 17)*, then measure and mark *(page 30)* cutting lines on it; if you are working on a wall, ensure there are no electrical wires or plumbing pipes behind it. Prepare to use a reciprocating saw *(page 52)*, consulting the owner's manual to set any speed selector switch for the material being cut; wear safety goggles *(page 25)* and respiratory protection *(page 26)*. Plug in the saw *(page 24)* using an extension cord, if necessary *(page 23)*.

For most materials, make a plunge entry. Holding the saw at one end of a cutting line with the teeth of the blade facing away from you, rest the edge of the shoe on the surface and align the blade with the cutting line just to the waste side. Then, pivot the saw on the edge of the shoe, raising the blade off the surface *(inset)*; ensure the power cord is clear of the blade. Gripping the saw firmly, depress and hold the trigger switch. When the blade is moving at full speed, carefully lower it straight into the workpiece at the cutting line *(left)*. If you cannot make a plunge entry, use a drill *(page 100)* to make a starting hole for the blade slightly larger than it just to the waste side of the cutting line.

When the shoe rests flat on the surface, guide the saw along the cutting line, letting the blade cut at its own speed and watching its position. If the blade veers from the cutting line, gently guide the saw ahead to it; avoid twisting the blade. When the blade reaches the end of the cutting line, release the trigger switch and let the blade stop, then lift the saw. Use the same procedure along each cutting line. Store your tools and clean up *(page 27)*.

## PREPARING TO USE A SABER SAW

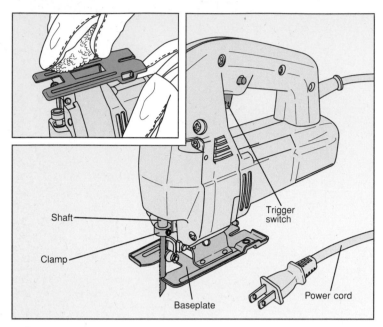

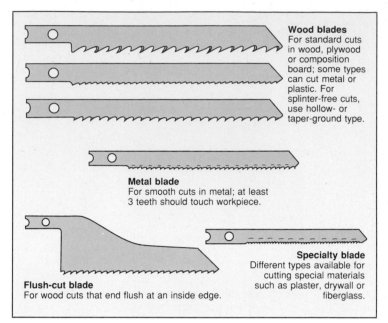

**Wood blades**
For standard cuts in wood, plywood or composition board; some types can cut metal or plastic. For splinter-free cuts, use hollow- or taper-ground type.

**Metal blade**
For smooth cuts in metal; at least 3 teeth should touch workpiece.

**Flush-cut blade**
For wood cuts that end flush at an inside edge.

**Specialty blade**
Different types available for cutting special materials such as plaster, drywall or fiberglass.

**1** **Inspecting a saber saw.** Check a saber saw before using it; with it unplugged, inspect its parts *(above)*, consulting your owner's manual. If the power cord or plug is loose or frayed, the handle, trigger switch or housing is cracked, or the clamp or shaft is damaged, do not use the saw. Tighten any loose screws. Use the saw only after any repair necessary is undertaken. To clean the saw, use a soft cloth dampened with a solution of mild household detergent and water. Use a file *(page 88)* to smooth any burrs on the baseplate; wearing work gloves *(page 25)*, use steel wool dampened with mineral spirits to clean any gum, pitch or glue off it *(inset)*. Use a stiff-bristled brush to remove any caked sawdust; on the vents and other surfaces difficult to reach, wear safety goggles *(page 25)* and use compressed air.

**2** **Choosing a saber saw blade.** Before using the saber saw, check that the blade is the right one for the job. Consult the chart *(above)* to determine the blade best suited to the type of material and type of cut; many specialty blades are also available. In general, use a blade just long enough to pass through the workpiece; for a curved cut, use the narrowest blade possible. Choose a blade with a high number of teeth per inch for a smooth cut; one with a low number of teeth per inch for a rough cut. When buying a blade for your saw, read the label carefully. Check that the blade can be used on the material you are cutting and that it fits your saw. Buy several blades to keep on hand in the event one breaks; choose a type made of sturdy bi-metal rather than of steel.

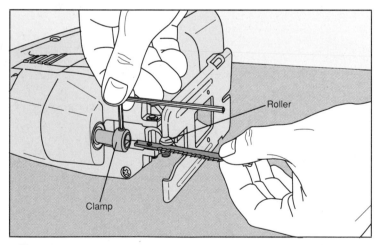

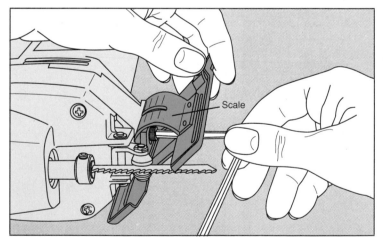

**3** **Inspecting, servicing and changing a blade.** Ensure the saber saw is unplugged, then remove the blade following the owner's manual instructions. On the model shown, loosen the clamp setscrew using the wrench supplied with the saw, then pull out the blade; if it is broken, use long-nose pliers to extract it. If the blade is bent or cracked or any teeth are chipped or missing, discard it. If the blade is not damaged, use a soft cloth dampened with mineral spirits to wipe any gum, pitch or glue off it; dry it using a clean cloth. To install a blade, orient the teeth toward the front of the saw. On the model shown, slide the blade into the clamp and seat it in the roller groove with its hole positioned below the setscrew, then use the wrench to tighten the setscrew *(above)*.

**4** **Adjusting the cutting angle of the blade.** Ensuring the saber saw is unplugged, follow the owner's manual instructions to set the cutting angle of the blade. For a straight or miter cut, set the blade at an angle of 90 degrees; for a bevel or compound cut, set the blade at the angle desired. On the model shown, loosen the setscrew under the baseplate using the wrench supplied with the saw, then pivot the baseplate until the edge of the housing is aligned with the desired numerical point on the bevel scale *(above)*. Tighten the setscrew to set the baseplate position. If you are making a precision cut, check that the blade is set at the exact angle necessary as you would with a circular saw *(page 49)*; if necessary, loosen the setscrew to readjust the cutting angle of the blade.

## USING A SABER SAW (STRAIGHT AND CURVED CUTS)

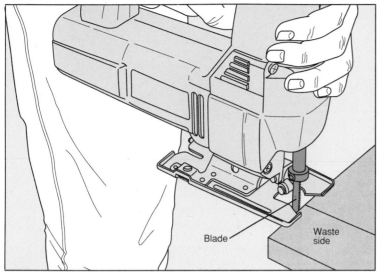

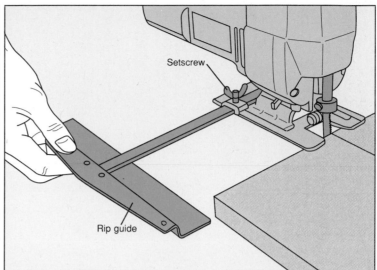

Setscrew

Blade

Waste side

Rip guide

**1** **Preparing to make a cut.** Set up the workpiece on a work surface *(page 17)* with its finished side facing down; measure and mark *(page 30)* a cutting line on it. Prepare to use a saber saw *(page 54)*, consulting the owner's manual to set any speed selector switch for the material being cut. For a precision straight cut, set up a cutting guide *(page 47)*. For a straight cut parallel to and less than 6 inches from a straight edge, buy a rip guide for your saw model and follow the manufacturer's instructions to install it; on the model shown, slide its arm into the baseplate slots. To position the saw, wear safety goggles *(page 25)* and respiratory protection *(page 26)*; if you are cutting metal, also wear work gloves *(page 25)*.

If you are not using a rip guide, plug in the saw *(page 24)* using an extension cord, if necessary *(page 23)*. Standing to one side of the cutting line, hold the saw by the handle and the front of the housing. If you have not installed a cutting guide, butt the blade against the cutting line just to the waste side and rest the baseplate on the surface; if you installed a cutting guide, butt the side of the baseplate against it. Then, pull the saw back slightly so the blade is not touching the workpiece *(above, left)*; keep the front edge of the baseplate flat on the surface. If you are using a rip guide, first slide it snug against the workpiece *(above, right)* and tighten its setscrew, then plug in the saw and position it. Ensure the power cord is clear of the blade.

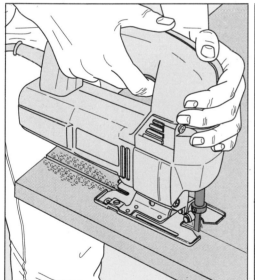

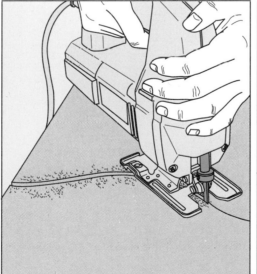

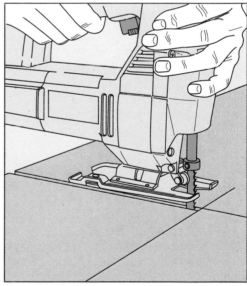

**2** **Making a cut.** Standing to one side of the saw and gripping it firmly, depress and hold the trigger switch; when the blade is moving at full speed, guide the saw slowly into the workpiece at the cutting line. For a straight cut, continue along the cutting line *(above, left)*, letting the blade cut at its own speed and watching its position. For a curved cut, use the same procedure *(above, center)*. If the curve is sharp, bypass it; cut straight to another point of the cutting line on the waste side, then complete the curve after the rest of the cut is finished.

If the blade veers from the cutting line, gently guide the saw ahead to it; avoid twisting the blade. If you are using a cutting guide, keep the baseplate pressed firmly against it; if you are using a rip guide, keep it pulled snug against the workpiece. If the blade slows or you have

difficulty keeping it aligned, release the trigger switch and let the blade stop, then change it *(page 54)*. If the blade binds, immediately release the trigger switch and let the blade stop; to continue, fit a small wedge in the cut behind the saw, then back up the saw slightly and start again. If the saw screeches or vibrates, immediately release the trigger switch; have the saw professionally inspected.

To finish the cut at an edge, keep the trigger switch depressed and guide the saw out of the workpiece. When the saw is clear, release the trigger switch and let the blade stop, then set the saw down. To finish the cut in the interior, release the trigger switch when the blade reaches the end of the cutting line, then let the blade stop and lift the saw *(above, right)*. Store your tools and clean up *(page 27)*.

## USING A SABER SAW (INTERIOR CUTS)

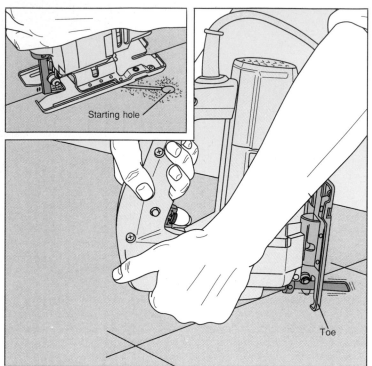

Starting hole

Toe

**1** **Starting a cut.** Set up the workpiece on a work surface *(page 17)* with its finished side facing down; measure and mark *(page 30)* cutting lines on it. Prepare to use a saber saw *(page 54)*, consulting the owner's manual to set any speed selector switch for the material being cut; if you are making a circular cut, buy a cutting guide for your saw model. To position the saw, wear safety goggles *(page 25)* and respiratory protection *(page 26)*; if you are cutting metal, also wear work gloves *(page 25)*. Plug in the saw *(page 24)* using an extension cord, if necessary *(page 23)*.

For most materials, make a plunge entry. Holding the saw near one end of a cutting line on the waste side, rest the toe of the baseplate on the surface and pivot the saw on it, raising the blade off the surface; ensure the power cord is clear of the blade. Gripping the saw firmly, depress and hold the trigger switch. When the blade is moving at full speed, carefully lower it straight into the workpiece *(left)*. If you cannot make a plunge entry, use a drill *(page 100)* to make a starting hole for the blade slightly larger than it near the cutting line just to the waste side. When the baseplate rests flat on the surface, guide the saw to the cutting line, releasing the trigger switch when the blade is aligned with it just to the waste side *(inset)*. Make the cut freehandedly *(step 2)* or using a cutting guide *(step 3)*.

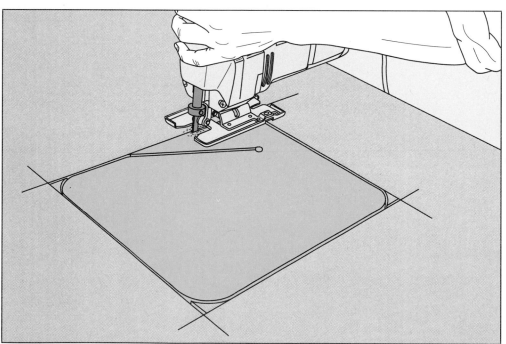

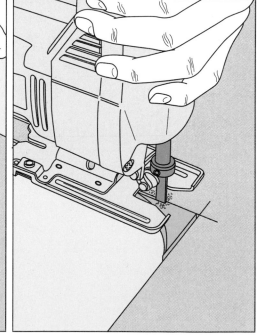

**2** **Making a freehanded cut.** Standing to one side of the saw and gripping it firmly, depress and hold the trigger switch. When the blade is moving at full speed, guide it slowly along the cutting line just to the waste side. For a straight cut, continue along the cutting line, letting the blade cut at its own speed and watching its position. For a curved cut, use the same procedure. If the curve is sharp, bypass it; cut straight to another point of the cutting line on the waste side, then complete the curve after the rest of the cut is finished.

If the blade veers from the cutting line, gently guide the saw ahead to it; avoid twisting the blade. If the blade slows or you have difficulty keeping it aligned, release the trigger switch and let the blade stop, then change it *(page 54)*. If the blade binds, immediately release the trigger

switch and let the blade stop; to continue, back up the saw slightly, then depress the trigger switch. If the saw screeches or vibrates, immediately release the trigger switch; have the saw professionally inspected.

For a square interior cut, continue until the blade reaches the end of the cutting line, then release the trigger switch and let the blade stop; back up the saw slightly and cut a curve that bypasses the corner, guiding the blade to the adjacent cutting line. Use the same procedure along each cutting line *(above, left)*, ensuring the workpiece center is supported; shift it on the work surface or drive a nail *(page 117)* into it to hold. Release the trigger switch when the blade reaches the end of the cut, then let the blade stop and lift the saw. Complete each corner the same way *(above, right)*. Store your tools and clean up *(page 27)*.

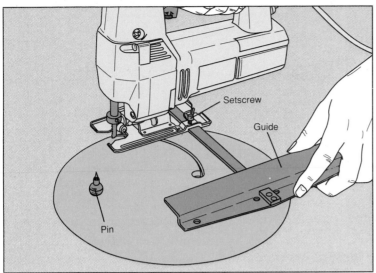

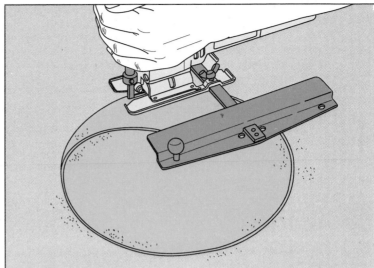

**3** **Making a circular cut with a cutting guide.** For a precision circular cut up to 14 inches in diameter, use a cutting guide; on the model shown, a rip guide can be turned over and used. Unplug the saw and install the cutting guide following the manufacturer's instructions; on the model shown, hold it with the arm down and slide it into the baseplate slots. Lifting the saw slightly, slide the cutting guide until a hole is positioned on the marked center point of the circle *(above, left)*; keeping the hole in position, lower the saw and rest the baseplate on the surface. Push the pin of the cutting guide through the hole into the marked center point; if necessary, tap it with a hammer. Then, tighten the setscrew to secure the cutting guide and plug in the saw.

Standing to one side of the saw and gripping it firmly, depress and hold the trigger switch. When the blade is moving at full speed, guide the saw slowly forward, letting the cutting guide draw it in an arc around the marked center point and watching the blade position. If the blade veers from the cutting line, release the trigger switch and let the blade stop, then adjust the cutting guide. Continue along the cutting line the same way *(above, right)*, ensuring the workpiece center is supported as you reach the end of the cut; shift it on the work surface or drive a nail *(page 117)* into it to hold. Release the trigger switch when the blade reaches the end of the cut, then let the blade stop and lift the saw. Store your tools and clean up *(page 27)*.

## PREPARING TO USE A HOLE SAW

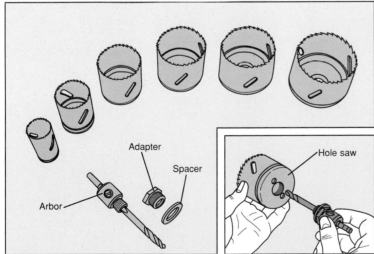

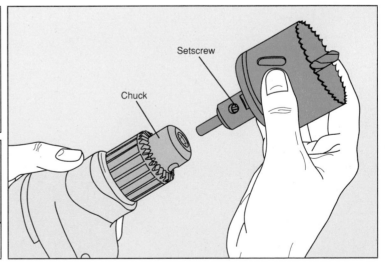

**Setting up a hole saw.** For a precision hole from 1 to 2 1/2 inches in diameter, use a hole saw of the same diameter as the cut and an electric drill. Hole saws for your drill model are usually available in kits; ensure a hole saw can be used on the material you are cutting and that its arbor fits the drill chuck. To assemble the hole saw, follow the manufacturer's instructions; on the model shown *(above, left)*, install a hole saw 1 1/2 inches or larger in diameter only on a drill with a side handle and a 3/8-inch or larger chuck. To install a hole saw 1 3/8 inches or larger in diameter, use an adapter; screw it onto the threaded end of the arbor and slip a spacer onto its threaded end, then fit the hole saw over the arbor *(inset)* and screw it in place. To install a hole saw less than 1 3/8 inches in diameter, screw it in place directly onto the threaded end of the arbor. The bit of the arbor should protrude about 1/4 inch beyond the teeth of the hole saw; if necessary, loosen the arbor setscrew to reposition the bit, then retighten it. Prepare to use the drill *(page 100)*, fitting it with a detachable side handle if there is no built-in one. Then, insert the bit of the arbor into the chuck *(above, right)*, installing it as you would any other bit *(page 101)*.

## USING A HOLE SAW

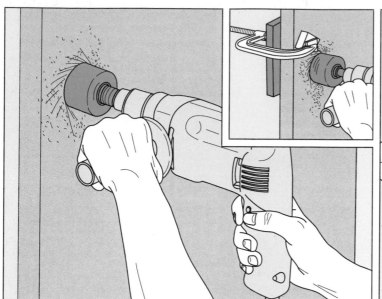

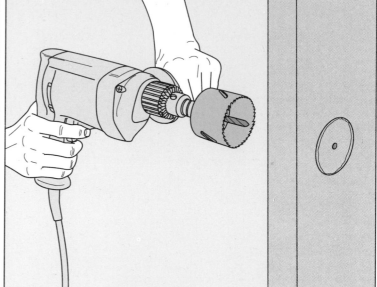

**Making a cut.** Set up the workpiece on a work surface, if necessary *(page 17)*; then, measure and mark *(page 30)* a center point for the cut. If the workpiece is 3/4 inch or less thick, secure a piece of wood behind it with C clamps *(page 22)* to keep it from splintering; use protective shims on the finished side, if necessary. Prepare to use a hole saw *(page 57)*, setting any drill speed switch to SLOW and reversing switch to FORWARD; wear safety goggles *(page 25)* and respiratory protection *(page 26)*. Plug in the drill *(page 24)* using an extension cord, if necessary *(page 23)*.

Gripping the drill firmly, hold it perpendicular to the workpiece and push the bit against the marked center point. Ensuring the power cord is clear of the hole saw, depress and hold the trigger switch to run the drill slowly; apply even pressure to sink the bit *(above, left)*. If the drill slows,

increase its speed; if it strains, decrease its speed or your pressure. To prevent overheating, periodically pull the drill straight back, then release the trigger switch and let the hole saw stop. Clear sawdust out of the cut, then continue when the hole saw is cool. If there is smoke or a burning odor, immediately pull the drill straight back. Continue the procedure until the hole saw exits the other side of the workpiece; if you secured a piece of wood behind it *(inset)*, ensure it can clear each C clamp. If the hole saw cannot cut deeper and has not exited the other side of the workpiece, pull it straight back. Replace the hole saw with a long twist bit *(page 101)*, then drill into the center point of the hole until the twist bit exits. Reinstall the hole saw and continue the procedure on the other side of the workpiece *(above, right)*; turn it over, if necessary. When the cut is finished, store your tools and clean up *(page 27)*.

## PREPARING TO USE A HANDSAW

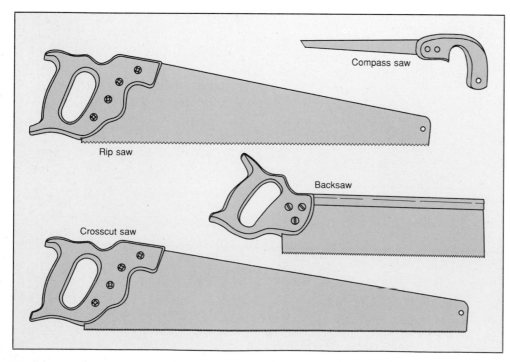

Compass saw

Rip saw

Backsaw

Crosscut saw

**Inspecting a handsaw.** Choose a handsaw *(page 43)* for the type of cut you are making, checking that the blade is the right one for the job; in general, use a blade with a high number of teeth or points per inch for a smooth cut; one with a low number of teeth or points per inch for a rough cut. Inspect the saw *(left)* before using it. If the handle is loose, tighten its screws or bolts; if it is broken, you may be able to replace it. If the blade is warped or any teeth are missing, buy a new saw; with a compass saw, it may be possible to replace the blade. If the blade is chipped or uneven or it cuts poorly, have it professionally sharpened. Use a soft cloth dampened with mineral spirits to wipe any gum, pitch or glue off the blade; wearing work gloves *(page 25)*, use steel wool dampened with light machine oil to remove any rust. When buying a new blade or handle, choose an exact duplicate; take the old one with you. To change the blade or handle, follow the manufacturer's instructions; with the saws shown, remove the bolts from the handle and slide out the blade, then reverse the procedure to install the new blade or handle.

## USING A CROSSCUT SAW

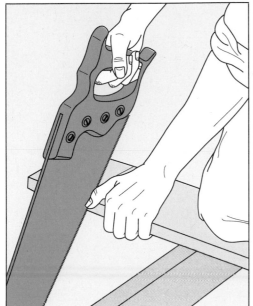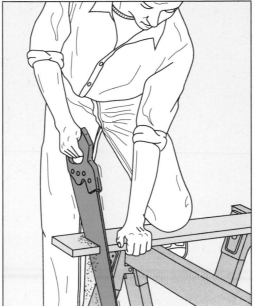

**Making a straight cut.** Set up the workpiece on a work surface *(page 17)* at knee level; measure and mark *(page 30)* a cutting line on it. For a precision cut, set up a cutting guide *(page 47)*. Prepare to use a crosscut saw *(page 58)*. Standing to one side of the cutting line, hold the saw almost perpendicular and butt the blade against the end of it just to the waste side; rest your knee on the workpiece to steady it, if necessary. Gripping the workpiece, rest your thumb against the blade to guide it and draw the saw toward you several times *(above, left)*, notching the edge; if it jumps, lower the angle. Lower the saw to a 45-degree angle, align your arm and shoulder with the blade, and start the cut with short strokes; push the saw down firmly and pull it up lightly. Gradually lengthen the strokes, fully extending your arm on the downstroke *(above, center)* and drawing it back on the upstroke. If the blade wanders from the cutting line, steadily guide it back; if it buckles or vibrates, realign your arm and shoulder with it. If the blade binds, inspect it *(page 58)*; it may need cleaning or sharpening. When the blade is 1 inch from the end of the cutting line, raise the saw almost perpendicular and finish the cut with short strokes, steadying any unsupported end of the workpiece *(above, right)*. If necessary, trim or smooth the cut edge *(page 78)*. Store your tools and clean up *(page 27)*.

## USING A RIP SAW

Wedge

**Making a straight cut.** Set up the workpiece on a work surface *(page 17)* at knee level; measure and mark *(page 30)* a cutting line on it. For a precision cut, set up a cutting guide *(page 47)*. Prepare to use a rip saw *(page 58)*. Standing to one side of the cutting line, hold the saw almost perpendicular and butt the blade against the end of it just to the waste side; steady the workpiece with your knee, if necessary. Gripping the workpiece, rest your thumb against the blade to guide it and draw the saw toward you several times, notching the edge; if it jumps, lower the angle. Lower the saw to a 60-degree angle, align your arm and shoulder with the blade, then start the cut with short, firm strokes, gradually lengthening them *(far left)*. If the blade wanders from the cutting line, steadily guide it back; if it buckles or vibrates, realign your arm and shoulder with it. If the blade binds, inspect it *(page 58)*; if necessary, fit a small wedge in the cut, as shown. When the blade is 1 inch from the end of the cutting line, raise the saw almost perpendicular and finish the cut with short strokes, steadying any unsupported end of the workpiece *(near left)*. If necessary, trim or smooth the cut edge *(page 78)*. Store your tools and clean up *(page 27)*.

## USING A BACKSAW

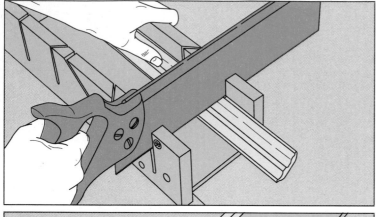

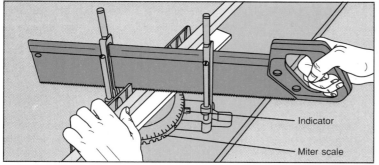

Indicator

Miter scale

Cutting guide

**Making a straight cut.** Set up the workpiece on a work surface *(page 17)*; measure and mark *(page 30)* a cutting line or point on it. For a precision cut, set up a miter box along an edge of the work surface; use C clamps *(page 22)* to secure it, if necessary. Position the workpiece flush against the back of the miter box, aligning the cutting line or point with the appropriate slot. If the workpiece is too large for a miter box, set up a cutting guide *(page 47)*. Prepare to use a backsaw *(page 58)*.

If you are using a wooden miter box, slide the saw into the slots appropriate for the cutting angle and rest the blade level on the workpiece at the cutting line or point just to the waste side; adjust the position of the workpiece, if necessary *(above left, top)*. If you are using a metal

miter box, follow the manufacturer's instructions to set the arm at the cutting angle desired; on the model shown, depress the lever, swivel the arm until its indicator intersects the numerical point on the miter scale and release the lever. Then, slide the saw into the slots and position the blade the same way *(above left, bottom)*. If you are using a cutting guide, set the saw against it, positioning the blade the same way.

Steadying the workpiece, draw the saw toward you several times to notch it. Aligning your arm and shoulder with the blade, use long, smooth strokes to make the cut *(above, right)*, pushing away firmly and pulling back lightly. If necessary, trim or smooth the cut edge *(page 78)*. Store your tools and clean up *(page 27)*.

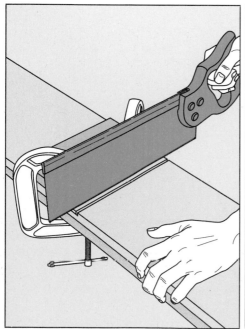

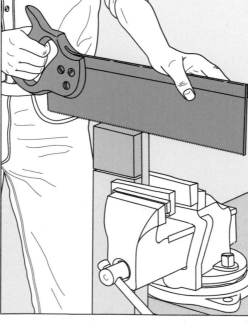

**Making a groove cut.** Set up the workpiece on a work surface *(page 17)*; measure and mark *(page 30)* a cutting line and a depth line at each end of it. For a precision cut, set up a cutting guide *(page 47)*. Prepare to use a backsaw *(page 58)*. Setting the saw against any cutting guide, rest the blade level on the workpiece at the cutting line just to the waste side. Steady the workpiece and draw the saw toward you several times to notch it. Aligning your arm and shoulder with the blade, use long, smooth strokes to make the cut, pushing away firmly and pulling back lightly. Continue until the blade reaches the depth line at each end of the cutting line. To make a series of parallel groove cuts, repeat the procedure at 1/8- to 1/4-inch intervals *(far left)*, then clear the waste material using a chisel *(page 71)*. To make a rabbet cut at an end of the workpiece, make two groove cuts: one across the width; the other at a 90-degree angle to it across the end grain. Steadying the saw, use the same procedure to cut across the end grain *(near left)* until the blade reaches each end of the first groove cut. Store your tools and clean up *(page 27)*.

## USING A COMPASS, KEYHOLE OR DRYWALL SAW

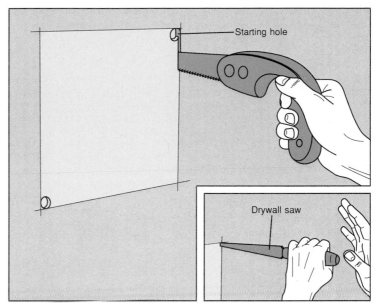

**Making a straight or curved cut.** If necessary, set up the workpiece on a work surface *(page 17)*, then measure and mark *(page 30)* a cutting line on it. Prepare to use a handsaw *(page 58)*. To make a straight cut with a compass saw, hold it at a 45-degree angle to the edge of the workpiece *(above)* and set the blade along any cutting line just to the waste side. Gripping the handle firmly with your thumb on one side to guide it, draw the saw toward you several times to notch the edge of the workpiece. Aligning your arm and shoulder with the blade, use long, smooth strokes to make the cut with its heel, pushing the saw away firmly and pulling it back lightly. To make a straight cut with a keyhole saw, use the same procedure. To make a curved cut, use the compass saw or keyhole saw the same way, using short strokes with its toe. If necessary, trim or smooth the cut edge *(page 78)*. Store your tools and clean up *(page 27)*.

**Making an interior cut.** If necessary, set up the workpiece on a work surface *(page 17)*, then measure and mark *(page 30)* cutting lines on it; if you are working on a wall, ensure there are no electrical wires or plumbing pipes behind it. Prepare to use a handsaw *(page 58)*. With a compass saw, use a drill *(page 100)* to make a starting hole: for a square cut, at two diagonally-opposite corners of the cutting lines just to the waste side; for a circular cut, at the cutting line just to the waste side. Fitting the blade into a hole and aligning your arm and shoulder with it, use short, smooth strokes to make the cut with its toe *(above)*; push away firmly and pull back lightly; for a square cut, repeat the procedure along each cutting line. With a keyhole saw, use the same procedure. With a drywall saw, align the tip of the blade with the cutting line just to the waste side and strike the handle sharply *(inset)*, plunging the blade; cut as you would with a knife. If necessary, trim or smooth any cut edge *(page 78)*. Store your tools and clean up *(page 27)*.

## PREPARING TO USE A COPING SAW

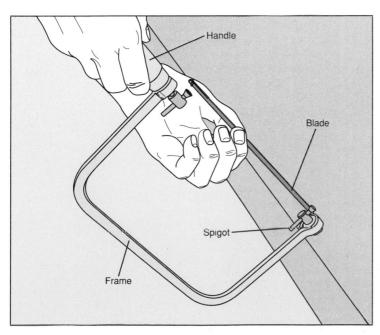

**Choosing, inspecting and changing a blade.** Inspect a coping saw before using it, checking that the blade is the right one for the type of material and type of cut. With a hard material such as ceramic tile or slate, use a specialty blade. In general, use a blade with a high number of teeth or points per inch for a smooth cut; one with a low number of teeth or points per inch for a fast, rough cut. If the blade is dirty, rusted, warped or broken or it cuts poorly, replace it.

To change the blade, follow the manufacturer's instructions. On the model shown, turn the handle counterclockwise to reduce the tension of the blade. Bracing the end of the frame against a fixed object, push the handle to loosen the blade, then lift it out of the spigot slots *(left)*. To install a new blade, orient it correctly: to cut on the pull stroke for a very smooth cut, with the teeth facing the handle; otherwise, with the teeth facing the end of the frame. Brace the end of the frame against a fixed object and push the handle, then slip the blade into the spigot slots; ensure the pin at each end of the blade is on the outer side of the spigot. Ease pressure on the handle and turn it clockwise to tighten the blade, keeping the spigots from turning with it.

## USING A COPING SAW

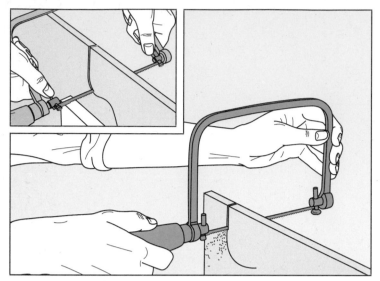

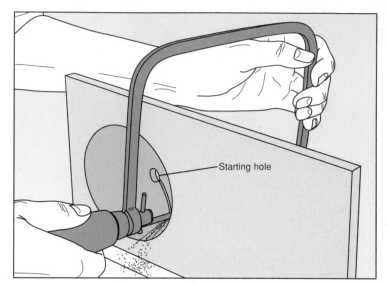

Starting hole

**Making a curved cut.** Set up the workpiece on a work surface *(page 17)*; measure and mark *(page 30)* a cutting line on it. Prepare to use a coping saw *(page 61)*, orienting the blade teeth toward the handle to work from the finished side of the workpiece; toward the end of the frame otherwise. Holding the saw across the edge of the workpiece and steadying the end of the frame, align the blade with the cutting line just to the waste side. Start the cut with short, smooth strokes, then gradually lengthen them; push the saw away firmly and pull it back lightly *(above)*, cutting on the appropriate stroke. Angle the frame to follow the cutting line; do not twist the blade. If a curve is sharp or the frame hits the workpiece, turn the handle to loosen the blade, then adjust the frame, holding the spigots to steady the blade *(inset)*; turn the handle to retighten the blade. If necessary, trim or smooth the cut edge *(page 78)*. Store your tools and clean up *(page 27)*.

**Making an interior cut.** Set up the workpiece on a work surface *(page 17)*; measure and mark *(page 30)* a cutting line on it. Use a drill *(page 100)* to make a starting hole for the blade of a coping saw near the cutting line on the waste side. Prepare to use the coping saw *(page 61)*, fitting the blade into the hole and then installing it on the frame; orient its teeth toward the handle to work from the finished side of the workpiece, toward the end of the frame otherwise. Holding the saw steady, use short, smooth strokes to guide the blade to the cutting line, then along it just to the waste side *(above)*; push away firmly and pull back lightly. Angle the frame to follow the cutting line; do not twist the blade. If the curve is sharp or the frame hits the workpiece, turn the handle to loosen the blade, then adjust the frame, holding the spigots to steady the blade; turn the handle to retighten the blade. If necessary, trim or smooth the cut edge *(page 78)*. Store your tools and clean up *(page 27)*.

## PREPARING TO USE A HACKSAW

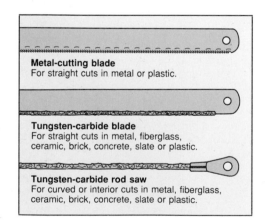

**Metal-cutting blade**
For straight cuts in metal or plastic.

**Tungsten-carbide blade**
For straight cuts in metal, fiberglass, ceramic, brick, concrete, slate or plastic.

**Tungsten-carbide rod saw**
For curved or interior cuts in metal, fiberglass, ceramic, brick, concrete, slate or plastic.

**1** **Choosing a blade.** Choose the right blade for the type of material using the chart *(above)*. In general, use a blade with a high number of teeth per inch (tpi) for a smooth cut; one with a low number of teeth per inch for a rough cut. As well, use the thickness of the workpiece as a guide: a 32 or 24 tpi blade to cut a thickness of less than 1/16 inch; a 24 or 18 tpi blade to cut a thickness of 1/16 to 1/4 inch; an 18 tpi blade to cut a thickness of more than 1/4 inch.

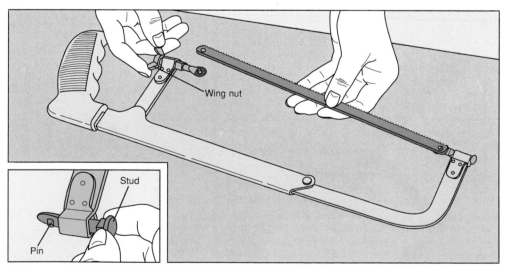

Wing nut

Stud

Pin

**2** **Changing and adjusting a blade.** To change or adjust a blade, follow the manufacturer's instructions. On the model shown, loosen the wing nut, then lift the blade off the studs *(above)*. To adjust the frame length, slide the back end until it catches in the appropriate notch of the front end. To adjust the blade angle, loosen the front stud and position its pin at the angle desired *(inset)*; then, loosen the back stud and position its pin at the same angle. With a metal-cutting blade, orient its teeth toward the front end of the frame, away from the handle. To install a blade, fit its holes onto the stud pins, then tighten the wing nut until it is rigid but not arched.

## USING A HACKSAW

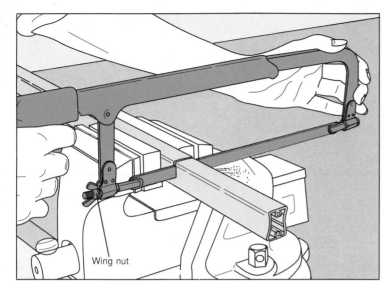

Wing nut

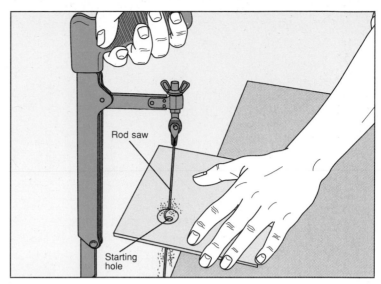

Rod saw

Starting hole

**Making a straight cut.** Set up the workpiece on a work surface *(page 17)*; measure and mark *(page 30)* a cutting line on it. Prepare to use a hacksaw *(page 62)*. Holding the saw steady, align the blade with the cutting line just to the waste side. With a metal-cutting blade, position at least 3 teeth on the workpiece, then push the saw away from you several times to notch it; lift the saw slightly to pull it back. Start the cut with short, smooth strokes, then gradually lengthen them; push away firmly *(above)* and pull back lightly. Angle the frame to follow the cutting line; do not twist the blade. If the frame hits the workpiece, adjust the blade *(page 62)*. With a tungsten-carbide blade or rod saw, use the same procedure, pushing away and pulling back firmly. If necessary, smooth the cut edge *(page 78)*. Store your tools and clean up *(page 27)*.

**Making an interior cut.** Set up the workpiece on a work surface *(page 17)*; measure and mark *(page 30)* a cutting line on it. Use a drill *(page 100)* to make a starting hole for the tungsten-carbide rod saw to be used as a blade with the hacksaw near the cutting line on the waste side. Then, prepare to use the hacksaw *(page 62)*, fitting the rod saw into the hole and then installing it on the frame. Holding the saw steady, use short, smooth strokes to guide the rod saw to the cutting line, then along it just to the waste side *(above)*; push away and pull back firmly. Swivel the frame to follow the cutting line along a curve or to change direction and follow an adjacent cutting line at a corner. If necessary, smooth the cut edge *(page 78)*. Store your tools and clean up *(page 27)*.

## USING A MINI-HACKSAW

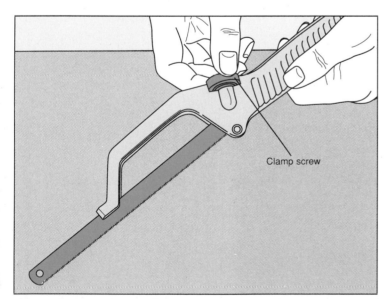

Clamp screw

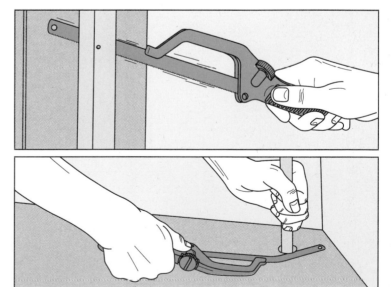

**1 Installing a blade.** If necessary, set up the workpiece on a work surface *(page 17)*; measure and mark *(page 30)* a cutting line on it. Use a mini-hacksaw when cutting with a standard hacksaw is impractical: access is obstructed or the workpiece is too small, for example. Choose a blade *(page 62)* and install it with its teeth facing away from the handle. Slide the blade into the slot of the handle, leaving enough extended to make the cut, then tighten the clamp screw *(above)*.

**2 Making a straight cut.** Gripping the handle of the saw, butt the blade against the workpiece along any cutting line just to the waste side. For example, fit the blade in a narrow opening *(above, top)* or set it flush with another surface, pressing the handle to bend it slightly *(above, bottom)*. Make the cut using short, smooth strokes, pushing the saw away firmly and pulling it back lightly. If necessary, smooth the cut edge *(page 78)*. Store your tools and clean up *(page 27)*.

## SETTING UP A GUIDE FOR A ROUTER

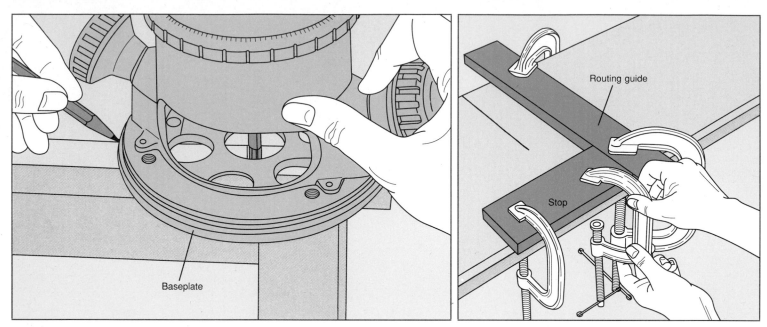

Baseplate

Routing guide

Stop

**Setting up a routing guide and a stop.** For a groove cut parallel to and less than 5 inches from a straight edge, set up an edge guide *(step below)*. Otherwise, set up a routing guide. To set up a routing guide, center the router at the starting end of the cutting line just to the waste side with its baseplate resting on the surface and the bit extended to the cutting depth. Turn the bit so its widest face is flush against the edge of the workpiece, then adjust the position of the router until the edge of the bit is aligned with the cutting line just to the waste side. Using a sharp pencil, mark a position point along the edge of the baseplate on the same side of the bit as the cutting line *(above, left)*. Mark a second position point equal in distance from the cutting line on the same side at the other end of it, then install a routing guide *(page 47)*. Set up a routing guide along any other parallel cutting line the same way.

For a stopped groove cut, also set up a stop. To set up a stop, use a carpenter's square *(page 36)* to measure the distance from the cutting line to the routing guide, then to measure the distance from one end to the other end of the cutting line. Add the two measurements together, then mark a position point along the inside edge of the routing guide equal to this total distance from the starting end of the cutting line. Using the carpenter's square, mark a position line perpendicular to the inside edge of the routing guide at the marked position point. To make a stop, use a straight-edged length of wood of the same thickness as the routing guide. To install the stop, set it against the inside edge of the routing guide with its straight edge aligned along the marked position line. Then, secure the stop with C clamps *(page 22)* along the edge farthest from the cutting line *(above, right)*; if necessary, use protective shims.

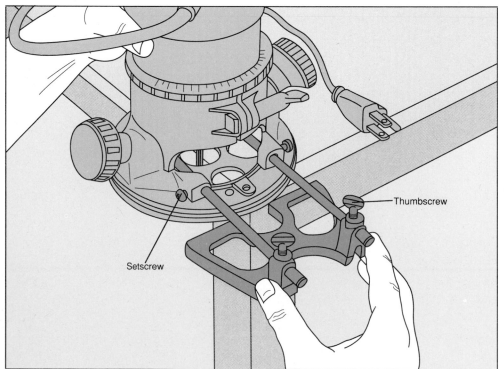

Thumbscrew

Setscrew

**Setting up an edge guide.** For a groove cut other than parallel to and less than 5 inches from a straight edge, set up a routing guide *(step above)*. Otherwise, buy an edge guide for your router model and install it following the manufacturer's instructions; on the model shown, slide the arms into the baseplate slots and tighten the setscrews. If necessary, smooth the edge of the workpiece *(page 78)* so the edge guide can travel easily along it. To adjust the edge guide, center the router at the starting end of the cutting line just to the waste side with its baseplate resting on the surface and the bit extended to the cutting depth. Turn the bit so its widest face is flush against the edge of the workpiece, then adjust the position of the router until the edge of the bit is aligned with the cutting line just to the waste side. Loosen the thumbscrews of the edge guide, then slide it snug against the workpiece *(left)* and tighten the thumbscrews.

# PREPARING TO USE A ROUTER

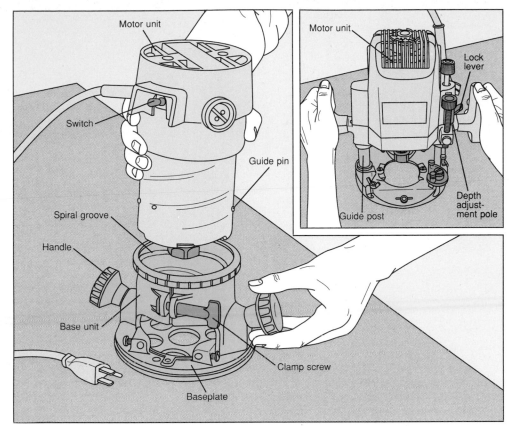

Motor unit
Switch
Guide pin
Spiral groove
Handle
Base unit
Clamp screw
Baseplate

Motor unit
Lock lever
Guide post
Depth adjustment pole

**1** **Inspecting a router.** Check a router before using it; with it unplugged, inspect its parts, consulting your owner's manual. If the power cord, plug or switch is faulty or the housing is damaged, do not use the router until any repair necessary is undertaken. Tighten any loose screws. Check also that the router is clean. With a conventional router, detach the motor unit from the base unit; on the model shown, loosen the clamp screw, then unscrew the motor unit and lift it out *(left)*, releasing its guide pins from the spiral grooves of the base unit. With a plunge router, raise its motor unit to maximum height; on the model shown, depress the lock lever to turn the height adjustment nut to its highest position, then flip it up to ease the motor unit up and down the guide posts *(inset)*. To clean dirt, gum or pitch off plastic parts, use a soft cloth dampened with a solution of mild household detergent and water; for metal parts, use a soft cloth dampened with mineral spirits, then apply a little silicone lubricant to any moving part you cleaned. If the motor unit of a plunge router slides poorly, apply a little silicone lubricant to the guide posts. If the baseplate is scratched, use sandpaper to smooth it. Remove any caked sawdust using a stiff-bristled brush; for vents and other surfaces difficult to reach, wear safety goggles *(page 25)* and use compressed air.

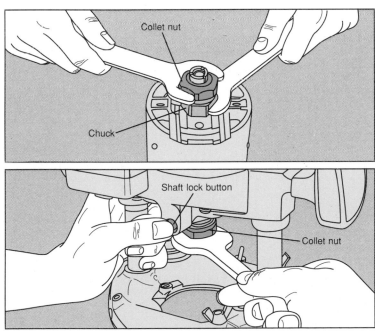

Collet nut
Chuck

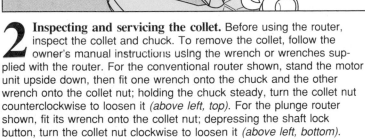

Shaft lock button
Collet nut

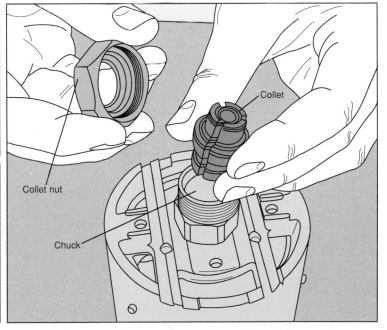

Collet nut
Chuck
Collet

**2** **Inspecting and servicing the collet.** Before using the router, inspect the collet and chuck. To remove the collet, follow the owner's manual instructions using the wrench or wrenches supplied with the router. For the conventional router shown, stand the motor unit upside down, then fit one wrench onto the chuck and the other wrench onto the collet nut; holding the chuck steady, turn the collet nut counterclockwise to loosen it *(above left, top)*. For the plunge router shown, fit its wrench onto the collet nut; depressing the shaft lock button, turn the collet nut clockwise to loosen it *(above left, bottom)*.

Unscrew the collet nut by hand and remove it, then lift the collet out of the chuck *(above right)*; on some models, you may need to snap it out of the collet nut. Inspect each part carefully; if it is worn, chipped or warped, replace it with an exact duplicate. Use a stiff-bristled brush to remove any caked sawdust. To clean gum, pitch or glue off a part, wear work gloves *(page 25)* and use steel wool dampened with mineral spirits, then apply a little silicone lubricant. To install the collet, reverse the sequence used to remove it; tighten the collet nut only a little by hand, then tighten it fully after choosing a bit *(step 3)* and installing it *(step 4)*.

## PREPARING TO USE A ROUTER (continued)

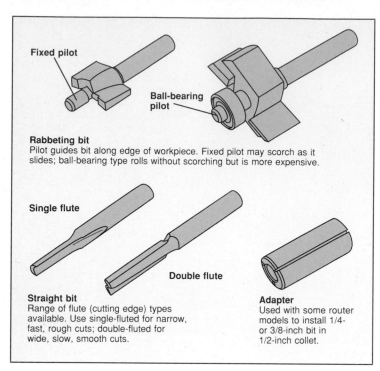

**Rabbeting bit**
Pilot guides bit along edge of workpiece. Fixed pilot may scorch as it slides; ball-bearing type rolls without scorching but is more expensive.

Fixed pilot

Ball-bearing pilot

Single flute

Double flute

**Straight bit**
Range of flute (cutting edge) types available. Use single-fluted for narrow, fast, rough cuts; double-fluted for wide, slow, smooth cuts.

**Adapter**
Used with some router models to install 1/4- or 3/8-inch bit in 1/2-inch collet.

**3** **Choosing a bit.** Before using the router, choose the right bit for the job, consulting the chart *(left)*; many specialty bits are also available. To make a groove cut or a stopped groove cut, use a straight bit; to make a rabbet cut, use a rabbeting bit. Choose a bit with a shank diameter that fits the chuck of your router. Use only a bit with a 1/4-inch shank for a router with a 1/4-inch chuck. For a router with a 1/2-inch chuck, you may be able to use bits with 1/4- or 3/8-inch shanks as well as with 1/2-inch shanks; follow the owner's manual instructions to install a smaller collet or use an adapter.

Choose a bit with a cutting depth equal to or greater than the depth of the cut you are making and with a cutting width equal to the width of the cut you are making. If a straight bit of the cutting width necessary is not available, choose one with a smaller cutting width and plan to use it to make overlapping parallel cuts; if a rabbeting bit of the cutting width necessary is not available, choose one with a smaller cutting width and plan to use a straight bit after it to widen the cut. For cuts in softwood, choose a high-speed steel bit; for cuts in hardwood, plywood or composition board or if you are buying a bit to be used frequently, choose a carbide-tipped type.

Inspect a bit before using it; if it is dull, warped or cracked or a flute is chipped, discard it. If there is caked sawdust, gum, pitch or glue on the tip of the bit, clean it using a soft cloth dampened with mineral spirits; on the shank of the bit, wear work gloves *(page 25)* and clean it using steel wool.

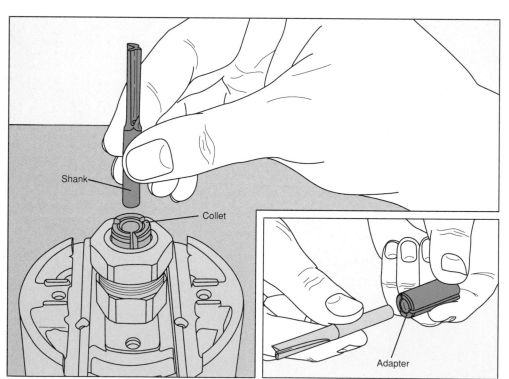

Shank

Collet

Adapter

**4** **Installing and tightening a bit.** Before installing a bit, check that the router is unplugged. Ensure a collet of the correct size is installed in the chuck and that its nut is screwed on loosely. If you are using a bit without an adapter, insert its shank into the collet *(above),* pushing it in as far as possible and then pulling it back out slightly—about 1/16 inch. If you are using a bit with an adapter, first slide the shank of the bit into the adapter *(inset),* then insert them together into the collet the same way. Holding the bit steady, tighten the collet nut fully by hand, then using the wrench or wrenches supplied with the router, reversing the procedure used to loosen it and inspect the collet *(step 2).* As a final check for a worn collet or chuck, carefully grasp the bit and try to shift it sideways; if it moves, the collet or chuck is worn and should be professionally serviced. If the collet nut is tight and the bit slips repeatedly while the router is in use, have the router professionally inspected.

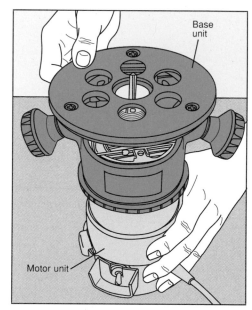

Base unit

Motor unit

**5** **Reassembling a conventional router.** If you are using a plunge router, set the cutting depth of the bit *(step 6).* To reassemble a conventional router, follow the owner's manual instructions, reversing the sequence used to disassemble and inspect it *(step 1).* With the model shown, stand the motor unit upside down and push the base unit as far as possible onto the bottom of it; then, screw the base unit onto the motor unit *(above),* the guide pins of the motor unit set firmly into the spiral grooves of the base unit. Tighten the clamp screw to secure the base unit to the motor unit.

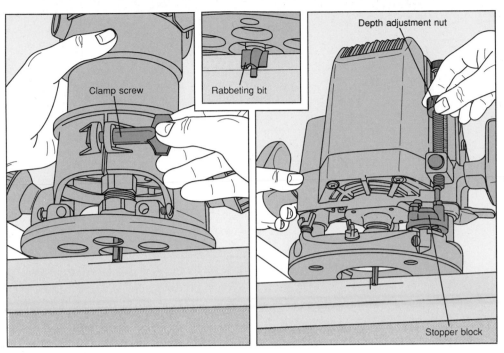

**6** **Setting the cutting depth of the bit.**
Measure and mark *(page 30)* a depth line on the edge of the workpiece at the starting end of the cutting line; cut no deeper than 1/4 inch at one time with softwood, 1/8 inch at one time with another material. To adjust the cutting depth of the bit, position the router at the starting end of the cutting line with its baseplate resting on the surface and follow the owner's manual instructions.

On the conventional router shown, loosen the clamp screw, then turn the motor unit to raise or lower it along with the bit. With a straight bit, align its tip with the depth line; with a rabbeting bit, align its bottom cutting edge with the depth line *(inset)*. To set the cutting depth of the bit, tighten the clamp screw *(far left)*.

On the plunge router shown, push the motor unit down until the bit is aligned with the depth line, then depress the lock lever. To set the router for plunging to the cutting depth, turn the depth adjustment pole until it butts a bolt on the stopper block under it *(near left)*; then, tighten the nut at the base of the bolt.

## USING A ROUTER (GROOVE CUTS)

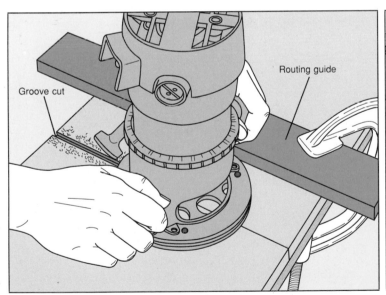

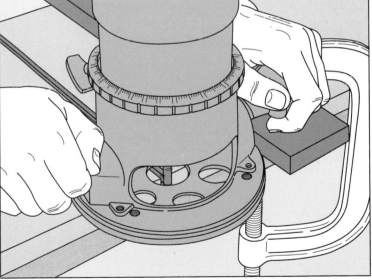

**1** **Making a cut.** Set up the workpiece on a work surface *(page 17)*; measure and mark *(page 30)* a cutting line, extending it down the edge at the starting end of the cut. Prepare to use a router *(page 65)*, then set up a routing guide or an edge guide *(page 64)*. Wearing safety goggles, hearing protection *(page 25)* and respiratory protection *(page 26)*, plug in the router *(page 24)* and make test cuts using scrap material; if necessary, unplug the router and adjust it. Position the router at the starting end of the cutting line with its baseplate resting on the surface; check the cutting depth of the bit *(step 6, above)*. If you are using a routing guide, butt the baseplate against it; if you are using an edge guide, set it snug against the workpiece. Then, pull the router back slightly so the bit is not touching the workpiece and ensure the power cord is out of the way. Grip the router firmly and turn it on. When the bit is turning at full speed, guide the router slowly into the workpiece.

Keeping the baseplate flat, move steadily along the cutting line *(above, left)*, watching the bit through the baseplate; it should move easily, throwing off small chips. If the bit veers from the cutting line, steer the router to it. If the bit scorches or powders the wood, move faster. If the bit strains and throws off big chips, move slower; if the bit still strains, turn off and unplug the router, then let the bit cool and decrease its cutting depth. If the router overheats, stop cutting until it cools, then turn off and unplug it to decrease the cutting depth of the bit. If the router vibrates noisily, have it professionally serviced. To finish the cut, guide the router out of the workpiece *(above, right)*, keeping the baseplate flat; then, tilt the router back, turn it off and let the bit stop. Before making another cut with the router, ensure the bit is tight *(page 66)*. If necessary, widen the cut *(step 2)*; to deepen it, increase the cutting depth of the bit and repeat the procedure. Otherwise, store your tools and clean up *(page 27)*.

## USING A ROUTER (GROOVE CUTS) (continued)

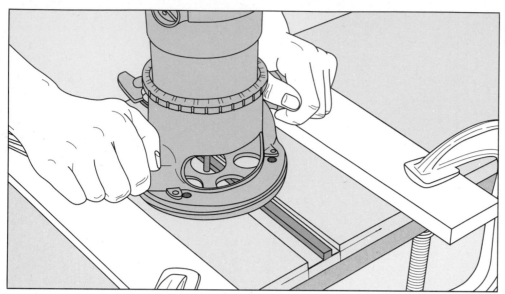

**2** **Widening the cut.** Measure and mark *(page 30)* a cutting line parallel to the first cut, extending it down the edge at the starting end of the cut; then, set up a second routing guide or an edge guide *(page 64)*. Wearing safety goggles, hearing protection *(page 25)* and respiratory protection *(page 26)*, use the router to make a second cut parallel to the first cut, following the procedure used to make it *(step 1)*. Then, use the router without a guide the same way to cut any waste material remaining between the two cuts *(left)*, working from the right to the left side of it and making as many consecutive, parallel cuts as necessary. To deepen the cuts, unplug the router to increase the cutting depth of the bit *(page 67)*; then, repeat the procedure, deepening the first cut and the second cut, then cutting any waste material remaining between the two cuts. Otherwise, store your tools and clean up *(page 27)*.

## USING A ROUTER (STOPPED GROOVE CUTS)

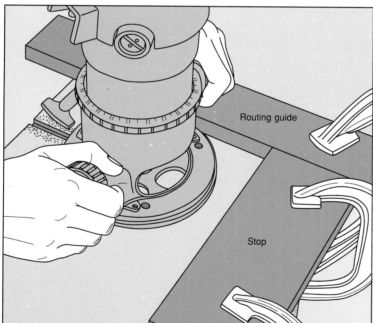

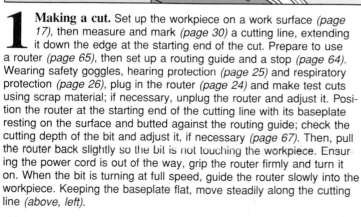

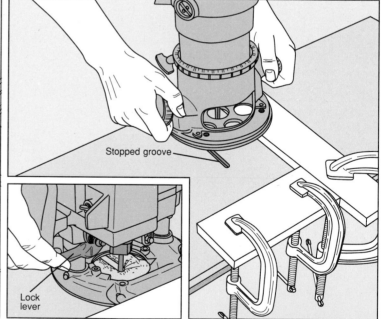

**1** **Making a cut.** Set up the workpiece on a work surface *(page 17)*, then measure and mark *(page 30)* a cutting line, extending it down the edge at the starting end of the cut. Prepare to use a router *(page 65)*, then set up a routing guide and a stop *(page 64)*. Wearing safety goggles, hearing protection *(page 25)* and respiratory protection *(page 26)*, plug in the router *(page 24)* and make test cuts using scrap material; if necessary, unplug the router and adjust it. Position the router at the starting end of the cutting line with its baseplate resting on the surface and butted against the routing guide; check the cutting depth of the bit and adjust it, if necessary *(page 67)*. Then, pull the router back slightly so the bit is not touching the workpiece. Ensuring the power cord is out of the way, grip the router firmly and turn it on. When the bit is turning at full speed, guide the router slowly into the workpiece. Keeping the baseplate flat, move steadily along the cutting line *(above, left)*.

Watch the bit through the baseplate; it should move easily, throwing off small chips. If the bit veers from the cutting line, steer the router to it. If the bit scorches or powders the wood, move faster. If the bit strains and throws off big chips, move slower; if the bit still strains, turn off and unplug the router, then let the bit cool and decrease its cutting depth. If the router overheats, stop cutting until it cools, then turn off and unplug it to decrease the cutting depth of the bit. If the router vibrates noisily, have it professionally serviced. Continue until the baseplate butts the stop firmly. With a conventional router, turn it off and let the bit stop, then lift it *(above, right)*; with a plunge router, flip up the lock lever *(inset)* and let the bit clear the workpiece, then turn it off and lift it. Before making another cut with the router, ensure the bit is tight *(page 66)*. If necessary, widen the cut *(step 2)*; to deepen it, increase the cutting depth of the bit and repeat the procedure. Otherwise, store your tools and clean up *(page 27)*.

## USING A ROUTER (STOPPED GROOVE CUTS) (continued)

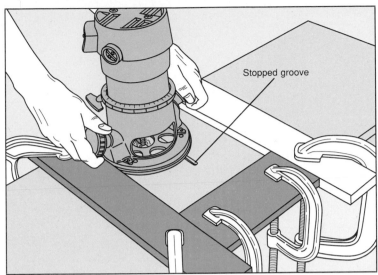

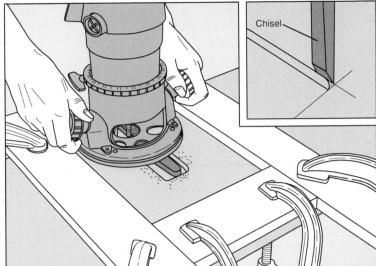

Chisel

Stopped groove

**2 Widening the cut.** Measure and mark *(page 30)* a cutting line parallel to the first cut, extending it down the edge at the starting end of the cut; then, set up a second routing guide *(page 64)*. Wearing safety goggles, hearing protection *(page 25)* and respiratory protection *(page 26)*, use the router to make a second cut parallel to the first cut *(above, left)*, following the procedure used to make it *(step 1)*. When the baseplate butts the stop, move steadily along it to the first routing guide, cutting between the ends of the two cuts perpendicular to them. Then, use the router without a guide the same way to cut any waste material remaining between the two cuts *(above, right)*, working

from the right to the left side of it and making as many consecutive, parallel cuts as necessary. To deepen the cuts, unplug the router to increase the cutting depth of the bit *(page 67)*; then, repeat the procedure, deepening the first cut and the second cut, then cutting any waste material remaining between the two cuts. Otherwise, remove the routing guides and the stop, then finish each side of the corners at the end of the cuts as you would to cut a deep mortise *(page 72)*; holding a chisel perpendicular to the surface with its cutting edge aligned along the cutting line just to the waste side and its bevel facing the waste material *(inset)*, strike its handle with a wooden mallet. Then, store your tools and clean up *(page 27)*.

## USING A ROUTER (RABBET CUTS)

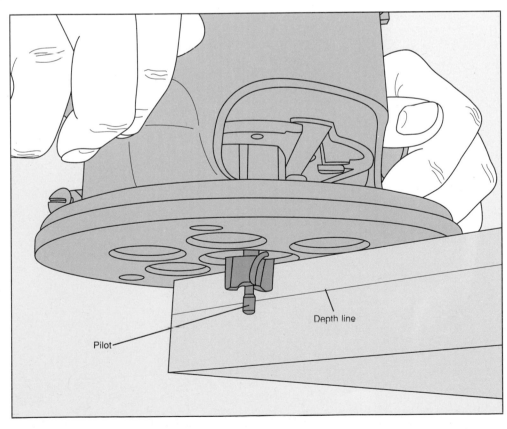

Depth line

Pilot

**1 Preparing to make a cut.** Set up the workpiece on a work surface *(page 17)*; if necessary, smooth any edge to be cut *(page 78)* so the router can travel easily along it. Prepare to use a router *(page 65)*, choosing and installing the right rabbeting bit for the job. Wearing safety goggles, hearing protection *(page 25)* and respiratory protection *(page 26)*, plug in the router *(page 24)* and make test cuts using scrap material; if necessary, unplug the router and adjust it. Then, position the router at the left end of the edge with its baseplate resting on the surface and the bit butted against the edge about 1 inch from the end *(left)*; if you are cutting more than one edge, start at any edge with end grain. Check the cutting depth of the bit and adjust it, if necessary *(page 67)*. Then, pull the router back slightly so the bit is not touching the workpiece and ensure the power cord is out of the way.

## USING A ROUTER (RABBET CUTS) (continued)

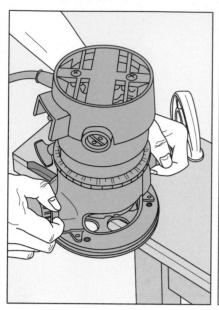
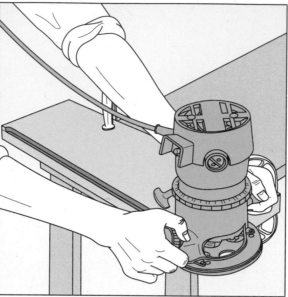
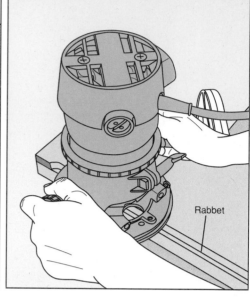

Rabbet

**2** **Making the cut.** Grip the router firmly and turn it on. When the bit is turning at full speed, guide the router slowly at a 90-degree angle straight into the edge, keeping the baseplate flat. When the pilot butts the edge and you can push no farther, move steadily to the right along the edge (above, left), keeping the pilot butted against it. Watch the bit through the baseplate; it should move easily, throwing off small chips. If the pilot veers away from the edge, steer the router to it. If the bit scorches or powders the wood, move faster. If the bit strains and throws off big chips, move slower; if the bit still strains, turn off and unplug the router, then let the bit cool and decrease its cutting depth (page 67). If the router overheats, stop cutting until it cools, then turn

off and unplug it to decrease the cutting depth of the bit. If the router vibrates noisily, have it professionally serviced. To finish the cut, guide the router off the end of the edge (above, center), keeping the baseplate flat. Then, tilt the router back, turn it off and let the bit stop. Finish cutting the starting end of the edge the same way, repositioning the router to the right of it and moving steadily to the left along (above, right) and then off it. To make a cut along any other edge, ensure the bit is tight (page 66) and use the same procedure. If necessary, choose and install a straight bit (page 66) to widen the cut as you would a groove cut (page 68). To deepen the cut, unplug the router to increase the cutting depth of the rabbeting bit, then repeat the procedure. Otherwise, store your tools and clean up (page 27).

## PREPARING TO USE A WOOD CHISEL

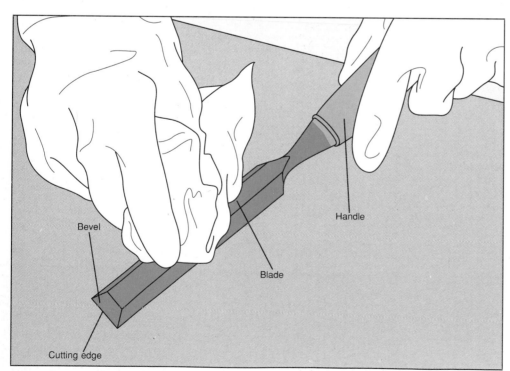

Bevel

Blade

Handle

Cutting edge

**1** **Inspecting and cleaning a wood chisel.** Inspect a chisel before using it. Check that the cutting edge is smooth. To remove a small nick, grind the chisel (step 2); for a nick wider than 1/32 inch, take the chisel for professional regrinding. If the cutting edge is smooth, test it for sharpness by dragging the tip of a fingernail very lightly along it. If your fingernail slides along easily rather than catching, hone the chisel (step 2); also grind it if it has already been honed several times.

Check also that the chisel is clean. If the handle is dirty, wipe it using a soft cloth dampened with a solution of mild household detergent and water. To clean stubborn residue off the blade, wear rubber gloves (page 25) and use a soft cloth dampened with mineral spirits (left); to remove rust, use steel wool dampened with light machine oil. Apply a little light machine oil to the blade of a chisel before storing it; wipe it with a soft cloth before using it.

## PREPARING TO USE A WOOD CHISEL (continued)

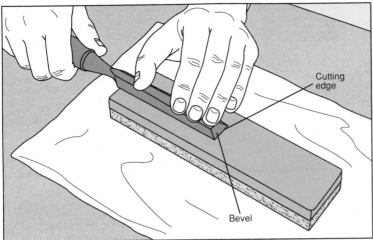

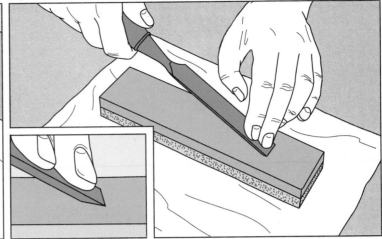

**2** **Grinding and honing the chisel.** To grind or hone a chisel, use a combination waterstone such as a 250-1000 grit model. Soak the waterstone in water for 5 minutes, then set it down on a rubber mat on a work surface; keep the coarse 250-grit surface face up for grinding, the fine 1000-grit surface face up for honing. Before grinding or honing the chisel, set the back of the blade on the waterstone to lap it. Gripping the handle with one hand and pressing the blade flat with your other hand, pull the chisel across the waterstone *(above, left)*, stopping before the cutting edge reaches the edge of it. Lift the chisel and lap the back of the blade again several times, then turn it over.

To grind the chisel, grip the handle with one hand and press the bevel flat against the 250-grit surface of the waterstone *(inset);* or, support the chisel using a grinding and honing guide, following the manufacturer's instructions to install the chisel at the correct angle in it. Then, draw the chisel across the waterstone *(above, right)*, stopping before the cutting edge reaches the edge of it. Lift the chisel and grind it again, continuing until any nick is removed and a thin line of metal is raised along the cutting edge. Stop periodically to splash water onto the waterstone; rinse it to remove accumulated grit. To remove the thin line of raised metal, turn over the chisel and lap the back again.

To hone the chisel, follow the same procedure used to grind it, working with the 1000-grit face of the waterstone. Continue honing the chisel until the angle between the bevel and the back of the blade is uniform and barely visible. Stop periodically to examine the cutting edge under a bright light and to test it for sharpness *(step 1)*. If honing does not sharpen the cutting edge, take the chisel for professional regrinding.

## USING A WOOD CHISEL (GROOVE CUTS)

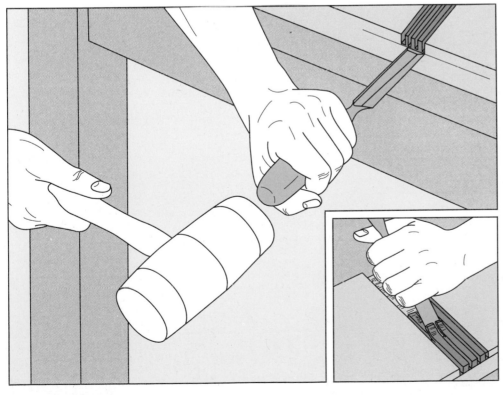

**1** **Cutting a groove.** Set up the workpiece on a work surface *(page 17)*, then measure and mark *(page 30)* cutting lines on it. Make a series of parallel groove cuts using a circular saw *(page 50)* or a backsaw *(page 60)*. Prepare to use a wood chisel *(page 70)*, then use it to score the bottom of the groove at each end. Holding the chisel perpendicular to the edge with its bevel facing the waste material, align its cutting edge with the depth line just to the waste side. Strike the handle of the chisel sharply using a wooden mallet *(left)*. Score the entire bottom of the groove along the depth line the same way.

Start at the center of the groove to cut the waste material. Holding the chisel at the top of its blade, position it at a 60-degree angle to the surface with its bevel facing the waste material. Resting the heel of your hand on the surface to guide the chisel, strike its handle gently with the mallet. Work to one end of the groove using the same procedure, repositioning the chisel 1/4 to 1/2 inch at a time. Starting again at the center of the groove, work to the other end the same way *(inset)*. If necessary, pare the bottom or sides of the groove *(page 73)*. Otherwise, store your tools and clean up *(page 27)*.

## USING A WOOD CHISEL (MORTISES)

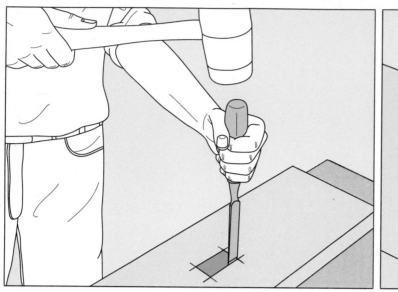

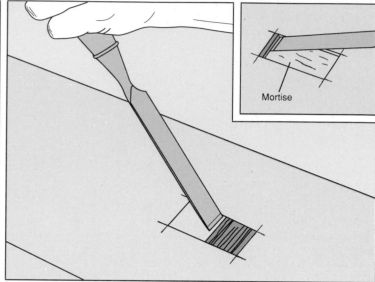

**Cutting a shallow mortise.** Set up the workpiece on a work surface *(page 17)*, then measure and mark *(page 30)* cutting lines on it. For a depth greater than 1/2 inch, cut a deep mortise *(step below)*. Otherwise, prepare to use a wood chisel *(page 70)*, then use it to score each side of the mortise; to avoid scoring too deeply, mark a depth line on the back of its blade with a straightedge and a sharp pencil. Holding the chisel perpendicular to the surface with its bevel facing the waste material, align its cutting edge with a cutting line just to the waste side. Strike the handle of the chisel sharply using a wooden mallet *(above, left)* until the depth line is aligned with the surface. Score the entire side of the mortise along the cutting line the same way. Work with the cutting edge of the chisel perpendicular to the wood grain to cut the waste material, starting about 3/8 inch from the side at one end of the mortise. Holding the chisel at a 60-degree angle to the surface with its bevel facing the waste material, strike its handle gently with the mallet; watch the depth line on the back of its blade to keep from cutting too deeply. Use the same procedure to work from one side to the other side across and along the mortise *(above, right)*, repositioning the chisel about 3/8 inch at a time. To cut the waste material along the side at the other end of the mortise, orient the chisel toward it about 3/8 inch from the scored line and work the same way *(inset)*. If necessary, pare the bottom or sides of the mortise *(page 73)*. Otherwise, store your tools and clean up *(page 27)*.

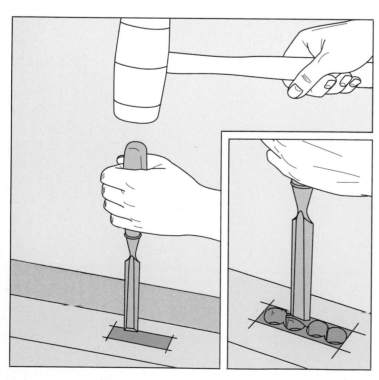

**Cutting a deep mortise.** Set up the workpiece on a work surface *(page 17)*, then measure and mark *(page 30)* cutting lines on it. For a depth up to 1/2 inch, cut a shallow mortise *(step above)*. Otherwise, prepare to use a wood chisel *(page 70)*, then use it to score each side of the mortise. Holding the chisel perpendicular to the surface with its bevel facing the waste material, align its cutting edge with a cutting line just to the waste side. Strike the handle of the chisel sharply using a wooden mallet *(left)*. Score the entire side of the mortise along the cutting line the same way.

Use a drill *(page 100)* to bore a series of holes in the waste material equal to the depth of the mortise; choose as large a bit as possible without its diameter exceeding the width of the mortise and mark the depth of the mortise on it with masking tape. To cut the remaining waste material, work from one side to the center of the mortise. Holding the chisel perpendicular to the surface with its bevel facing the waste material, align its cutting edge with a scored line and strike its handle gently with the mallet *(inset)*. Use the same procedure to work in turn from each other side to the center of the mortise. If necessary, pare the bottom or sides of the mortise *(page 73)*. Otherwise, store your tools and clean up *(page 27)*.

## USING A WOOD CHISEL (PARING)

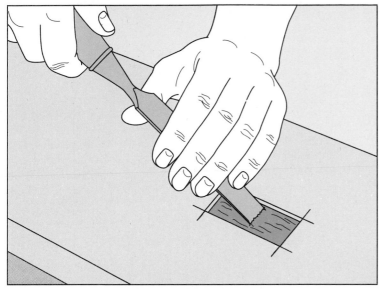

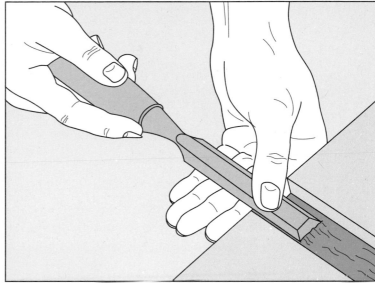

**Paring the bottom of a mortise or groove.** To pare the bottom of a mortise or groove, use a wood chisel; work with its cutting edge perpendicular to the wood grain. Holding the chisel by its handle with one hand, position it at a 60-degree angle to the surface with its bevel flat on the bottom of the mortise or groove and its cutting edge against the waste material. If the chisel is obstructed, scrape the bottom of the mortise or groove *(step below, left)*. Otherwise, grip the top of the blade with your other hand and rest its heel on the surface to guide the chisel. Pressing against the blade, push the handle firmly to cut the waste material *(above, left)*.

If necessary, pare the bottom of a groove further using the chisel. Holding the chisel by its handle in the palm of one hand with your thumb and forefinger extended, position it horizontally with the back of its blade flat on the bottom of the groove and its cutting edge against the waste material. Use your other hand to guide the chisel, pressing against the blade with your thumb. Then, push the top of the handle gently with the palm of your hand, using smooth strokes to cut the waste material *(above, right)*. If necessary, pare the sides of the mortise or groove *(step below, right)*. Otherwise, store your tools and clean up *(page 27)*.

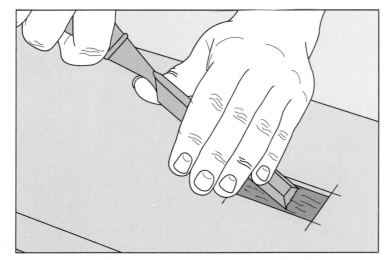

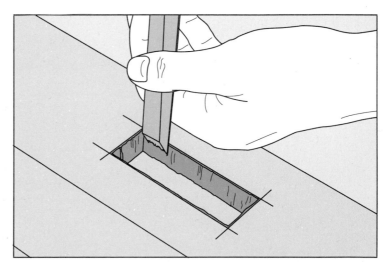

**Scraping the bottom of a mortise or groove.** To scrape the bottom of a mortise or groove, use a wood chisel; work with its cutting edge perpendicular to the wood grain. Holding the chisel by its handle with one hand, position it at a 60-degree angle to the surface with the back of its blade facing the waste material. Grip the top of the blade with your other hand and rest its heel on the surface to guide the chisel. Pressing against the blade, pull the handle firmly, dragging the cutting edge smoothly along the bottom of the mortise or groove to cut the waste material *(above)*. If necessary, pare the sides of the mortise or groove *(step right)*. Otherwise, store your tools and clean up *(page 27)*.

**Paring the sides of a mortise or groove.** To pare the sides of a mortise or groove, use a wood chisel. Holding the chisel by its handle in the palm of one hand with your thumb and forefinger extended, position it perpendicular to the surface with its bevel facing the waste material and its cutting edge aligned with the side of the mortise or groove. Use your other hand to guide the chisel, pressing against the blade with your thumb. Then, push the top of the handle gently with the palm of your hand, cutting the waste material *(above)*. If necessary, pare the bottom of the mortise or groove *(step above)*. Otherwise, store your tools and clean up *(page 27)*.

## USING A MASONRY CHISEL

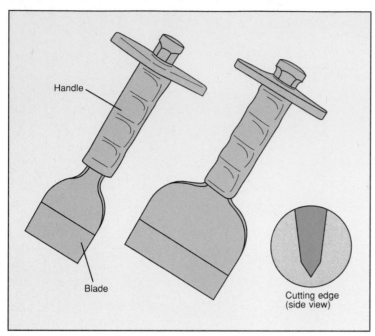

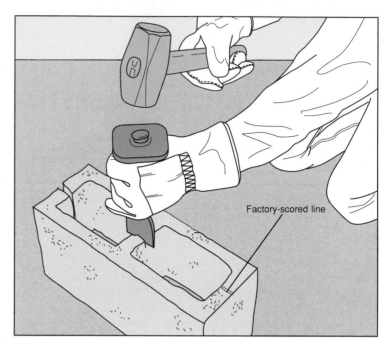

**Choosing and inspecting a masonry chisel.** Choose the right masonry chisel for the job; types with wide blades are called brick chisels. Use a chisel with a cutting edge equal to or greater than the cut you are making; if one is not available, use a circular saw *(page 50)*. Inspect a chisel *(above)* before using it. If the handle or the blade is damaged, discard the chisel. The blade of the chisel should have a smooth, sharp cutting edge, its bevels tapered evenly into a point; otherwise, take the chisel for professional regrinding. Check also that the chisel is clean. To clean off dirt, use a soft cloth dampened with a solution of household detergent and water; for stubborn residue, use a soft cloth dampened with mineral spirits. To remove rust, wear work gloves *(page 25)* and use steel wool dampened with light machine oil. Apply a little light machine oil to the blade of a chisel before storing it; wipe it with a soft cloth before using it.

**Cutting a concrete block.** Set up the workpiece on a work surface *(page 17)* protected with plywood, if necessary. Have extra blocks on hand; a clean cut can take more than one try. To cut the block along a factory-scored line or perforation on its webs, choose a chisel and inspect it *(step left)*; otherwise, first measure and mark *(page 30)* a cutting line on the top, bottom and each side of the block, then score along each cutting line as you would the top and bottom of a brick *(step below)*. Wearing safety goggles and work gloves *(page 25)*, hold the chisel perpendicular to the surface and align the cutting edge with a scored line, then tap the handle using a hand drilling hammer *(page 116)*; let its weight do the work. Use the same procedure on each scored line *(above)*, then turn over the block and work the same way; continue until it cuts cleanly. If the block does not cut cleanly, repeat the procedure. Otherwise, store your tools and clean up *(page 27)*.

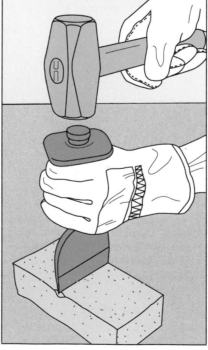

**Cutting a brick.** Set up the workpiece on a work surface *(page 17)* protected with plywood, if necessary. Have extra bricks on hand; a clean cut can take more than one try. Measure and mark *(page 30)* a cutting line on the top and bottom of the brick, then choose a chisel and inspect it *(step above, left)*.

Wearing safety goggles and work gloves *(page 25)*, start at one end of the cutting line to score along it. Holding the chisel at a 45-degree angle to the surface, align a corner of the cutting edge with the cutting line and tap the handle using a hand drilling hammer *(page 116)*, scoring to a depth of at least 1/8 inch *(far left)*. Work to the other end of the cutting line using the same procedure, then turn over the brick and score along the other cutting line the same way.

To cut the brick, hold the chisel perpendicular to the surface and align the cutting edge with the scored line; then, strike the handle once sharply with the hammer *(near left)*. If the brick does not cut cleanly, repeat the procedure. Otherwise, store your tools and clean up *(page 27)*.

## USING TIN SNIPS

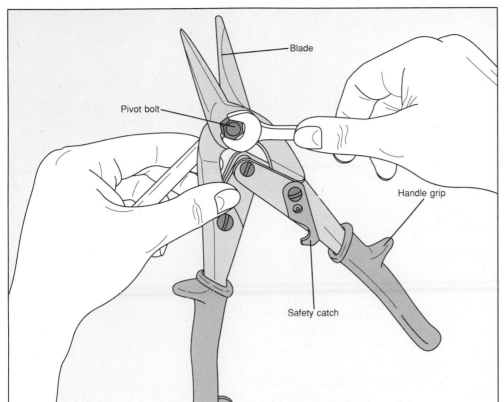

**Choosing and inspecting tin snips.** Choose the right tin snips for the job. For most straight or curved cuts in sheet metal, the straight, aviation type of tin snips with compound leverage action is easiest to use; for clean cuts in thick metal or along tight curves, the left- or right-oriented type is best. The straight conventional type of tin snips can be used for straight or wide-curved cuts, but it can be difficult to manipulate. Specialty types of tin snips are also available.

Inspect a tin snips before using it. The blades should spring apart easily when the handles are released. If the pivot bolt is loose, tighten it; with the aviation type shown, use wrenches *(left)*. If the blades are dull, take the tin snips for professional sharpening. If the grips of the handles are dirty, clean them using a soft cloth dampened with a solution of mild household detergent and water. Periodically lubricate each pivot point of the tin snips using light machine oil. To remove rust from the blades, wear work gloves *(page 25)* and use steel wool dampened with light machine oil. Apply a little light machine oil to the blades of a tin snips before storing it; wipe it with a soft cloth before using it.

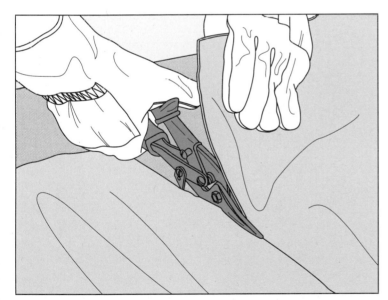

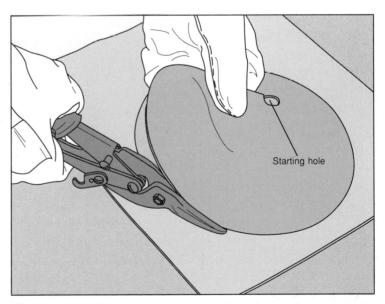

**Making a straight or curved cut.** Set up the workpiece on a work surface *(page 17)*; measure and mark *(page 30)* a cutting line on it. Prepare to use a tin snips *(step above)*. Wearing safety goggles and work gloves *(page 25)*, position the tin snips at one end of the cutting line and align the cutting edges of the blades with it just to the waste side. Holding the waste material out of the way, squeeze the handles together to close the blades, then release the handles to open the blades and reposition the cutting edges; to avoid dimpling or tearing the metal, do not close the blades completely. Continue cutting along the cutting line the same way *(above)*. Use the same procedure along a curve, cutting slowly only a little at a time; to avoid dimpling or tearing the metal along a tight curve, change to a matching left- or right-oriented type of aviation tin snips. Store your tools and clean up *(page 27)*.

**Making an interior cut.** Set up the workpiece on a work surface *(page 17)*; measure and mark *(page 30)* a cutting line on it. Prepare to use a tin snips *(step above)*. Use a drill *(page 100)* to make a starting hole large enough for a blade near the cutting line on the waste side. Wearing safety goggles and work gloves *(page 25)*, fit the blade into the hole and cut as wide a curve as possible to the cutting line, then slowly a little at a time along it just to the waste side. Holding the waste material out of the way, squeeze the handles together to close the blades *(above)*, then release the handles to open the blades and reposition the cutting edges; to avoid dimpling or tearing the metal, do not close the blades completely. To avoid dimpling or tearing the metal along a tight curve, change to a matching left- or right-oriented type of aviation tin snips. Store your tools and clean up *(page 27)*.

## USING A PIPE OR TUBING CUTTER

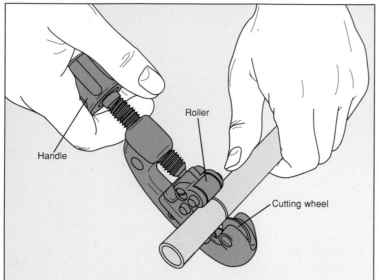

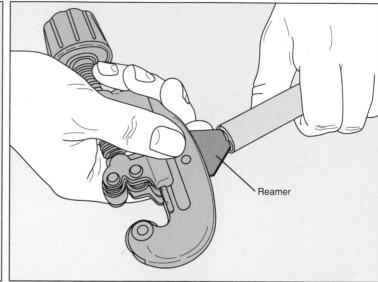

**Cutting pipe or tubing.** Set up the workpiece on a work surface *(page 17)*; measure and mark *(page 30)* a cutting line on it. Choose a pipe or tubing cutter of an appropriate size with the correct cutting wheel for the material; if the wheel is dull or damaged, replace it. Wearing safety goggles *(page 25)*, fit the jaws around the pipe and align the cutting wheel with the cutting line. Keeping the cutter perpendicular to the pipe, turn the handle to tighten the rollers. Rotate the cutter once around the pipe *(above, left)*, ensuring the cutting wheel is aligned correctly. If neces-

sary, loosen the rollers to reposition the cutting wheel, then repeat the procedure. If the cutting wheel still veers from the cutting line, it may be dull; replace it and repeat the procedure. Otherwise, tighten the rollers and rotate the cutter, continuing until the pipe is cut. To deburr the inside cut edges, use a file *(page 88)* or ream the pipe; on the cutter shown, there is a built-in reamer that pulls out. Insert the reamer into the cut end of the pipe, then rotate the cutter several times *(above, right)* to deburr it. Store your tools and clean up *(page 27)*.

## USING A UTILITY KNIFE

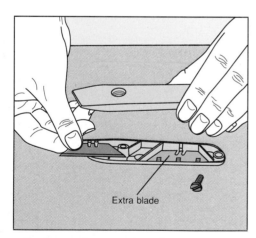

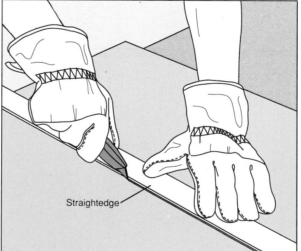

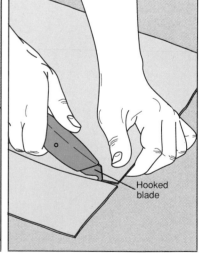

**1** **Inspecting and changing a blade.** Choose the right blade for the job: a standard type for most scoring or cutting; a hooked type for cutting materials such as linoleum. If the blade is dull or damaged, replace it. To change the blade of a utility knife, unscrew the handle and separate the sections, then carefully lift it out *(above)*. Before disposing of a blade, wrap masking tape around it. To install a new blade, fit its notches onto the interior projections, then reassemble the handle.

**2** **Making a cut.** Set up the workpiece on a work surface *(page 17)*; measure and mark *(page 30)* a cutting line on it. Wearing work gloves *(page 25)*, use a utility knife to score or cut from one end to the other end along the cutting line. With a standard blade, align the cutting edge with the cutting line just to the waste side, then position a metal straightedge along it just opposite to the waste side; butt the straightedge against the blade. Holding the straightedge steady with your fingers out of the way, draw the utility knife along it, keeping the blade butted against it *(above, left)*. To score lightly, hold the handle at a low angle to the surface and apply light pressure; to cut deeply, hold the handle at a high angle to the surface and apply moderate pressure. If necessary, repeat the procedure, pressing the blade deeper. With a hooked blade, align the cutting edge the same way; then, draw the utility knife along the cutting line, holding the waste material out of the way *(above, right)*. Store your tools and clean up *(page 27)*.

## USING A GLASS CUTTER

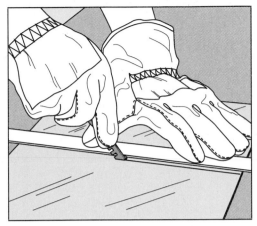 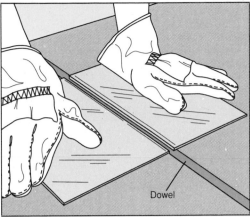 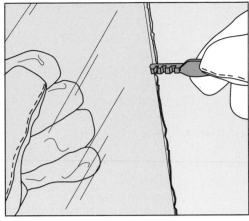

Dowel

**Making a straight cut.** Set up the workpiece on a work surface *(page 17)* padded with newspapers or old carpeting; measure and mark *(page 30)* the end points of a cutting line on it using a china marker. Prepare to use a glass cutter, lubricating its cutting wheel with a little light machine oil. Wearing work gloves and safety goggles *(page 25)*, position the cutting wheel at one end point just to the waste side, then align a straightedge with each end point just opposite to the waste side; butt the straightedge against the cutting wheel. To score the cutting line, hold the straightedge steady with your fingers out of the way and draw the cutter along it in one continuous stroke, keeping the cutting wheel butted against it *(above, left)*; do not roll the cutting wheel back and forth. Slow the cutter as you reach the other end point to avoid chipping the edge of the glass.

Carefully raise the glass enough to tap the bottom of it along the scored line with the end of the cutter handle. Then, position a wooden dowel at least as long as the scored line directly under it. Positioning your hands on opposite sides of the scored line at the same distance from it, apply balanced, uniform pressure straight down to snap the glass cleanly along it *(above, center)*. If there is too little waste material to snap off using a dowel or if waste material remains along the snapped edge, use the cutter notches to break it off one small piece at a time. Fit a notch of an appropriate size onto an edge of the waste material *(above, right)* and snap downward, breaking off a piece. Continue breaking off pieces of the waste material the same way until you reach the scored line; avoid trying to break off a large piece at one time. Then, store your tools and clean up *(page 27)*.

## USING A TILE NIPPER

 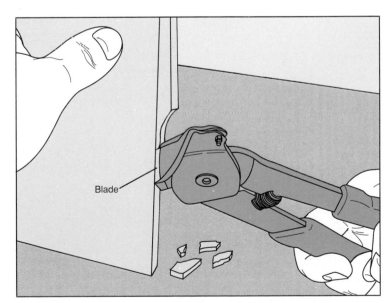

Blade

**Making a curved cut.** Set up the workpiece on a work surface *(page 17)*, then measure and mark *(page 30)* a cutting line on it. Wearing safety goggles *(page 25)*, use a tile nipper to remove the waste material. Hold the tile with one hand and use the nippers to notch an edge of the waste material, positioning the tips of blades around it and squeezing the handles. Starting at the notch, work with the nippers to bite off one small chip of the waste material at a time; if there is a large amount of waste material, bite off large chips of it until you are near the cutting line, then bite off small chips of it until you reach the cutting line *(above)*. Then, store your tools and clean up *(page 27)*.

**Making a straight cut near an edge.** Set up the workpiece on a work surface *(page 17)*, then measure and mark *(page 30)* a cutting line on it. Wearing safety goggles *(page 25)*, first score the cutting line using a glass cutter equipped with a carbide-type cutting wheel *(step above)*; press down firmly to break the glaze of the tile with as few strokes of the cutting wheel as possible. Then, use a tile nipper to remove the waste material. Holding the tile with one hand, work with the full blade length to bite off pieces of the waste material up to the scored line. Continue biting off pieces of the waste material along the scored line the same way *(above)*. Then, store your tools and clean up *(page 27)*.

# TRIMMING AND SMOOTHING

Trimming and smoothing, separately or together in the progression from rough work to final product, typically are performed after cutting operations and before finishing. Trimming techniques are exacting adjustments for removing relatively small amounts of material, usually to make a piece fit; a plane *(page 80)*, a surface-forming tool or a file *(page 87)* should be used only when a cutting tool *(page 42)* is no longer effective. And while an abrasive often can be used to shave off tiny amounts of material for a perfect fit, smoothing in general is done after cutting and trimming on surfaces or edges that will be visible. To smooth the edge of a board, for instance, use a sanding block *(page 91)* or a file; although files also can be used on metal or plastic, keep separate sets. To remove paint, follow the techniques in Finishing *(page 126)* to take off most of it, then work with an abrasive to complete the job.

Smoothing techniques are themselves a continuum, with each successive stage removing the imperfections left by the preceding stage. As a general rule, continue smoothing a surface or an edge until you achieve the results you desire; avoid oversmoothing wood in particular, however, which can raise the fibers and leave it rough or close the pores and reduce the adherence of a finish to it. After using a belt sander *(page 95)*, follow up with an orbital sander *(page 92)*, starting with sandpaper of the same grit as the last sanding belt you used; provide the piece with a final sanding using a sanding block if finishing is the next step. Consult the abrasives chart *(page 90)* to help you choose the right grit of sandpaper to start, continuing with it until the surface or edge is uniformly smooth and then proceeding to a finer grit to remove the imperfections left by it.

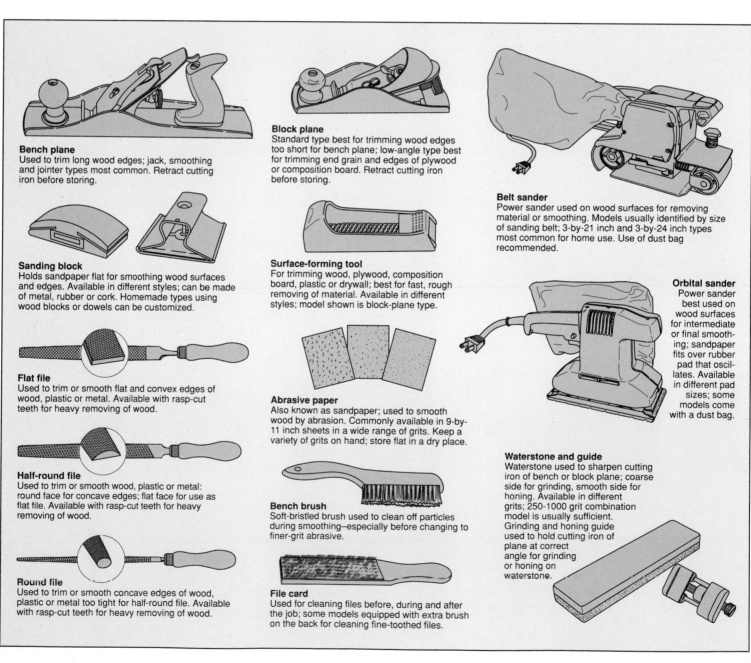

**Bench plane**
Used to trim long wood edges; jack, smoothing and jointer types most common. Retract cutting iron before storing.

**Sanding block**
Holds sandpaper flat for smoothing wood surfaces and edges. Available in different styles; can be made of metal, rubber or cork. Homemade types using wood blocks or dowels can be customized.

**Flat file**
Used to trim or smooth flat and convex edges of wood, plastic or metal. Available with rasp-cut teeth for heavy removing of wood.

**Half-round file**
Used to trim or smooth wood, plastic or metal: round face for concave edges; flat face for use as flat file. Available with rasp-cut teeth for heavy removing of wood.

**Round file**
Used to trim or smooth concave edges of wood, plastic or metal too tight for half-round file. Available with rasp-cut teeth for heavy removing of wood.

**Block plane**
Standard type best for trimming wood edges too short for bench plane; low-angle type best for trimming end grain and edges of plywood or composition board. Retract cutting iron before storing.

**Surface-forming tool**
For trimming wood, plywood, composition board, plastic or drywall; best for fast, rough removing of material. Available in different styles; model shown is block-plane type.

**Abrasive paper**
Also known as sandpaper; used to smooth wood by abrasion. Commonly available in 9-by-11 inch sheets in a wide range of grits. Keep a variety of grits on hand; store flat in a dry place.

**Bench brush**
Soft-bristled brush used to clean off particles during smoothing—especially before changing to finer-grit abrasive.

**File card**
Used for cleaning files before, during and after the job; some models equipped with extra brush on the back for cleaning fine-toothed files.

**Belt sander**
Power sander used on wood surfaces for removing material or smoothing. Models usually identified by size of sanding belt; 3-by-21 inch and 3-by-24 inch types most common for home use. Use of dust bag recommended.

**Orbital sander**
Power sander best used on wood surfaces for intermediate or final smoothing; sandpaper fits over rubber pad that oscillates. Available in different pad sizes; some models come with a dust bag.

**Waterstone and guide**
Waterstone used to sharpen cutting iron of bench or block plane; coarse side for grinding, smooth side for honing. Available in different grits; 250-1000 grit combination model is usually sufficient. Grinding and honing guide used to hold cutting iron of plane at correct angle for grinding or honing on waterstone.

To choose the most appropriate trimming or smoothing tool for the job, refer to the inventory presented on page 78 and the Troubleshooting Guide *(below)*, checking the section on the type of material you are using. In general, any power tool is recommended only for large workpieces due to the set-up time that can be involved. Proper preparation and accuracy are essential to a quality trimming or smoothing job. Read the chapter on Setting Up To Work *(page 14)* to determine the best way to secure your workpiece; planing it, for instance, is virtually impossible unless it is immovable. Consult Measuring And Marking *(page 30)* to measure and mark precisely; when trimming, closely watch any cutting lines for a result tailored to the specifications for the job. Practice using any trimming or smoothing tool on a scrap piece of your workpiece material before using it on the workpiece.

Safety in the workshop is an important part of any trimming or smoothing task; work carefully and wear the safety gear *(page 25)* recommended for the job: safety goggles to keep particles out of your eyes; respiratory protection to prevent breathing in harmful particles or dusts; and hearing protection with a noisy power tool such as a belt sander. Some materials that may have sharp edges or be chemically-treated—such as wood that is pressure-treated with preservatives—require skin protection when you handle them; as a rule, wear work gloves if you have any safety concerns about the material being used. If you are using a power sander, inspect it first and repair it, if necessary. Consult your owner's manual for instructions on its safe use; choose only the accessories recommended and work slowly and carefully, keeping your fingers away from any moving parts.

## TROUBLESHOOTING GUIDE

| PROBLEM | PROCEDURE |
| --- | --- |
| **WOOD** | |
| **Removing large amount of material from an edge** | For a long, flat edge, use a bench plane *(p. 80)* to trim equal or unequal amount *(p. 85)*; or, use a surface-forming tool *(p. 87)* |
| | For a short, flat edge, use a block plane *(p. 80)* to trim equal or unequal amount or end grain *(p. 85)*; use a surface-forming tool *(p. 87)*; or, use a flat or half-round file *(p. 87)* to cross-file *(p. 88)* |
| | For a contoured edge, use a surface-forming tool *(p. 87)*; if concave, use a half-round or round file *(p. 87)* to cross-file *(p. 88)*; or, if convex, use a flat or half-round file *(p. 87)* to cross-file *(p. 89)* |
| **Removing small amount of material from an edge** | For a long, flat edge, use a bench plane *(p. 80)* to trim equal or unequal amount *(p. 85)* |
| | For a short, flat edge, use a block plane *(p. 80)* to trim equal or unequal amount or end grain *(p. 85)*; or, use a flat or half-round file *(p. 87)* to cross-file *(p. 88)* |
| | For a contoured edge: if concave, use a half-round or round file *(p. 87)* to cross-file *(p. 88)*; or, if convex, use a flat or half-round file *(p. 87)* to cross-file *(p. 89)* |
| **Removing material from a surface** | Remove material from surface *(p. 94)* using a belt sander *(p. 93)* |
| **Smoothing an edge** | Use a file *(p. 87)* to draw-file *(p. 89)*; sand edge *(p. 91)* using a sanding block *(p. 90)* |
| **Smoothing a surface** | For a large surface, sand *(p. 95)* using a belt sander *(p. 93)*, then sand *(p. 92)* using an orbital sander *(p. 92)*; if necessary, then sand *(p. 91)* using a sanding block *(p. 90)* |
| | For a small surface, sand *(p. 91)* using a sanding block *(p. 90)* |
| **Rounding an edge** | Round edge *(p. 91)* using a sanding block *(p. 90)* |
| **METAL** | |
| **Removing material from an edge** | For a flat edge, use a flat or half-round file *(p. 87)* to cross-file *(p. 88)* |
| | For a contoured edge: if concave, use a half-round or round file *(p. 87)* to cross-file *(p. 88)*; or, if convex, use a flat or half-round file *(p. 87)* to cross-file *(p. 89)* |
| **Smoothing an edge** | Use a file *(p. 87)* to draw-file *(p. 89)* |
| **Deburring an edge** | Use a file *(p. 87)* to deburr metal edge *(p. 89)* |
| **PLASTIC** | |
| **Removing large amount of material from an edge** | Use a surface-forming tool *(p. 87)* |
| **Removing small amount of material from an edge** | For a flat edge, use a flat or half-round file *(p. 87)* to cross-file *(p. 88)* |
| | For a contoured edge: if concave, use a half-round or round file *(p. 87)* to cross-file *(p. 88)*; or, if convex, use a flat or half-round file *(p. 87)* to cross-file *(p. 89)* |
| **Smoothing an edge** | Use a file *(p. 87)* to draw-file *(p. 89)* |
| **DRYWALL** | |
| **Removing material from an edge** | Use a surface-forming tool *(p. 87)* |

## CHOOSING AND PREPARING TO USE A PLANE

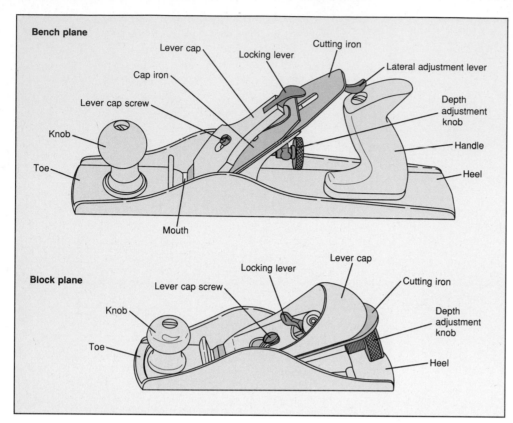

**Bench plane**

Lever cap · Locking lever · Cutting iron · Lateral adjustment lever · Cap iron · Depth adjustment knob · Lever cap screw · Knob · Handle · Toe · Heel · Mouth

**Block plane**

Locking lever · Lever cap · Lever cap screw · Cutting iron · Knob · Depth adjustment knob · Toe · Heel

**1** **Choosing and inspecting a plane.**
Choose the right plane for the job. For work on most wood edges more than 12 inches long, use a bench plane. For work on wood edges up to 12 inches long, on end grain, or on plywood or composition board, use a block plane—with its more suitable low cutting angle.

Inspect a bench plane or a block plane before using it *(left)*. Tighten any loose handle or knob screws. Service the cutting iron of the bench plane *(page 81)* or the block plane *(page 82)* if it is nicked, rusty or otherwise damaged, as well as to remove any clogged wood chips. To lubricate the threads of the depth adjustment screw or the locking lever, apply a small amount of light machine oil.

Check also that the sole of the plane is clean and undamaged. To clean off gum, pitch or glue, wear work gloves *(page 25)* and use steel wool dampened with mineral spirits; remove rust using steel wool dampened with light machine oil. If there are burrs on the sole, use a file *(page 87)* to deburr it *(page 89)*. Before storing a plane, apply a thin film of light machine oil to the sole; before using a plane you have stored, wipe the sole with a soft cloth.

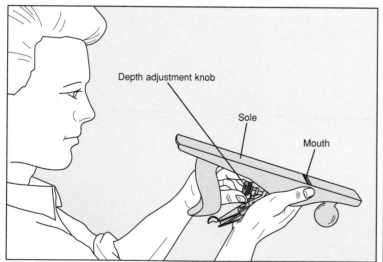

Depth adjustment knob · Sole · Mouth

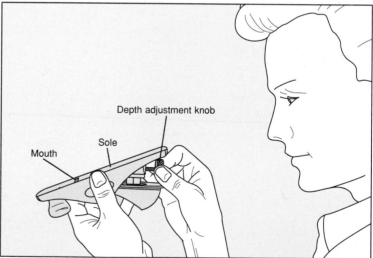

Depth adjustment knob · Mouth · Sole

**2** **Adjusting the cutting iron.** To adjust the depth and the lateral position of the cutting iron on a bench plane, hold the plane upside down under a good source of light. Sighting along the sole from the heel or the toe of the plane, turn the depth adjustment knob *(above left)* until the cutting edge of the cutting iron projects slightly from the mouth; it should be just barely visible. Then, move the lateral adjustment lever until the cutting edge of the cutting iron is aligned squarely within the mouth. Check the depth of the cutting iron; readjust it, if necessary. If the depth or lateral position of the cutting iron cannot be adjusted properly, check that the bench plane is assembled correctly *(page 81)*.

To adjust the depth and the lateral position of the cutting iron on a block plane, follow the owner's manual instructions. On the block plane shown, adjust the depth of the cutting iron the same way as on a bench plane; its cutting edge should project slightly from the mouth and be just barely visible. To adjust the lateral position of the cutting iron, loosen the locking lever and move the cutting iron by hand until its cutting edge is aligned squarely within the mouth, then tighten the locking lever. Check the depth of the cutting iron; readjust it, if necessary *(above, right)*. If the depth or lateral position of the cutting iron cannot be adjusted properly, check that the block plane is assembled correctly *(page 82)*.

## SERVICING THE CUTTING IRON (BENCH PLANE)

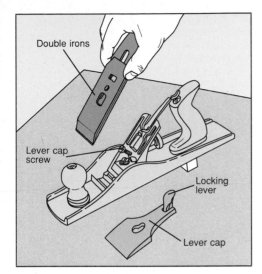

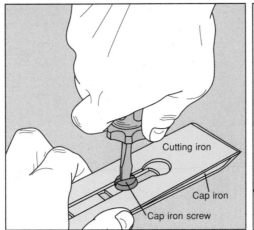

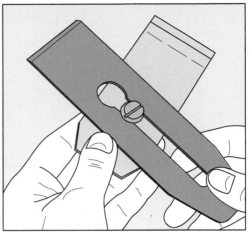

**1 Disassembling the bench plane.** To disassemble the bench plane, follow the owner's manual instructions. On the bench plane shown, release the locking lever, then slide the lever cap up and over the lever cap screw. Carefully lift the double irons (the cutting iron and the cap iron) out of the plane *(above)* and set them down gently on a flat surface; avoid cutting yourself on the cutting edge of the cutting iron or hitting it against a hard surface.

**2 Inspecting and cleaning the cutting iron.** Inspect the cutting iron closely; its cutting edge should be clean, smooth and sharp. To test the cutting iron for sharpness, drag the tip of a fingernail very lightly along its cutting edge; your fingernail should catch rather than slide easily. If the cutting edge of the cutting iron is clean, smooth and sharp, check that the double irons are aligned correctly and adjust them, if necessary *(step 3)*. Otherwise, take the double irons apart. First, loosen the screw of the cap iron with a screwdriver *(above, left)*, then turn the cutting iron perpendicular to the cap iron and slide it along the screw *(above, right)* until it can be lifted off; note its orientation for reassembly.

To remove a small nick, grind the cutting iron *(page 82)*; for a nick wider than 1/32 inch, take the cutting iron for professional regrinding. To sharpen the cutting iron, hone it *(page 82)*; also grind it if it has already been honed several times. To clean gum, pitch or glue off the cutting iron, wear work gloves *(page 25)* and use steel wool dampened with mineral spirits; to remove rust, use steel wool dampened with light machine oil. Reassemble the double irons, reversing the procedure used to take them apart.

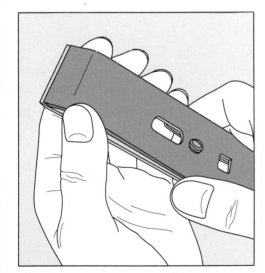

**3 Adjusting the double irons.** Check that the double irons are aligned correctly; the cutting edge of the cutting iron should extend 1/16 inch from and parallel to the edge of the cap iron with the sides of the irons perfectly flush against each other. If necessary, loosen the screw of the cap iron using a screwdriver with a large flat-tipped blade, then align the double irons *(above)*. Holding the double irons aligned, tighten the screw of the cap iron securely.

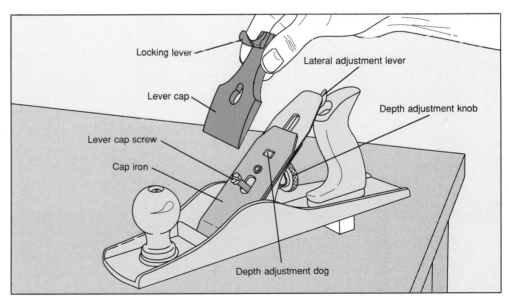

**4 Reassembling the bench plane.** To reassemble the bench plane, turn the depth adjustment knob to the midpoint of its travel and center the lateral adjustment lever. With the cap iron facing upward, position the double irons into the plane, fitting them over the lever cap screw. Check that the slot of the double irons is seated correctly over the depth adjustment dog; the double irons should shift as the lateral adjustment lever is moved. Reinstall the lever cap *(above)*, sliding it down over the lever cap screw, then close the locking lever. If the locking lever cannot be closed, remove the lever cap and the double irons to reposition them; if it still cannot be closed, loosen the lever cap screw slightly and try again. If the locking lever closes too easily, tighten the lever cap screw slightly and try again. When the locking lever is closed tightly, adjust the depth and lateral position of the cutting iron *(page 80)*.

## SERVICING THE CUTTING IRON (BLOCK PLANE)

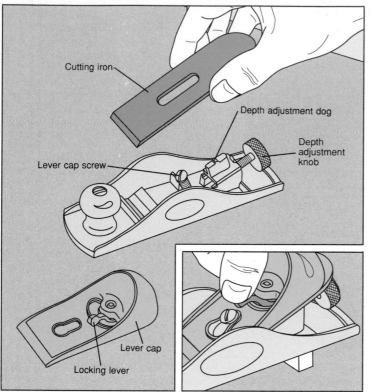

**Removing, inspecting and reinstalling the cutting iron.** To disassemble the block plane, follow the owner's manual instructions. On the block plane shown, release the locking lever, then slide the lever cap up and over the lever cap screw. Carefully lift the cutting iron out of the plane *(left)* to inspect it; note its orientation for reassembly. The cutting edge of the cutting iron should be clean, smooth and sharp. To test the cutting edge for sharpness, drag the tip of a fingernail very lightly along it; your fingernail should catch rather than slide easily. To remove a small nick, grind the cutting iron *(steps below)*; for a nick wider than 1/32 inch, take the cutting iron for professional regrinding. To sharpen the cutting iron, hone it *(steps below)*; also grind it if it has already been honed several times. To clean off gum, pitch or glue, wear work gloves *(page 25)* and use steel wool dampened with mineral spirits; to remove rust, use steel wool dampened with light machine oil.

To reassemble the block plane, turn the depth adjustment knob to the midpoint of its travel. Position the cutting iron into the plane, fitting it over the lever cap screw; its cutting edge should be aligned and centered in the mouth with one slot seated securely on the depth adjustment dog. Reinstall the lever cap, sliding it down over the lever cap screw, then close the locking lever *(inset)*. If the locking lever cannot be closed, take off the lever cap and the cutting iron to reposition them; if it still cannot be closed, loosen the lever cap screw slightly and try again. If the locking lever closes too easily, tighten the lever cap screw slightly and try again. When the locking lever is closed tightly, adjust the depth and lateral position of the cutting iron *(page 80)*.

## GRINDING AND HONING THE CUTTING IRON

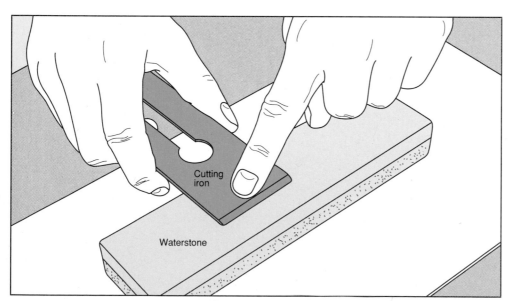

**1** **Lapping the cutting iron.** To grind or hone a cutting iron, use a combination waterstone such as a 250-1000 grit model. Soak the waterstone in water for 5 minutes, then set it down on a rubber mat on a work surface; keep the coarse 250-grit surface face up for grinding, the fine 1000-grit surface face up for honing. Before grinding or honing the cutting iron, set the back of it on the waterstone to lap it. Gripping the cutting iron by its sides with one hand and pressing it flat with your other hand, draw it across the waterstone *(above)*, stopping before its cutting edge reaches the edge. Lift the cutting iron and lap the back of it again several times, then turn it over. Set up a grinding and honing guide for the cutting iron *(step 2)* or support the cutting iron by hand to grind or hone it *(step 3)*.

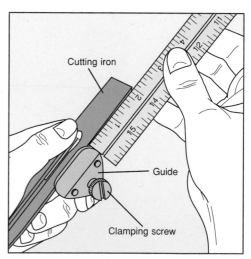

**2** **Setting up a grinding and honing guide.** Buy a grinding and honing guide, then follow the manufacturer's instructions to install the cutting iron at the correct angle in it. On the guide shown, markings indicate the distance to extend the cutting iron for the angle desired. Set the cutting iron in the guide with the bevel of the cutting edge facing it; using a ruler to measure, extend the cutting iron the distance necessary *(above)* and tighten the clamping screw. Set the guide on a flat surface; if the bevel of the cutting edge does not sit even, adjust the cutting iron.

## GRINDING AND HONING THE CUTTING IRON (continued)

Guide

**3** **Grinding and honing the cutting iron.** To grind the cutting iron, set the bevel of its cutting edge on the 250-grit surface of the waterstone. If you are using a guide, control its movement with your thumbs and press the bevel of the cutting edge flat against the surface with your index fingers *(left)*. If you are not using a guide, grip the cutting iron by its sides with one hand and press the bevel of the cutting edge flat against the surface with your other hand. Draw the cutting iron across the waterstone, stopping before the cutting edge reaches the edge of it. Lift the cutting iron and grind it again, continuing until any nick is removed and a thin line of metal is raised along the cutting edge. Stop periodically to splash water onto the waterstone; rinse it to remove accumulated grit. To remove the thin line of raised metal, turn over the cutting iron and lap the back again *(step 1)*.

To hone the cutting iron, follow the same procedure used to grind it, working with the 1000-grit face of the waterstone. Continue honing the cutting iron until the angle between the bevel of the cutting edge and the back of the cutting iron is uniform and barely visible. Stop periodically to examine the cutting edge under a bright light and to test it for sharpness, dragging the tip of a fingernail very lightly along it. If your fingernail slides easily rather than catching, continue honing. After honing the cutting iron, also grind it if it has already been honed several times. If honing does not sharpen the cutting edge, take the cutting iron for professional regrinding. Otherwise, reinstall the cutting iron in the bench plane *(page 81)* or the block plane *(page 82)*.

## PREPARING TO PLANE

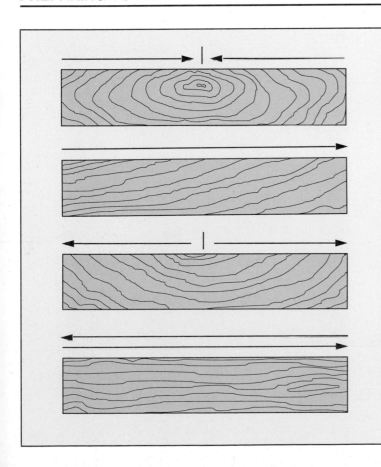

**Determining the best direction to plane.** Trim end grain with a block plane *(page 86)*. Otherwise, plan to set up your workpiece using the grain pattern of the surface adjacent to the edge to be planed in determining the best direction to plane. As a general rule, position the workpiece with the edge to be planed facing upward and plane horizontally; otherwise, leave the workpiece in place and plane vertically.

With the workpiece positioned, examine the grain pattern along the surface adjacent to the edge to be planed; the diagram *(left)* shows several typical grain patterns with arrows indicating the best direction to plane. To prevent the cutting edge of the plane from catching the grain and tearing or roughening the wood, always plane in the "uphill" grain direction. On a workpiece, the "uphill" grain direction may change, requiring a change in the direction to plane; or, it may be consistently horizontal, allowing a choice in the direction to plane.

After determining the best direction to plane, set up the workpiece on a work surface *(page 17)*, measuring and marking *(page 30)* cutting lines on it, if necessary; orient it for comfortable, easy access to the edge to be planed in the best direction to plane. On a workpiece with different "uphill" grain directions, work from both sides of it or turn it around to maintain comfortable, easy access to the edge to be planed in the best direction to plane. When the workpiece is set up, choose and prepare to use a plane *(page 80)*, then ensure you know how to use it properly to work horizontally *(page 84)* or vertically *(page 85)*.

## PREPARING TO PLANE (continued)

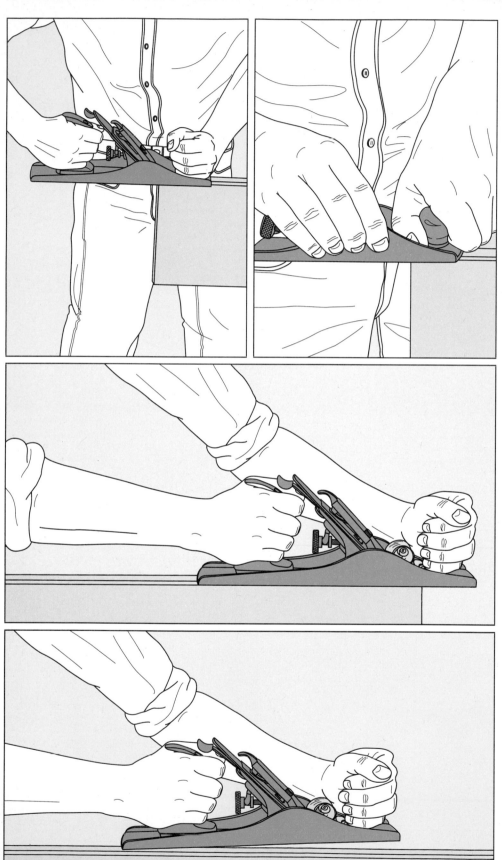

**Using a plane horizontally.** To use a bench plane or a block plane for horizontal strokes, maintain a well-balanced stance; keep your feet apart and your shoulders over the edge you are planing. Hold the plane with both hands, placing your non-dominant hand in front on the knob and your dominant hand in back: on the handle of a bench plane; on the lever cap of a block plane. Always work in the best direction to plane *(page 83)* and keep the sole of the plane centered on the edge.

To start a stroke at the end of an edge, position the plane level with the edge and rest the toe of the sole flat on it—without the cutting iron of the bench plane *(far left, top)* or the block plane *(near left, top)* touching it. Pressing down firmly with the hand in front to keep the sole flat on the edge, use the hand in back to push the plane forward for a full cutting stroke; apply only forward pressure on the handle of the bench plane or the lever cap of the block plane to start, then apply equal downward pressure with both hands to keep the sole flat as soon as most of it is on the edge. To start a stroke away from the end of an edge, position the plane on the edge and push it forward for a full cutting stroke, constantly applying equal downward pressure with both hands.

To continue the stroke, maintain your balanced stance and lean forward, using the momentum of your upper body as much as the strength of your arms to achieve a smooth, even cut with the plane. Move with the plane alongside the workpiece, if necessary, rather than trying to overextend your reach with it along the edge. To finish the stroke at the end of the edge, continue applying equal downward pressure with both hands until the toe of the sole leaves the edge, then reduce it in front on the knob and maintain it in back: on the handle of the bench plane *(left, center)*; on the lever cap of the block plane. As soon as the cutting iron leaves the edge, lift the plane smoothly and without stopping, returning it for another stroke in a circular motion. To finish the stroke before the end of the edge, continue applying equal downward pressure with both hands until your arms are fully extended, then lift the plane smoothly and without stopping the same way *(left, bottom)*.

Repeat the procedure as many times as necessary to trim the edge of the workpiece, moving to the other side of it or turning it around as required to plane in the best direction. If the cutting iron of the plane catches, cuts poorly or cuts off more than a thin shaving, adjust it *(page 80)*; if the problem persists, service the cutting iron of the bench plane *(page 81)* or the block plane *(page 82)*. When you stop planing, protect the cutting iron by setting the plane down on its side—not on its sole.

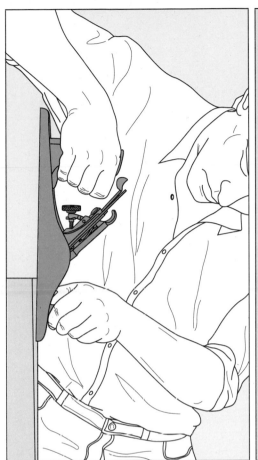 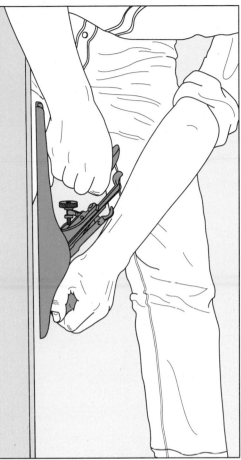

**Using a plane vertically.** To use a bench plane or a block plane for vertical strokes, hold it with both hands, placing your dominant hand in back: on the handle of a bench plane; on the lever cap of a block plane. Always work in the best direction to plane *(page 83)* and keep the sole of the plane centered on the edge.

To start at the end of an edge, align the plane and rest the toe of the sole flat on it *(far left)*. Pressing firmly into the edge with the hand in front to keep the sole flat, use the hand in back to push the plane; apply equal pressure with both hands into the edge as soon as most of the sole is on it. To start away from the end of an edge, align the plane on the edge and push it, constantly applying equal pressure with both hands into the edge.

To finish before the end of the edge, continue until your arms are fully extended, then lift the plane away smoothly and without stopping *(near left)*. To finish at the end of the edge, reduce pressure into the edge in front as soon as the toe of the sole leaves the edge, then lift the plane away the same way.

Move yourself or the workpiece as necessary to repeat the procedure. If the cutting iron catches, cuts poorly or cuts off more than a thin shaving, adjust it *(page 80)*; if the problem persists, service the cutting iron of the bench plane *(page 81)* or the block plane *(page 82)*. Protect the cutting iron when you stop by setting the plane down on its side—not on its sole.

## TRIMMING WITH A PLANE

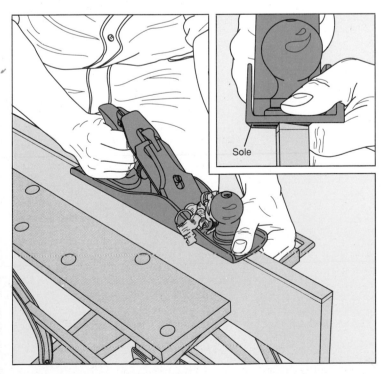

Sole

**Trimming an equal amount off an edge.** Trim end grain with a block plane *(page 86)*. Otherwise, determine the best direction to plane *(page 83)* and set up the workpiece on a work surface *(page 17)*, measuring and marking *(page 30)* cutting lines on each side of it. Choose and prepare to use a plane *(page 80)*, then use it horizontally *(page 84)* or vertically *(step above)* to trim an equal amount of material off the edge up to about 1/8 inch from the cutting lines. Stop periodically to check your progress, marking areas where you have cut off enough to avoid trimming them farther.

To trim the last 1/8 inch of material off the edge, change the position of the hand in front and use the plane the same way. Pressing firmly into the edge in front with your thumb, slide your fingers lightly along an adjacent surface under the sole to keep a sense of its position and angle *(left)*. If the cutting iron catches, cuts poorly or cuts off more than a thin shaving, adjust it *(page 80)*; if the problem persists, service the cutting iron of the bench plane *(page 81)* or the block plane *(page 82)*. Stop periodically to check your progress, measuring the angle between the edge and the adjacent surfaces *(page 30)*. To correct any deviation, use the fingers of your hand in front to raise the sole off the low side of the edge *(inset)*, keeping it at the proper angle. Continue trimming the same way until you reach the cutting lines. Store your tools and clean up *(page 27)*.

## TRIMMING WITH A PLANE (continued)

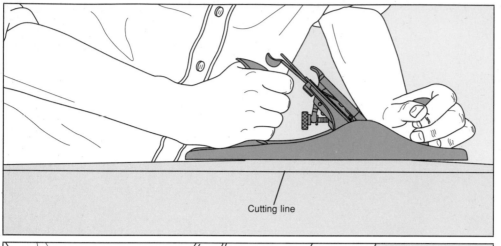

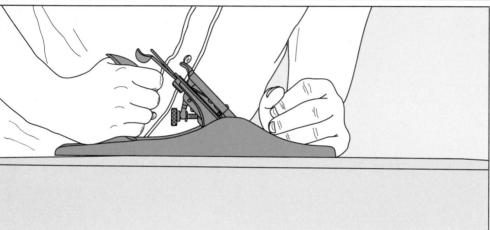

Cutting line

**Trimming an unequal amount off an edge.**
Trim end grain with a block plane *(page 86)*.
Otherwise, determine the best direction to plane *(page 83)* and set up the workpiece on a work surface *(page 17)*, measuring and marking *(page 30)* cutting lines on each side of it. Choose and prepare to use a plane *(page 80)*, then use it horizontally *(page 84)* or vertically *(page 85)* to trim an unequal amount of material off the edge up to about 1/8 inch from the cutting lines. Start trimming where the most material needs to be cut, using short strokes at first *(left, top)*, then gradually longer strokes to keep trimming parallel to the cutting lines *(left, bottom)*. If the cutting iron catches, cuts poorly or cuts off more than a thin shaving, adjust it *(page 80)*; if the problem persists, service the cutting iron of the bench plane *(page 81)* or the block plane *(page 82)*. Stop periodically to check your progress, marking areas where you have cut off enough to avoid trimming them farther. To trim the last 1/8 inch of material off the edge, use the plane horizontally or vertically as you would to trim an equal amount of material off any edge *(page 85)*. Store your tools and clean up *(page 27)*.

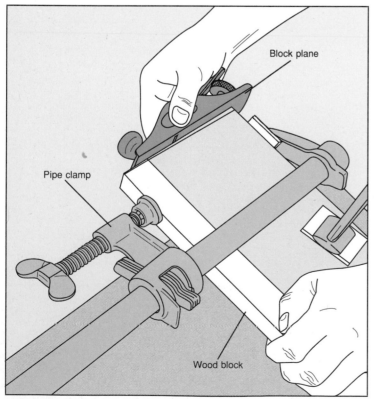

Block plane

Pipe clamp

Wood block

**Trimming end grain.** Set up the workpiece on a work surface *(page 17)* with the end to be trimmed facing upward, if possible; to keep from tearing or splintering the wood, secure a wood block along one side flush with the end to be trimmed and plan to plane toward it. If the workpiece is long, as in the instance shown, set it up with the end to be trimmed overhanging the work surface; to secure the wood block, use a pipe clamp, as shown, or C clamps *(page 124)*. Measure and mark *(page 30)* cutting lines on each side of the workpiece; plan to start trimming where the most material needs to be cut.

Prepare to use a block plane *(page 80)*. If the end to be trimmed is facing upward, use the plane horizontally as you would for any edge, applying greater downward pressure *(page 84)*. Otherwise, hold the plane by the sides with one hand, your palm in back on the lever cap and your forefinger in front just behind or on the knob. To start at the edge, align the plane and rest the toe of the sole flat on the end. Pressing firmly into the end in front to keep the sole flat, push the plane toward the wood block; apply uniform pressure into the end as soon as most of the sole is on it. To start away from the edge, align the plane on the end and push it, constantly applying uniform pressure into the end *(left)*. To finish before the edge of the wood block, lift the plane away smoothly and without stopping. To finish at the edge of the wood block, reduce pressure into the end in front as soon as the toe of the sole leaves the edge, then lift the plane away the same way.

If the cutting iron catches or cuts poorly, plane toward the wood block at an angle using short strokes. If the problem persists, adjust the cutting iron *(page 80)*; if it still persists, service the cutting iron *(page 82)*. Protect the cutting iron when you stop by setting the plane down on its side—not on its sole. Continue trimming the same way until you reach the cutting lines. Store your tools and clean up *(page 27)*.

## USING A SURFACE-FORMING TOOL

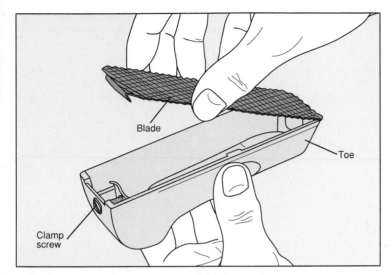

Blade

Toe

Clamp screw

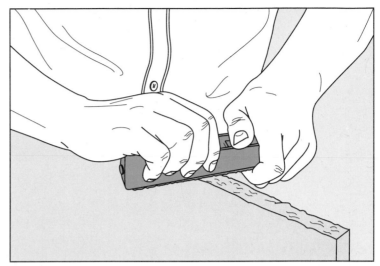

**1** **Preparing to use a surface-forming tool.** Check a surface-forming tool before using it. If the blade is dull or damaged, follow the manufacturer's instructions to replace it. On the model shown, loosen the clamp screw enough to lift off the blade. Install a new blade with the teeth oriented toward the toe of the tool, hooking it in place *(above)* and tightening the clamp screw. Use a stiff-bristled brush to remove shavings from the blade. To clean gum, pitch or glue off the blade, use a clean cloth dampened with mineral spirits; to remove rust, wear work gloves *(page 25)* and use steel wool.

**2** **Trimming an edge.** Set up the workpiece on a work surface *(page 17)*; if necessary, measure and mark *(page 30)* cutting lines on each side of it. Hold the surface-forming tool with both hands, your dominant hand on the heel. For fast, rough trimming of material, position the tool flat on the edge at a 45-degree angle to it. Pressing into the edge with both hands, push the tool along it *(above)*. For smoother trimming of material, gradually shift the angle of the tool, moving its toe and heel closer to the edge. For final trimming of material, center the tool on the edge. Store your tools and clean up *(page 27)*.

## PREPARING TO USE A FILE

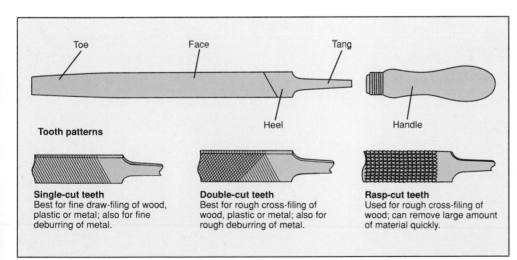

Toe

Face

Tang

Heel

Handle

**Tooth patterns**

**Single-cut teeth**
Best for fine draw-filing of wood, plastic or metal; also for fine deburring of metal.

**Double-cut teeth**
Best for rough cross-filing of wood, plastic or metal; also for rough deburring of metal.

**Rasp-cut teeth**
Used for rough cross-filing of wood; can remove large amount of material quickly.

**Choosing a file.** Choose the correct file for the job. Refer to page 78 to choose a file of an appropriate shape: a flat type for flat or convex edges; a half-round type for flat or convex edges (flat-faced portion) or concave edges (round-faced portion); or a round type for tight concave edges. Use a half-round or round file that matches the curve of the edge as closely as possible. To choose a file with an appropriate tooth pattern, consult the diagram *(above)*. The tooth patterns shown are usually available in three grades of coarseness: bastard cut for the fastest, roughest filing of material; second cut for finer filing of material; and smooth cut for the finest filing of material. A long file typically has proportionately larger, coarser teeth than a small file. In general, use a bastard-cut file for soft material; its coarse teeth are least prone to clogging. Use a smooth-cut file on hard material; its fine teeth are least prone to gouging. Always use a handle with a file—for safety and control. To install the handle, push the file tang into its hole; then, hold the handle with the file upright and rap the bottom of it sharply on a sturdy surface until the file is securely in place. To remove the handle, grip the file firmly and tap the ferrule of the handle using a wood block.

**Cleaning a file.** Before, periodically during and after using a file, clean filings out of its teeth with a file card or a wire brush. To use a file card, scrub across the file along the rows of teeth, keeping the wires of the brush parallel to them *(above)*; use a wire brush the same way. To remove any stubborn filings, use a small nail. To help decrease the accumulation of filings, rub chalk over the file teeth after cleaning them; never oil the file. Store your files separately in a drawer with dividers, inside a tool roll or wrapped in a cloth.

## USING A FILE

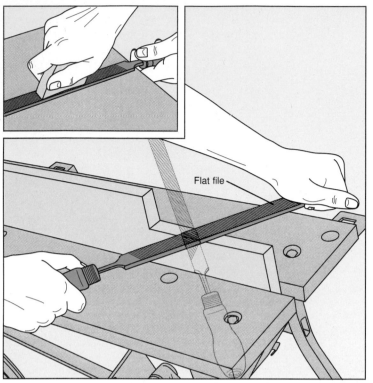

**Cross-filing a flat edge.** Set up the workpiece on a work surface, if possible *(page 17)*; if necessary, measure and mark cutting lines on each side of it. Prepare to use a file *(page 87)*; if you are working with metal, wear work gloves *(page 25)*. If the workpiece is too small to set up securely, use a flat filing technique on the edge, setting the file flat on the work surface with the handle overhanging it. Holding the handle, position the edge flat on the file at the toe, then pull the workpiece straight along the face *(inset)*, applying enough uniform pressure into it to cut the material. When the workpiece reaches the heel, lift it away smoothly and without stopping, returning it to continue, if necessary. If the file does not cut off enough material, position the edge diagonally across it and pull the workpiece straight along its face the same way. To further smooth a wood edge, use a sanding block *(page 91)*.

Otherwise, hold the file by the handle in one hand and by the toe in the other hand to work across the edge from one end to the other end of it. To start a stroke, position the toe of the file flat on the edge diagonally across it, orienting the toe in the direction you are working. Keeping the file flat, push it straight across the edge *(left)*, applying enough uniform pressure into the edge to cut the material. When the heel of the file reaches the edge at the end of the stroke, lift the file away smoothly and without stopping in a circular motion. Continue filing the same way, overlapping each stroke slightly. If the file rides over rather than cuts the material, clean it *(page 87)*. Then, file along the edge diagonally across it the same way, orienting the heel in the direction you are working *(ghosted file)*. For a fine-finished edge, draw-file *(page 89)*. Otherwise, store your tools and clean up *(page 27)*.

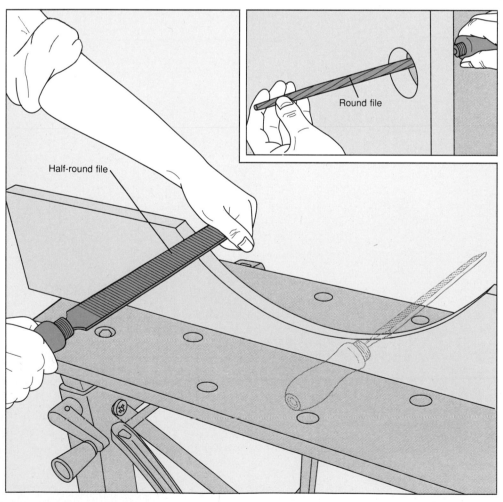

**Cross-filing a concave edge.** Set up the workpiece on a work surface *(page 17)*; if necessary, measure and mark cutting lines on each side of it. Prepare to use a file *(page 87)*; if you are working with metal, wear work gloves *(page 25)*. Holding the file by the handle in one hand and by the toe in the other hand, work across and along the edge at the same time from one end to the other end of it.

To start a stroke, position the toe of the file flat on the edge at a 90-degree angle across it. Keeping the file flat, push it simultaneously across and along the edge *(left)*, turning it back and forth slightly and applying enough uniform pressure into the edge to cut the material; if you are using a round file, let the toe turn fully in your hand *(inset)*. When the heel of the file reaches the edge at the end of the stroke *(ghosted file)*, lift the file away smoothly and without stopping in a circular motion.

Continue filing the same way, overlapping each stroke slightly. If the file rides over rather than cuts the material, clean it *(page 87)*. For a fine-finished edge, draw-file *(page 89)*. Otherwise, store your tools and clean up *(page 27)*.

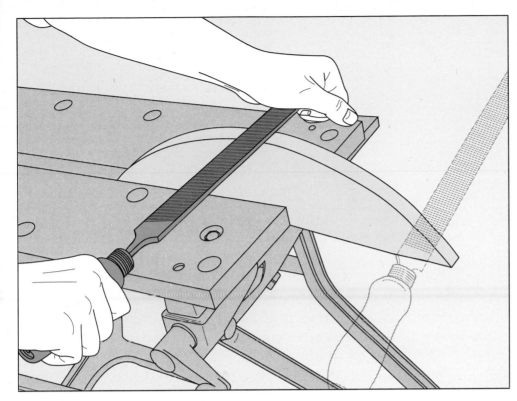

**Cross-filing a convex edge.** Set up the workpiece on a work surface *(page 17)*; if necessary, measure and mark cutting lines on each side of it. Prepare to use a file *(page 87)*; if you are working with metal, wear work gloves *(page 25)*. Holding the file by the handle in one hand and by the toe in the other hand, work across and along the edge at the same time from one end to the other end of it.

To start a stroke, position the toe of the file flat on the edge at a 90-degree angle across it. Keeping the file flat, push it simultaneously across and along the edge *(left)*, applying enough uniform pressure into the edge to cut the material. When the heel of the file reaches the edge at the end of the stroke *(ghosted file)*, lift the file away smoothly and without stopping in a circular motion.

Continue filing the same way, overlapping each stroke slightly. If the file rides over rather than cuts the material, clean it *(page 87)*. For a fine-finished edge, draw-file *(page 89)*. Otherwise, store your tools and clean up *(page 27)*.

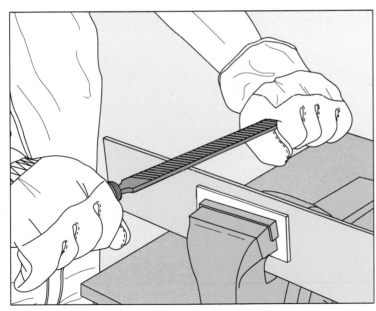

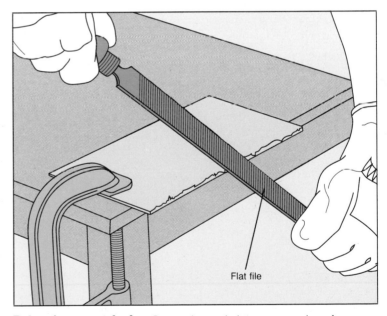

Flat file

**Draw-filing.** Set up the workpiece on a work surface *(page 17)* and prepare to use a file *(page 87)*; if you are working with metal, wear work gloves *(page 25)*. Holding the file by the handle in one hand and by the toe in the other hand, work straight along the edge from one end to the other end of it. To start a stroke, position the toe of the file flat on the edge at a 90-degree angle across one end of it. Keeping the file flat, push it straight along the edge *(above)*, applying enough uniform pressure into the edge to cut the material. When the file reaches the other end of the edge at the end of the stroke, pull it straight back smoothly and without stopping. Continue filing the same way, using a different part of the face to prevent it from clogging. If the file rides over rather than cuts the material, clean it *(page 87)*. To further smooth a wood edge, use a sanding block *(page 91)*. Otherwise, store your tools and clean up *(page 27)*.

**Deburring a metal edge.** Set up the workpiece on a work surface *(page 17)* with the burred edge facing upward and overhanging the work surface. Prepare to use a file *(page 87)*, choosing a single-cut type for fine deburring of tools; a double-cut type otherwise. Wearing work gloves *(page 25)*, hold the file by the handle in one hand and by the toe in the other hand. To start a stroke, position the file across the edge at a 45-degree angle to it. Keeping the file in position, push it straight across the edge *(above)*, applying enough uniform pressure into the edge to cut the material; if you are deburring the inside of a pipe or tube with a round file, hold it by the handle and turn it as you push it. When the heel of the file reaches the edge at the end of the stroke, lift it away smoothly and without stopping. Continue filing the same way, overlapping each stroke slightly. If the file rides over rather than cuts the material, clean it *(page 87)*. Store your tools and clean up *(page 27)*.

# CHOOSING AN ABRASIVE

### ABRASIVES

| Sandpaper | Grit | Grade | Uses |
|---|---|---|---|
| Very coarse | 36<br>40<br>50 | 2<br>1½<br>1 | Fast, heavy removing of material or many thick layers of paint; rough sanding with belt sander. |
| Coarse | 60<br>80 | ½<br>1/0 or 0 | Moderate to light removing of material or thick layers of paint; preliminary smoothing; leveling of deep depressions and scratches; smoothing with belt sander. |
| Medium | 100<br>120 | 2/0<br>3/0 | Intermediate smoothing; leveling of shallow depressions and scratches; final smoothing with belt sander. |
| Fine | 150<br>180 | 4/0<br>5/0 | Final smoothing before applying paint; light sanding between coats of paint. |
| Very fine | 220<br>240 | 6/0<br>7/0 | Final smoothing before applying clear finish; light sanding between coats of clear finish. |
| Extra fine | 280<br>320 | 8/0<br>9/0 | Fine sanding to remove air bubbles between coats of clear finish. |

| Steel wool | Grade | Uses |
|---|---|---|
| Medium fine | 1/0 (0) | General smoothing of most materials; removing rust or finish. |
| Very fine | 2/0 (00) | Deglossing of finish. |
| Extra fine | 3/0 (000) | Removing of paint spots; polishing of metal. |
| Super fine | 4/0 (0000) | Smoothing of finish; fine polishing of metal. |

**Choosing the right abrasive for the job.**
To choose an abrasive appropriate to the material and task, refer to the chart *(left)*; presented are types of sandpaper for use on wood and steel wool for use primarily on wood, metal or plastic. Sandpaper is usually identified by its coarseness, expressed as grit or grade; depending on the manufacturer, it may be named differently. In general, judge the condition of the surface to choose the sandpaper of the coarsest grit you need to start, then progress to successively finer grits.

Of the various types of grit available, flint is the least durable—best used for rough sanding or removing paint. Garnet is recommended for hand-sanding; aluminum oxide or silicon carbide for machine-sanding. For rough work, soft wood or removing paint, use an open-coat type; its dispersed grit is least prone to clogging. For fine work, hard wood or hand-sanding, use a closed-coat type; its dense grit cuts quickly. The weight of backing material ranges from A (lightest) to E (sturdiest) for paper; for cloth, X is sturdier than J.

Steel wool is identified by grade. Choose the steel wool of the grade you need for the job; wear work gloves *(page 25)* to rub the surface with it. For an irregular-shaped surface, mold the steel wool to match its contours.

# PREPARING TO USE A SANDING BLOCK

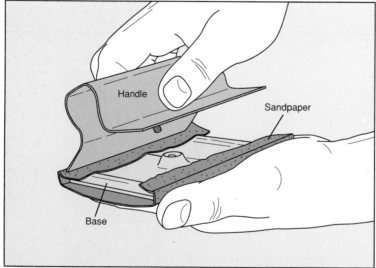

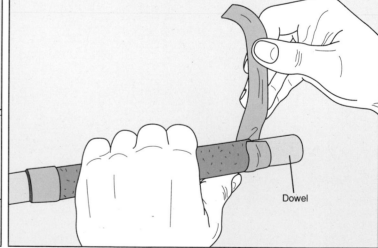

**Changing sandpaper.** To sand a flat or convex surface, buy a sanding block; or, use a small wood block, gluing a thick piece of felt or cork onto the bottom of it for padding. For a concave surface, use a wood dowel as a sanding stick. Choose a grit of sandpaper *(step above)*, then determine the size of sheet you need; a manufactured sanding block typically can hold a 1/4-sheet of sandpaper.

To change the sandpaper on the sanding block shown, loosen the screw and lift the handle off the base. Remove any old sandpaper, then use scissors or a utility knife and straightedge to trim a new sheet

of sandpaper to size: as long and as wide as the base with enough overlap for it to be held snugly in place by the handle. Wrap the sandpaper around the bottom of the base, folding the edges over the top of it, then reposition the handle *(above, left)* and tighten the screw.

For a homemade sanding block, trim a sheet of sandpaper as wide as it and long enough to wrap around it snugly with a bit of overlap on the top to hold while sanding. For a sanding stick, trim a sheet of sandpaper to fit snugly around the dowel with a bit of overlap, then use masking tape to secure the edges to it *(above, right)*.

## USING A SANDING BLOCK

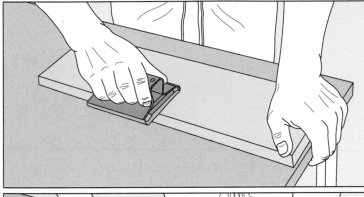

**Sanding the surface of a board.** Set up the workpiece on a work surface *(page 17)*, securing it by hand, if desired. Prepare to use a sanding block *(page 90)*. Holding the sanding block firmly in your hand, work parallel to the wood grain from one end to the other end of the surface. Position the sanding block flat on the surface and move it straight back and forth in long, smooth strokes, applying enough uniform pressure into the surface for the sandpaper to cut evenly; if the sandpaper cuts too deeply, reduce your pressure. To reposition the sanding block, lift it rather than sand across the wood grain, overlapping parallel strokes.

If a leading edge of the sandpaper catches, lift the sanding block and turn it 90 degrees to sand with a secured edge. To prevent the rounding of an edge along the length of the surface, keep most of the sanding block flat on the surface, overhanging the edge by less than half its width *(left, top)*. To prevent the rounding of an edge across the width of the surface, stop the sanding block before it leaves the surface, overhanging the edge by less than half its length *(left, bottom)*.

Stop sanding periodically to brush particles off the surface. To clear the sandpaper, tap an edge of the sanding block against a hard surface; if it is clogged, worn or torn, change it *(page 90)*. Check your work at a low angle under a good light source; as well as your eyes, use your fingers. Change to a finer-grit sandpaper as necessary. When you finish sanding, store your tools and clean up *(page 27)*.

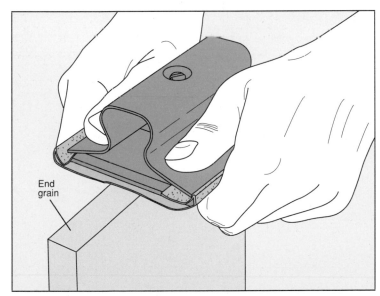

End grain

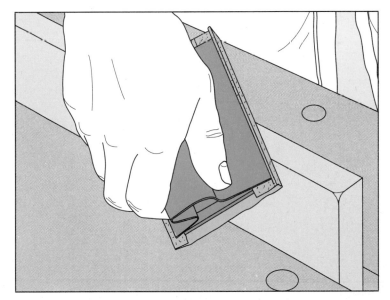

**Sanding the edge of a board.** Set up the workpiece on a work surface *(page 17)* with the edge facing upward, if possible. Prepare to use a sanding block *(page 90)*. Holding the sanding block firmly by its sides in both hands, work from one end to the other end along the edge. Position the sanding block flat on the edge and move it straight back and forth in smooth strokes without tilting it *(above)*; apply enough uniform pressure into the edge for the sandpaper to cut evenly. To avoid rounding an end of the edge, stop the sanding block before it leaves the edge, overhanging the end by less than half its length. Stop sanding periodically to brush particles off the edge. To clear the sandpaper, tap an edge of the sanding block against a hard surface; if it is clogged, worn or torn, change it *(page 90)*. Check your work at a low angle under a good light source; as well as your eyes, use your fingers. Change to a finer-grit sandpaper as necessary. When you finish sanding, store your tools and clean up *(page 27)*.

**Rounding the edge of a board.** Set up the workpiece on a work surface *(page 17)* and prepare to use a sanding block *(page 90)*. Holding the sanding block firmly in your hand, work from one end to the other end along the edge. Position the sanding block at a 45-degree angle to the edge almost flat on an adjacent surface, then move it straight back and forth in long, smooth strokes; apply enough uniform pressure into the edge for the sandpaper to cut evenly. Keeping the sanding block at a 45-degree angle to the edge, raise it farther off the adjacent surface and repeat the procedure, continuing *(above)* until it is almost flat on the other adjacent surface. Stop sanding periodically to brush particles off the edge. To clear the sandpaper, tap an edge of the sanding block against a hard surface; if it is clogged, worn or torn, change it *(page 90)*. Check your work at a low angle under a good light source; as well as your eyes, use your fingers. Change to a finer-grit sandpaper as necessary. When you finish sanding, store your tools and clean up *(page 27)*.

## PREPARING TO USE AN ORBITAL SANDER

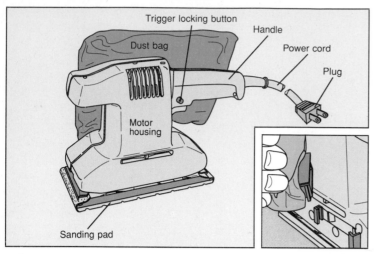

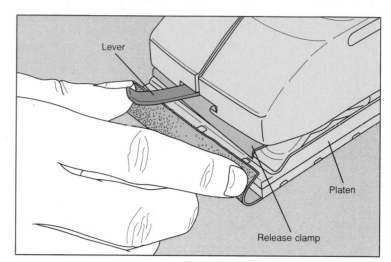

**1** **Inspecting an orbital sander.** Check an orbital sander before using it: with it unplugged, inspect its parts *(above)*, consulting your owner's manual. If the power cord or plug is loose or frayed or the handle, trigger switch or motor housing is cracked, do not use the sander until it is repaired. Tighten any loose screws. Empty any dust bag if it is more than half full, following the owner's manual instructions; on the model shown, slide the intake up off the brackets *(inset)*, then unzip the dust bag and empty it. If there is a hole in the dust bag, repair it with duct tape or buy a replacement. Zip up the dust bag and fit the intake into the brackets. Check also that the sander is clean. If the handle is greasy, wipe it using a soft cloth dampened with a solution of mild household detergent and water; do not wet any internal parts. Use a stiff-bristled brush to remove any caked dust; on surfaces difficult to reach, wear safety goggles *(page 25)* and use compressed air.

**2** **Changing sandpaper.** Ensuring the sander is unplugged, follow the owner's manual instructions to change the sandpaper if it is clogged, worn, torn or the wrong grit for the job. On the model shown, pull out the lever of a release clamp, then center it and pull it up to free one end of the old sandpaper; use the same procedure at the other end of the platen. If the pad on the bottom of the platen is glazed, roughen it slightly with fine sandpaper; if it is damaged, have it replaced. Choose a grit of sandpaper *(page 90)*, then use scissors or a utility knife and straightedge to trim the sheet to the size specified by the manufacturer. Holding up the lever of a release clamp, fold one end of the sandpaper over the edge of the platen *(above)*, then release the lever and push it back into place under the housing. Ensuring the sandpaper is flush with the sides of the pad, pull the other end of it snugly to the other end of the platen and install it the same way.

## USING AN ORBITAL SANDER

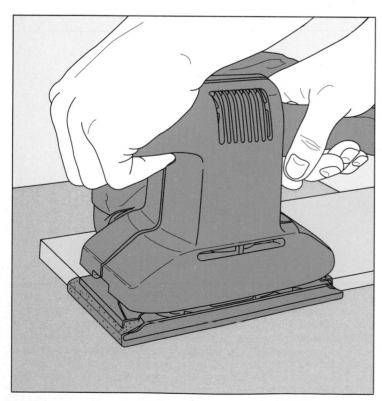

**Sanding the surface of a board.** Set up the workpiece on a work surface *(page 17)*, then prepare to use an orbital sander *(steps above)*. Wearing safety goggles *(page 25)* and respiratory protection *(page 26)*, plug in the sander *(page 24)* using an extension cord, if necessary *(page 23)*. Ensuring the power cord is out of the way, grip the sander firmly with both hands and lift it, then depress the trigger switch. When the sander is running at full speed, gently set it down flat on the surface—and immediately move it slowly, working back and forth along or from side to side across the surface in long, smooth, overlapping strokes; on a small surface, use a circular motion. Let the weight of the sander provide the uniform pressure into the surface for the sandpaper to cut evenly; never let the sander rest on one spot. Depress any trigger lock, if desired; to release it, depress the trigger switch.

To prevent the rounding of an edge along the length of the surface, orient the sander parallel to it and keep most of the sander flat on the surface, never overhanging it more than slightly *(left)*. To prevent the rounding of an edge across the width of the surface, be ready to move the sander back as you reach it; reorient the sander parallel to it, if necessary. Keep the sander back from any obstruction to avoid damaging the pad. To stop sanding, lift the sander straight off the surface, then release the trigger switch; let the pad stop moving before setting the sander down. Stop sanding periodically to empty the dust bag *(step 1, above)* and brush particles off the surface. Unplug the sander to clear the sandpaper, tapping or brushing it gently; if it is clogged, worn or torn, change it *(step 2, above)*. Check your work at a low angle under a good light source; as well as your eyes, use your fingers. Unplug the sander and change to a finer-grit sandpaper as necessary. When you finish sanding, store your tools and clean up *(page 27)*.

## PREPARING TO USE A BELT SANDER

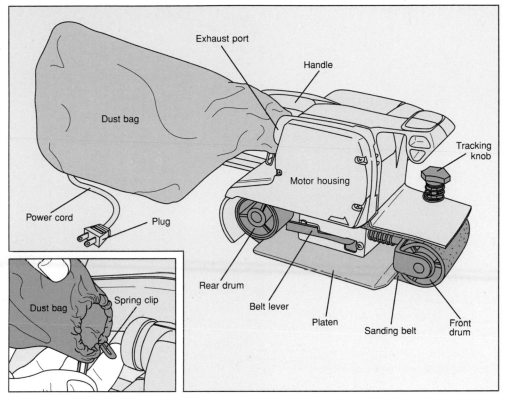

Dust bag

Exhaust port

Handle

Tracking knob

Motor housing

Power cord

Plug

Rear drum

Belt lever

Platen

Sanding belt

Front drum

Dust bag

Spring clip

**1** **Inspecting a belt sander.** Check a belt sander before using it: with it unplugged, inspect its parts *(left)*, consulting your owner's manual. If the power cord or plug is loose or frayed or the handle, trigger switch or motor housing is cracked, do not use the sander until it is repaired. Tighten any loose screws.

Empty any dust bag if it is more than half full, following the owner's manual instructions; on the model shown, compress the ends of the spring clip on the intake and pull off the dust bag *(inset)*, then unzip and empty it. If there is a hole in the dust bag, repair it with duct tape or buy a replacement. Zip up the dust bag and fit the intake onto the exhaust port, compressing the ends of the spring clip enough to open it and slide it into the groove.

Check also that the sander is clean. If the handle is greasy, wipe it using a soft cloth dampened with a solution of mild household detergent and water; do not wet any internal parts. Use a stiff-bristled brush to remove any caked dust; on the vents of the motor housing and other surfaces difficult to reach, wear safety goggles *(page 25)* and use compressed air.

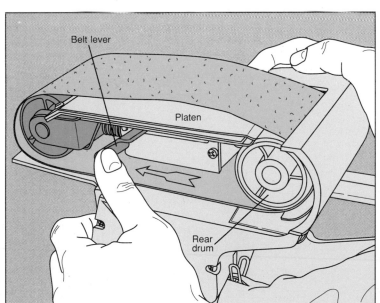

Belt lever

Platen

Rear drum

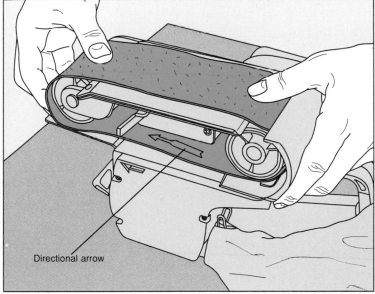

Directional arrow

**2** **Changing a sanding belt.** Ensuring the sander is unplugged, follow the owner's manual instructions to change the sanding belt if it is clogged, worn, torn or the wrong grit for the job; if necessary, turn it by hand to inspect its entire length. On the model shown, turn the sander upside down and pull the belt lever all the way out, locking it open *(above, left)*; then, slide the old sanding belt off the front and rear drums. To remove caked dust from the housing around the rear drum, use an old toothbrush; on any surface difficult to reach, wear safety goggles *(page 25)* and use compressed air. If the platen, the front drum or the rear drum is worn or otherwise damaged, have it replaced.

Choose a grit of sandpaper *(page 90)*, ensuring you use a sanding belt of the correct size for your sander; if you are removing material from plywood or veneer, choose a finer grit of sandpaper than you would for another type of wood to avoid sanding through the top layer of it. Install the sanding belt with the sander upside down, sliding it into place around the front and rear drums *(above, right)*; use the arrows marked on it to orient it in the direction of rotation specified by the manufacturer. Position the sanding belt parallel to the edge of the platen and align its outside edge with the outside edge of the rear drum, then push the belt lever all the way back into place, locking it closed.

## PREPARING TO USE A BELT SANDER (continued)

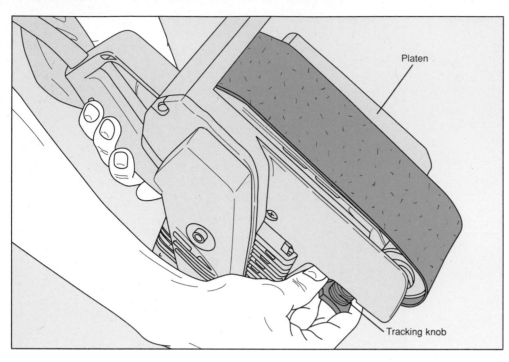

Platen

Tracking knob

**3** **Adjusting the tracking of the sanding belt.** If your sander has manual tracking, wear safety goggles *(page 25)* and plug in the sander *(page 24)* to check it. Setting the sander upside down on a work surface, grip the handle securely and depress the trigger switch, then examine the travel of the sanding belt. The sanding belt should stay centered on the front and rear drums, traveling parallel to the edge of the platen with its outside edge aligned with the outside edge of the rear drum. If the sanding belt travels laterally outward or in toward the housing, adjust its tracking.

Keeping away from the sanding belt, rotate the tracking knob back and forth a little at a time *(left)*, adjusting the angle of the front roller and the travel of the sanding belt. When the travel of the sanding belt is adjusted correctly, allow the sander to run for several minutes to ensure the sanding belt stays locked on track. Take the sander for professional service if its sanding belt does not stay locked on track or it has automatic tracking and its sanding belt travels laterally outward or in toward the housing.

## USING A BELT SANDER

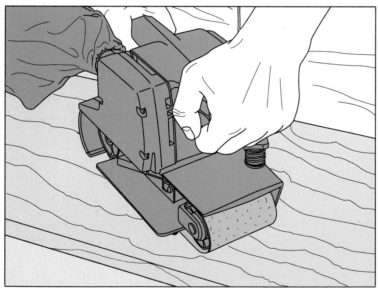

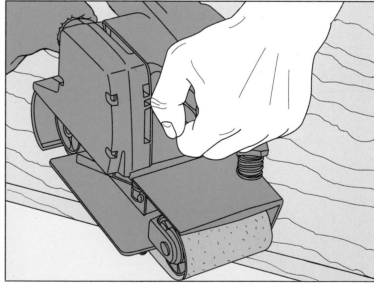

**Removing material from the surface of a board.** Set up the workpiece on a work surface *(page 17)*, then prepare to use a belt sander *(page 93)*. Wearing safety goggles, hearing protection *(page 25)* and respiratory protection *(page 26)*, plug in the sander *(page 24)* using an extension cord, if necessary *(page 23)*. Ensuring the power cord is out of the way, grip the sander firmly with both hands and lift it, then depress the trigger switch. When the sanding belt is traveling at full speed, orient the sander at a 45-degree angle to the wood grain and gently set it down flat on the surface—and immediately move it slowly, working back and forth along the surface parallel to the wood grain in long, smooth, overlapping strokes *(above, left)*. Let the weight of the sander provide the uniform pressure into the surface for the sanding belt to cut evenly; never let the sander rest on one spot. Depress any trigger lock, if desired; to release it, depress the trigger switch.

To prevent the rounding of an edge along the length of the surface, keep most of the sander flat on it, never overhanging a drum completely *(above, right)*. To prevent the rounding of an edge across the width of the surface, be ready to move the sander back as you reach it. Keep the sander back from any obstruction to avoid damaging the platen. To stop sanding, lift the sander straight off the surface, then release the trigger switch; let the sanding belt stop before setting the sander down. Stop sanding periodically to empty the dust bag *(page 93)* and brush particles off the surface. Unplug the sander to clear the sanding belt, tapping or brushing it gently or using an abrasive cleaner; if it is clogged, worn or torn, change it *(page 93)*. If necessary, adjust the tracking of the sanding belt *(step 3, above)*. Sand again the same way, orienting the sander in the opposite 45-degree angle to the wood grain. When you finish sanding, store your tools and clean up *(page 27)*.

## USING A BELT SANDER (continued)

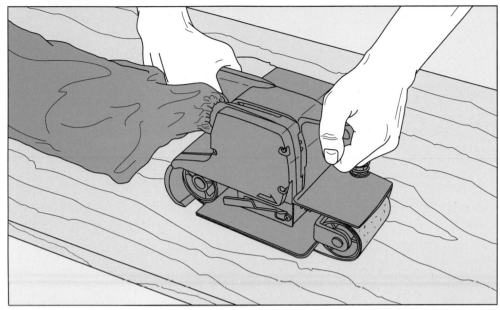

**Sanding the surface of a board.** Set up the workpiece on a work surface *(page 17)*, then prepare to use a belt sander *(page 93)*; if you removed material from the surface using the belt sander, start with a sanding belt of the same grit as the last sanding belt you used. Wearing safety goggles, hearing protection *(page 25)* and respiratory protection *(page 26)*, plug in the sander *(page 24)* using an extension cord, if necessary *(page 23)*. Ensuring the power cord is out of the way, grip the sander firmly with both hands and lift it, then depress the trigger switch.

When the sanding belt is traveling at full speed, orient the sander parallel to the wood grain and gently set it down flat on the surface— and immediately move it slowly, working back and forth along the surface in long, smooth, overlapping strokes *(left, top)*. Let the weight of the sander provide the uniform pressure into the surface for the sanding belt to cut evenly; never let the sander rest on one spot. Depress any trigger lock, if desired; to release it, depress the trigger switch.

To prevent the rounding of an edge along the length of the surface, keep most of the sander flat on it, never overhanging a drum completely *(left, center)*. To prevent the rounding of an edge across the width of the surface, be ready to move the sander back as you reach it *(left, bottom)*. Keep the sander back from any obstruction to avoid damaging the platen. To stop sanding, lift the sander straight off the surface, then release the trigger switch; let the sanding belt stop before setting the sander down.

Stop sanding periodically to empty the dust bag *(page 93)* and brush particles off the surface. Unplug the sander to clear the sanding belt, tapping or brushing it gently or using an abrasive cleaner; if it is clogged, worn or torn, change it *(page 93)*. If necessary, adjust the tracking of the sanding belt *(page 94)*. Check your work at a low angle under a good light source; as well as your eyes, use your fingers. Unplug the sander and change to a finer-grit sandpaper as necessary. For fine-sanding of the surface, continue sanding using an orbital sander *(page 92)*, starting with sandpaper of the same grit as the last sanding belt you used. When you finish sanding, store your tools and clean up *(page 27)*.

# FASTENING

Fasteners and fastening tools perform continually in the home workshop. For every repair project, fasteners are needed to assemble carefully measured and cut materials, ready for finishing or use. And whenever two pieces must be joined, a fastening tool must be chosen. This chapter covers the most common fastening techniques: nailing, screwing, bolting, pop riveting and gluing—each involving a wide array of tools. Although the hammers, screwdrivers and wrenches of basic fastening are probably the most familiar tools in the home workshop, their use always entails special considerations.

To choose the fastening technique and tool best suited to your task, consult the Troubleshooting Guide *(page 99)* and the inventory presented below and on page 98. For fastening certain materials, you may be given a choice of fastening techniques and tools. Refer to the specific repair acts in the chapter to help make your choice, selecting the fastener that can provide the holding strength, permanence and appearance appropriate to the job. In general, choose nails for rough work such as framing or for jobs requiring many fasteners. Screws, threaded fasteners that are driven by their heads, require more

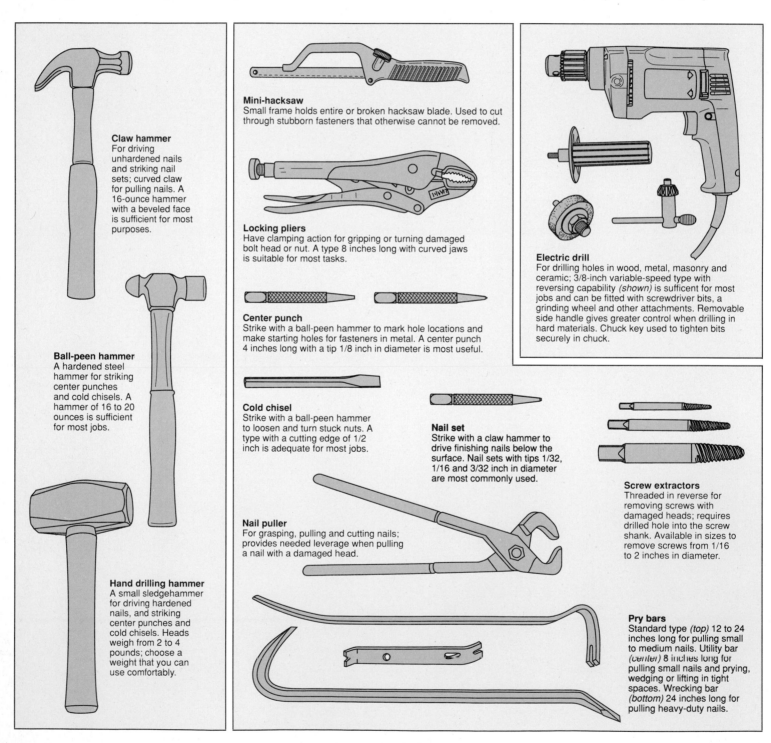

**Claw hammer**
For driving unhardened nails and striking nail sets; curved claw for pulling nails. A 16-ounce hammer with a beveled face is sufficient for most purposes.

**Ball-peen hammer**
A hardened steel hammer for striking center punches and cold chisels. A hammer of 16 to 20 ounces is sufficient for most jobs.

**Hand drilling hammer**
A small sledgehammer for driving hardened nails, and striking center punches and cold chisels. Heads weigh from 2 to 4 pounds; choose a weight that you can use comfortably.

**Mini-hacksaw**
Small frame holds entire or broken hacksaw blade. Used to cut through stubborn fasteners that otherwise cannot be removed.

**Locking pliers**
Have clamping action for gripping or turning damaged bolt head or nut. A type 8 inches long with curved jaws is suitable for most tasks.

**Center punch**
Strike with a ball-peen hammer to mark hole locations and make starting holes for fasteners in metal. A center punch 4 inches long with a tip 1/8 inch in diameter is most useful.

**Cold chisel**
Strike with a ball-peen hammer to loosen and turn stuck nuts. A type with a cutting edge of 1/2 inch is adequate for most jobs.

**Nail puller**
For grasping, pulling and cutting nails; provides needed leverage when pulling a nail with a damaged head.

**Nail set**
Strike with a claw hammer to drive finishing nails below the surface. Nail sets with tips 1/32, 1/16 and 3/32 inch in diameter are most commonly used.

**Electric drill**
For drilling holes in wood, metal, masonry and ceramic; 3/8-inch variable-speed type with reversing capability *(shown)* is sufficent for most jobs and can be fitted with screwdriver bits, a grinding wheel and other attachments. Removable side handle gives greater control when drilling in hard materials. Chuck key used to tighten bits securely in chuck.

**Screw extractors**
Threaded in reverse for removing screws with damaged heads; requires drilled hole into the screw shank. Available in sizes to remove screws from 1/16 to 2 inches in diameter.

**Pry bars**
Standard type *(top)* 12 to 24 inches long for pulling small to medium nails. Utility bar *(center)* 8 inches long for pulling small nails and prying, wedging or lifting in tight spaces. Wrecking bar *(bottom)* 24 inches long for pulling heavy-duty nails.

effort to install but hold better than nails—and can be easily and neatly removed for disassembly later. Bolts, threaded fasteners that are held tightly by nuts, are used for fastening large or heavy materials and for pieces that require regular disassembly and reassembly. Glues provide a strong, permanent bond that leaves no trace of the fastener. For joining thin sheet materials that do not need to be separated later, pop rivets are usually the best fastener choice.

When the choice of fastener has been made, use the information provided on techniques to help you do a good job with it. Refer to the charts on each category of fastener to choose the specific fastener best suited to your needs. The inventories of screws *(page 104)*, bolts *(page 111)* and nails *(page 117)*, and the chart on glues *(page 122)* present common general- and special-purpose types within each category.

Consult Measuring And Marking *(page 30)* to measure and mark fastener position points accurately. Many fasteners require drilled holes before they can be installed; use an electric drill *(page 100)* to bore holes in wood *(page 102)* or drill holes in metal, ceramic or masonry *(page 103)*. You will

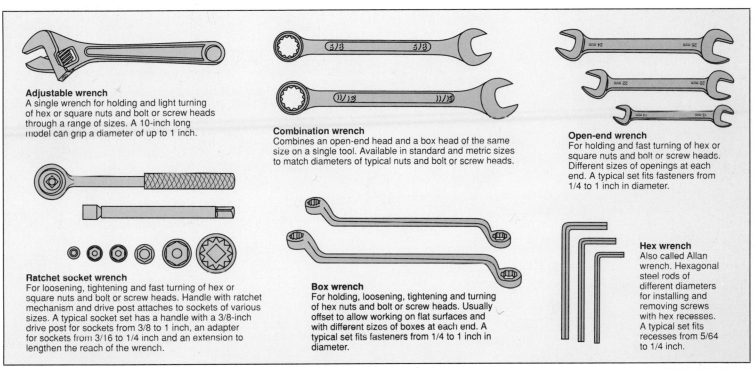

**Adjustable wrench**
A single wrench for holding and light turning of hex or square nuts and bolt or screw heads through a range of sizes. A 10-inch long model can grip a diameter of up to 1 inch.

**Combination wrench**
Combines an open-end head and a box head of the same size on a single tool. Available in standard and metric sizes to match diameters of typical nuts and bolt or screw heads.

**Open-end wrench**
For holding and fast turning of hex or square nuts and bolt or screw heads. Different sizes of openings at each end. A typical set fits fasteners from 1/4 to 1 inch in diameter.

**Ratchet socket wrench**
For loosening, tightening and fast turning of hex or square nuts and bolt or screw heads. Handle with ratchet mechanism and drive post attaches to sockets of various sizes. A typical socket set has a handle with a 3/8-inch drive post for sockets from 3/8 to 1 inch, an adapter for sockets from 3/16 to 1/4 inch and an extension to lengthen the reach of the wrench.

**Box wrench**
For holding, loosening, tightening and turning of hex nuts and bolt or screw heads. Usually offset to allow working on flat surfaces and with different sizes of boxes at each end. A typical set fits fasteners from 1/4 to 1 inch in diameter.

**Hex wrench**
Also called Allan wrench. Hexagonal steel rods of different diameters for installing and removing screws with hex recesses. A typical set fits recesses from 5/64 to 1/4 inch.

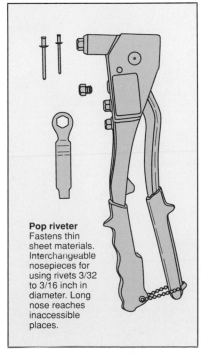

**Pop riveter**
Fastens thin sheet materials. Interchangeable nosepieces for using rivets 3/32 to 3/16 inch in diameter. Long nose reaches inaccessible places.

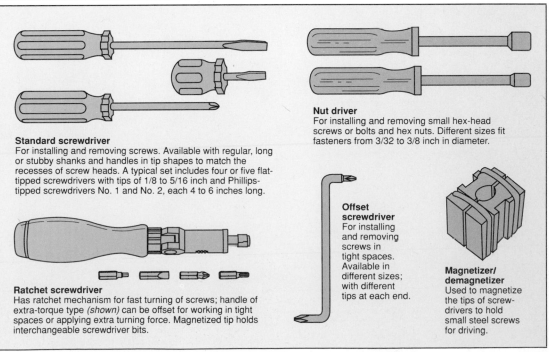

**Standard screwdriver**
For installing and removing screws. Available with regular, long or stubby shanks and handles in tip shapes to match the recesses of screw heads. A typical set includes four or five flat-tipped screwdrivers with tips of 1/8 to 5/16 inch and Phillips-tipped screwdrivers No. 1 and No. 2, each 4 to 6 inches long.

**Ratchet screwdriver**
Has ratchet mechanism for fast turning of screws; handle of extra-torque type *(shown)* can be offset for working in tight spaces or applying extra turning force. Magnetized tip holds interchangeable screwdriver bits.

**Nut driver**
For installing and removing small hex-head screws or bolts and hex nuts. Different sizes fit fasteners from 3/32 to 3/8 inch in diameter.

**Offset screwdriver**
For installing and removing screws in tight spaces. Available in different sizes; with different tips at each end.

**Magnetizer/demagnetizer**
Used to magnetize the tips of screwdrivers to hold small steel screws for driving.

need sets of fastening tools to match the vast range of fastener types and sizes. Choose a tool that can reach the fastener and is large enough to supply the needed force. Inspect your tools before using them; do not use damaged tools. Only use a tool for its intended purpose. Using the wrong tool because it is conveniently at hand can ruin it for its proper function.

Always wear the safety gear recommended for each tool. Safety goggles should be worn for all drilling and hammering operations to protect your eyes from flying particles. Wear work gloves when handling materials that have sharp edges or rough surfaces; rubber gloves when handling materials that have been treated with chemical preservatives. Work slowly and carefully while using any fastening tool. If a fastening task causes frustration, take time to evaluate the problem. When you have finished working, store your tools and spare fasteners in an assigned place in the workshop, organized by type and size for quick retrieval when next needed. Clean your tools using a soft cloth dampened with a solution of mild household detergent and water, then dry them thoroughly; on metal parts, you can clean with mineral spirits.

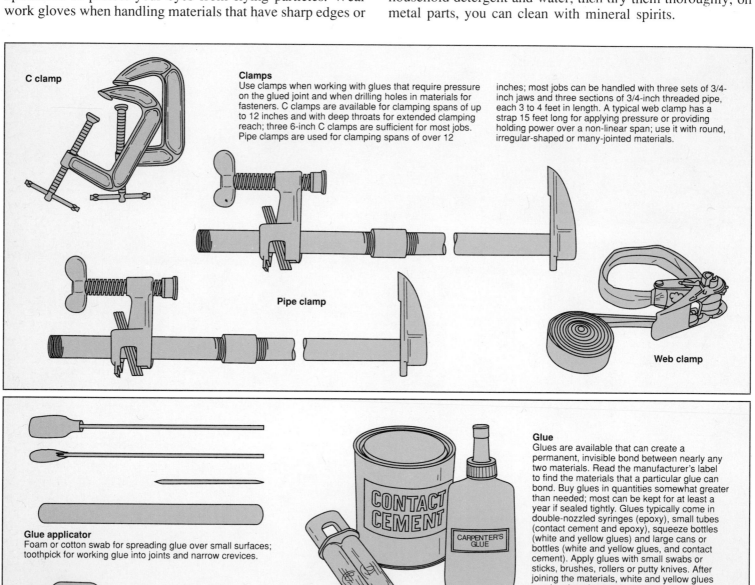

**C clamp**

**Clamps**
Use clamps when working with glues that require pressure on the glued joint and when drilling holes in materials for fasteners. C clamps are available for clamping spans of up to 12 inches and with deep throats for extended clamping reach; three 6-inch C clamps are sufficient for most jobs. Pipe clamps are used for clamping spans of over 12 inches; most jobs can be handled with three sets of 3/4-inch jaws and three sections of 3/4-inch threaded pipe, each 3 to 4 feet in length. A typical web clamp has a strap 15 feet long for applying pressure or providing holding power over a non-linear span; use it with round, irregular-shaped or many-jointed materials.

**Pipe clamp**

**Web clamp**

**Glue applicator**
Foam or cotton swab for spreading glue over small surfaces; toothpick for working glue into joints and narrow crevices.

**Glue**
Glues are available that can create a permanent, invisible bond between nearly any two materials. Read the manufacturer's label to find the materials that a particular glue can bond. Buy glues in quantities somewhat greater than needed; most can be kept for at least a year if sealed tightly. Glues typically come in double-nozzled syringes (epoxy), small tubes (contact cement and epoxy), squeeze bottles (white and yellow glues) and large cans or bottles (white and yellow glues, and contact cement). Apply glues with small swabs or sticks, brushes, rollers or putty knives. After joining the materials, white and yellow glues require clamping; contact cement requires smoothing with a pressure roller.

**Pressure roller**
Wooden or plastic roller for smoothing and applying pressure to thin material after glue is applied to it and it is positioned.

**Putty knife**
For applying glue to large surfaces and cleaning up excess glue squeezed out of joints.

**Glue syringe**
Forces glue into joints and narrow crevices. Best used with water-soluble glues. When filled, store with protective cap to prevent glue from drying out.

# TROUBLESHOOTING GUIDE

| PROBLEM | PROCEDURE |
|---|---|
| **Making a pilot hole or a clearance hole for a fastener** | Use a drill (p. 100) to bore into wood (p. 102) or drill into metal, ceramic or masonry (p. 103) |
| **Boring a countersink hole for a fastener in wood** | Use a drill (p. 100) with a combination bit or a countersink bit (p. 102) |
| **Fastening wood, plywood or composition board to wood** | Fasten with screws (p. 106) using a hand screwdriver (p. 105) or a screwdriver bit with an electric drill (p. 106); with lag bolts, using a wrench (p. 109) |
| | Fasten with nails (p. 118) using a claw hammer (p. 115) |
| | Fasten with carriage bolts, machine bolts (p. 112) or stove bolts (p. 113) using a wrench (p. 109) |
| | Fasten with glue (p. 122) |
| **Fastening wood veneer or plastic laminate to wood** | Fasten with glue (p. 122) |
| **Fastening wood to metal** | Fasten with carriage bolts, machine bolts (p. 112) or stove bolts (p. 113) using a wrench (p. 109) |
| **Fastening wood to masonry** | Fasten with screws (p. 107) using a hand screwdriver (p. 105) or a screwdriver bit with an electric drill (p. 106); with lag bolts, using a wrench (p. 109) |
| | Fasten with nails (p. 119) using a hand drilling hammer (p. 116) |
| **Fastening wood to a hollow wall (including concrete block and ceramic tile)** | Fasten with screws (p. 108) using a hand screwdriver (p. 105) or a screwdriver bit with an electric drill (p. 106) |
| | Fasten with toggle bolts (p. 113) or expansion anchors (p. 114) using a hand screwdriver (p. 105) |
| | Fasten with glue (p. 122) |
| **Fastening metal to wood** | Fasten with screws (p. 106) using a hand screwdriver (p. 105) or a screwdriver bit with an electric drill (p. 106); with lag bolts, using a wrench (p. 109) |
| | Fasten with machine bolts (p. 112) or stove bolts (p. 113) using a wrench (p. 109) |
| **Fastening metal to metal** | Fasten with screws (p. 107) using a hand screwdriver (p. 105) or a screwdriver bit with an electric drill (p. 106) |
| | Fasten with machine bolts (p. 112) or stove bolts (p. 113) using a wrench (p. 109) |
| | Fasten with pop rivets using a pop riveter (p. 120) |
| | Fasten with glue (p. 122) |
| **Fastening metal to masonry** | Fasten with screws (p. 107) using a hand screwdriver (p. 105) or a screwdriver bit with an electric drill (p. 106); with lag bolts, using a wrench (p. 109) |
| | Fasten with nails (p. 119) using a hand drilling hammer (p. 116) |
| **Fastening metal to a hollow wall (including concrete block and ceramic tile)** | Fasten with screws (p. 108) using a hand screwdriver (p. 105) or a screwdriver bit with an electric drill (p. 106) |
| | Fasten with toggle bolts (p. 113) or expansion anchors (p. 114) using a hand screwdriver (p. 105) |
| | Fasten with glue (p. 122) |
| **Fastening drywall to wood** | Fasten with nails (p. 118) using a claw hammer (p. 115) |
| | Fasten with screws (p. 106) using a hand screwdriver (p. 105) or a screwdriver bit with an electric drill (p. 106) |
| **Removing screws** | For undamaged screws, use a hand screwdriver or a screwdriver bit with an electric drill (p. 108); with lag bolts, use a wrench (p. 109) |
| | For damaged screws, use a screw extractor (p. 109) |
| | If no other tool works, cut through screw shank using a mini-hacksaw (p. 63) |
| **Removing carriage bolts, machine bolts or stove bolts** | For undamaged bolts, use a wrench (p. 114) |
| | For damaged bolts, use locking pliers or a cold chisel (p. 115) |
| | If no other tool works, cut through bolt shank using a mini-hacksaw (p. 63) |
| **Removing nails** | For nails with undamaged and accessible heads, use a claw hammer or a pry bar (p. 119) |
| | For nails with damaged heads, use a nail puller (p. 120) |
| | For nails with inaccessible heads, use a nail set (p. 120) |
| | If no other tool works, cut through nail shank using a mini-hacksaw (p. 63) |
| **Removing pop rivets** | Drill out or grind off pop rivet using an electric drill (p. 121) |

## PREPARING TO USE AN ELECTRIC DRILL

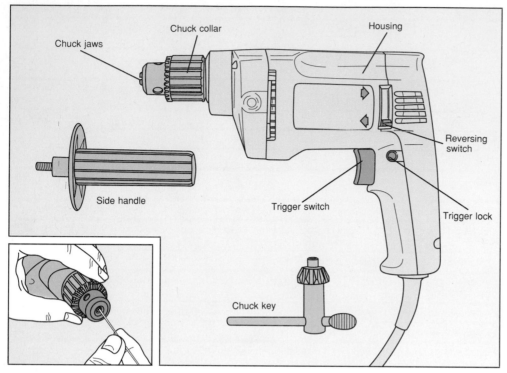

Chuck collar

Chuck jaws

Housing

Side handle

Reversing switch

Trigger switch

Trigger lock

Chuck key

**1** **Inspecting a drill.** An electric drill is sized by the largest diameter bit shank its chuck can hold; a 3/8-inch, variable-speed reversing drill, as shown, is sufficient for most purposes. Check the drill before using it; with it unplugged, inspect its parts *(left)*, consulting the owner's manual. If the power cord or plug is loose or frayed or the handle, trigger switch or housing is cracked, do not use the drill. Tighten any loose screws. Rotate the chuck collar to ensure the jaws open and close freely. If there is any friction or blockage, open the jaws as far as possible, then rotate the chuck collar back and forth, tapping it with your hand or using a wire to dislodge any particles *(inset)*. Use the drill only after any repair necessary is undertaken.

Check also that the drill is clean. If the handle or housing is dirty or greasy, wipe it using a soft cloth dampened with a solution of mild household detergent and water; do not wet any internal parts. Use a stiff-bristled brush to remove any caked sawdust; on the housing vents and other surfaces difficult to reach, wear safety goggles *(page 25)* and use compressed air.

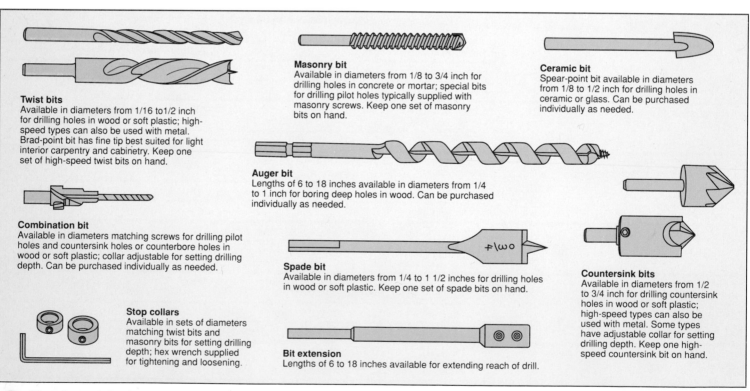

**Twist bits**
Available in diameters from 1/16 to 1/2 inch for drilling holes in wood or soft plastic; high-speed types can also be used with metal. Brad-point bit has fine tip best suited for light interior carpentry and cabinetry. Keep one set of high-speed twist bits on hand.

**Masonry bit**
Available in diameters from 1/8 to 3/4 inch for drilling holes in concrete or mortar; special bits for drilling pilot holes typically supplied with masonry screws. Keep one set of masonry bits on hand.

**Ceramic bit**
Spear-point bit available in diameters from 1/8 to 1/2 inch for drilling holes in ceramic or glass. Can be purchased individually as needed.

**Auger bit**
Lengths of 6 to 18 inches available in diameters from 1/4 to 1 inch for boring deep holes in wood. Can be purchased individually as needed.

**Combination bit**
Available in diameters matching screws for drilling pilot holes and countersink or counterbore holes in wood or soft plastic; collar adjustable for setting drilling depth. Can be purchased individually as needed.

**Spade bit**
Available in diameters from 1/4 to 1 1/2 inches for drilling holes in wood or soft plastic. Keep one set of spade bits on hand.

**Countersink bits**
Available in diameters from 1/2 to 3/4 inch for drilling countersink holes in wood or soft plastic; high-speed types can also be used with metal. Some types have adjustable collar for setting drilling depth. Keep one high-speed countersink bit on hand.

**Stop collars**
Available in sets of diameters matching twist bits and masonry bits for setting drilling depth; hex wrench supplied for tightening and loosening.

**Bit extension**
Lengths of 6 to 18 inches available for extending reach of drill.

**2** **Choosing a drill bit.** Consult the chart *(above)* to determine the bit best suited to the material and the hole; note that its shank cannot be larger than 3/8 inch in diameter for a 3/8-inch drill. Many types of bits are available in sets of standard sizes; some types of bits can be purchased individually. For most drilling with wood or plastic, a set of twist bits from 1/16 to 3/8 inch in diameter is sufficient; the high-speed type are most expensive but can also be used with metal. To drill to a set depth, also use a stop collar. To extend the reach of the drill, use a bit extension.

For beveled hole edges that match a flat-head screw or bolt, use a countersink bit; to drill to a set depth, use an adjustable type. Use a combination bit for a pilot hole and countersink or counterbore hole. For a hole with a diameter of 1/4 to 1 1/2 inches up to 4 inches deep in wood or plastic, use a spade bit. For a hole deeper than 4 inches in wood, use an auger bit; it drills quickly with only slight pressure. For fine woodworking, choose a brad-point bit; it ensures starting accuracy, splinterless hole edges and a flat hole bottom. With concrete or mortar, use a masonry bit. With ceramic or glass, use a spear-point bit.

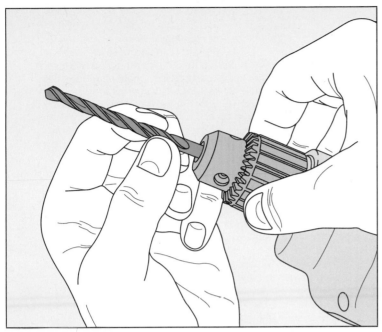

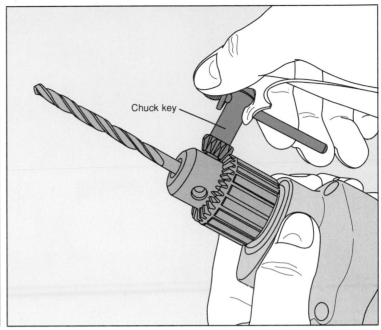

**3** **Inspecting, servicing and changing a bit.** To inspect, service or change a bit, ensure the drill is unplugged. To remove a bit, open the chuck jaws using the chuck key supplied with the drill. Fit the chuck key into a chuck hole and turn it counterclockwise until the bit is loose enough to slide out of the chuck. If the bit is dull, warped or cracked or a flute is chipped, discard it. Clean any caked sawdust, gum, pitch or glue off the bit using a soft cloth dampened with mineral spirits. If you are changing the bit, apply a little light machine oil to it before storing it. Before installing a bit you have stored, wipe it with a soft cloth.

To install a bit, use the chuck key to open the chuck jaws enough to slide it in. With a large bit, push its shank into the chuck as far as possible and then pull it out slightly—about 1/8 inch. With a small bit, push its shank fully into the chuck; keep its flutes exposed. Steadying the bit with one hand and twisting it 1/4 turn back and forth to keep it aligned, turn the chuck collar clockwise with your other hand to close the chuck jaws *(above, left)*. Tighten the chuck jaws with the chuck key, fitting it in turn into each chuck hole and turning it clockwise *(above, right)*. To check the bit, run the drill at low speed; if the bit wobbles, reinstall it.

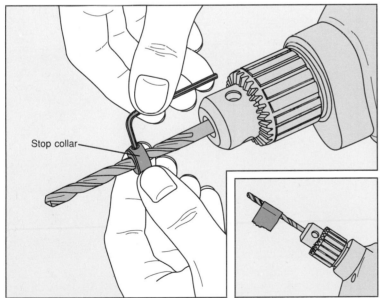

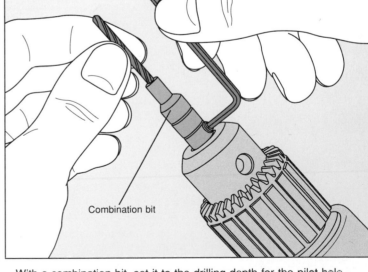

**4** **Setting the drilling depth of the bit.** To set the drilling depth of the bit, ensure the drill is unplugged. With a twist bit or a masonry bit, choose a stop collar that fits snugly onto it, then slide the stop collar into position at the drilling depth. Steadying the stop collar with one hand, use your other hand to turn its setscrew clockwise with its hex wrench *(above, left)*, gently tightening it against a flute of the bit. Or, mark the drilling depth on the bit using masking tape; wrap a strip of the masking tape tightly around the bit to create a short flag *(inset)* that is clearly visible when the drill is running.

With a combination bit, set it to the drilling depth for the pilot hole. Using the hex wrench supplied with the combination bit, turn the setscrew counterclockwise to loosen the collar, then adjust the bit position to the screw length: to its full length for drilling into hardwood; to 2/3 its length for drilling into softwood. Steadying the bit with one hand, use your other hand to turn the setscrew clockwise with the hex wrench *(above, right)*, gently tightening it. With an adjustable countersink bit, set it to the drilling depth the same way, adjusting the bit position to the fastener head thickness.

## BORING INTO WOOD

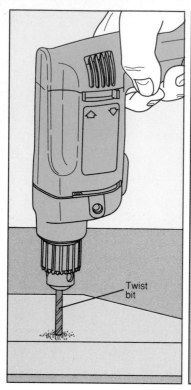 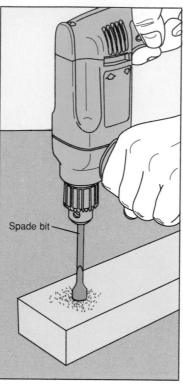

Twist bit

Spade bit

**Boring a hole.** Set up on a work surface *(page 17)*; measure and mark *(page 30)* a hole position point. Prepare to use a drill *(page 100)*, choosing a bit for wood of an appropriate diameter: with a 3/8-inch drill, a combination bit for a pilot hole and countersink or counterbore hole *(step below, left)*; a twist bit for a hole up to 3/8 inch in diameter and 4 inches deep; a spade bit for a hole more than 3/8 inch in diameter and up to 4 inches deep; an auger bit for a hole from 1/4 to 1 inch in diameter and more than 4 inches deep. If necessary, set the drilling depth of a twist bit with a stop collar or masking tape. If you are using a spade bit or an auger bit, fit the drill with its side handle. Wearing safety goggles *(page 25)* and respiratory protection *(page 26)*, plug in the drill *(page 24)* and set any reversing switch to FORWARD, then set the tip of the bit at the marked position point.

Holding the drill steady, apply light pressure and depress the trigger switch slightly, running the drill at low speed. Keeping the bit perpendicular to the surface, gradually increase your pressure and the drill speed as the bit starts to cut *(far left)*; if the drill is fitted with a side handle, keep one hand on it *(near left)*. If the drill strains or the bit heats up, decrease your pressure and the drill speed. If the bit still heats up, withdraw it from the hole, then release the trigger switch; let the bit cool and brush or blow particles out of the hole before continuing. If the bit makes no progress, it may be dull; replace it *(page 101)*. When the bit reaches the drilling depth desired, withdraw it from the hole and then release the trigger switch. Let the bit cool, then replace it with a countersink bit to bore a countersink hole *(step below, right)*, if necessary.

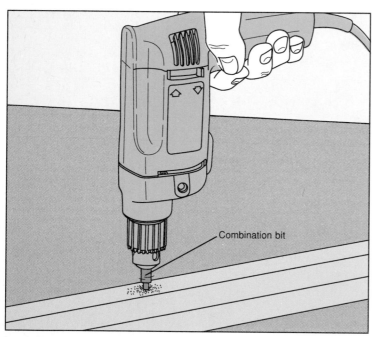

Combination bit

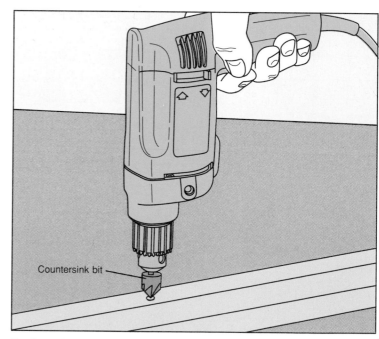

Countersink bit

**Boring with a combination bit.** Set up on a work surface *(page 17)*; measure and mark *(page 30)* a hole position point. Prepare to use a drill *(page 100)*, choosing a combination bit of an appropriate diameter and setting the drilling depth. Wearing safety goggles *(page 25)* and respiratory protection *(page 26)*, plug in the drill *(page 24)* and set any reversing switch to FORWARD, then set the tip of the bit at the marked position point. Holding the drill steady, apply light pressure and depress the trigger switch slightly, running the drill at low speed. Keeping the bit perpendicular to the surface, gradually increase your pressure and the drill speed as the bit starts to cut *(above)*. When the bit reaches the countersink or counterbore depth desired, withdraw it from the hole and then release the trigger switch.

**Boring with a countersink bit.** Set up on a work surface *(page 17)*; measure and mark *(page 30)* a hole position point. Prepare to use a drill *(page 100)*, making a pilot or clearance hole *(step above)*, then choosing a countersink bit; if it is adjustable, set the drilling depth. Wearing safety goggles *(page 25)* and respiratory protection *(page 26)*, plug in the drill *(page 24)* and set any reversing switch to FORWARD, then set the tip of the bit at the hole. Holding the drill steady, apply light pressure and depress the trigger switch slightly, running the drill at low speed. Keeping the bit perpendicular to the surface, gradually increase your pressure and the drill speed as the bit starts to cut *(above)*. When the bit reaches the countersink depth desired, withdraw it from the hole and then release the trigger switch.

# DRILLING INTO METAL, MASONRY OR CERAMIC

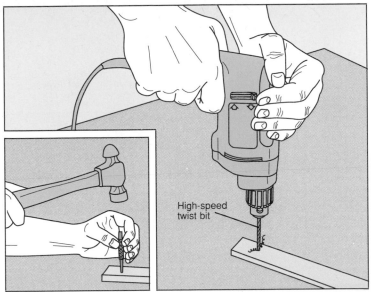

High-speed twist bit

**Drilling into metal.** Set up on a work surface *(page 17)*; measure and mark *(page 30)* a hole position point. Prepare to use a drill *(page 100)*, choosing a high-speed twist bit for metal of an appropriate diameter; for chrome, have any hole needed machine-drilled professionally. To keep the bit from wandering, use a center punch and a ball-peen hammer *(page 115)* to make a starting point. Wearing safety goggles *(page 25)*, set the tip of the center punch at the marked position point and strike the top of it lightly with the hammer *(inset)*. Plug in the drill *(page 24)* and set any reversing switch to FORWARD, then set the tip of the bit at the starting point.

Holding the drill steady with both hands, apply moderate pressure and depress the trigger switch slightly, running the drill at low speed. Keeping the bit perpendicular to the surface, maintain your pressure and the drill speed as the bit starts to cut *(left)*. If the drill strains or the bit heats up, decrease your pressure. If the bit still heats up, withdraw it from the hole, then release the trigger switch; let the bit cool and brush or blow particles out of the hole before continuing. If the bit makes no progress, it may be dull; replace it *(page 101)*. When the bit reaches the drilling depth desired, withdraw it from the hole and then release the trigger switch.

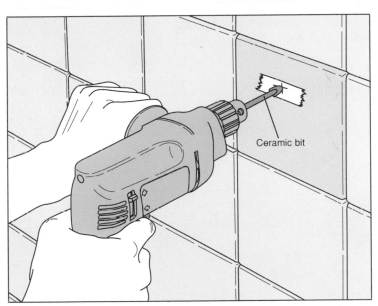

Ceramic bit

**Drilling into ceramic.** If necessary, set up on a work surface *(page 17)*; measure and mark *(page 30)* a hole position point using masking tape as padding, as shown. Prepare to use a drill *(page 100)* with a side handle, choosing a spear-point bit for ceramic of an appropriate diameter; for a hole wider than 1/4 inch, plan to drill first with a bit 1/4 inch in diameter, then successively with bits up to 1/8 inch in diameter larger. Wearing safety goggles *(page 25)*, plug in the drill *(page 24)* and set any reversing switch to FORWARD, then set the tip of the bit at the marked position point.

Holding the drill steady with both hands, apply light pressure and depress the trigger switch slightly, running the drill at low speed *(left)*. Keeping the bit perpendicular to the surface, gradually increase your pressure and the drill speed as the bit starts to cut. If the drill strains or the bit heats up, decrease your pressure and the drill speed. If the bit still heats up, withdraw it from the hole, then release the trigger switch; let the bit cool and brush or blow particles out of the hole before continuing. If the bit makes no progress, it may be dull; replace it *(page 101)*. When the bit reaches the drilling depth desired, withdraw it from the hole and then release the trigger switch. Let the bit cool, then replace it to drill again, if necessary.

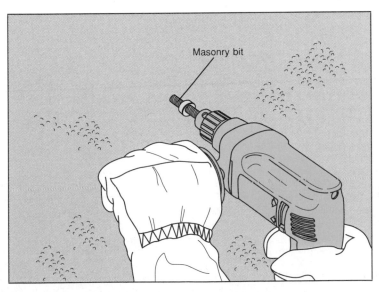

Masonry bit

**Drilling into masonry.** If necessary, set up on a work surface *(page 17)*; measure and mark *(page 30)* a hole position point. Prepare to use a drill *(page 100)* with a side handle, choosing a masonry bit for concrete or mortar of an appropriate diameter; for a hole wider than 1/4 inch, plan to drill first with a bit 1/4 inch in diameter, then successively with bits up to 1/4 inch in diameter larger. Wearing safety goggles, work gloves *(page 25)* and respiratory protection *(page 26)*, plug in the drill *(page 24)* and set any reversing switch to FORWARD, then set the tip of the bit at the marked position point.

Holding the drill steady with both hands, apply light pressure and depress the trigger switch slightly, running the drill at low speed. Keeping the bit perpendicular to the surface, gradually increase your pressure and the drill speed as the bit starts to cut *(left)*. If the drill strains or the bit heats up, decrease your pressure and the drill speed. If the bit still heats up, withdraw it from the hole, then release the trigger switch; let the bit cool and brush or blow particles out of the hole before continuing. If the bit makes no progress, it may be dull; replace it *(page 101)*. When the bit reaches the drilling depth desired, withdraw it from the hole and then release the trigger switch. Let the bit cool, then replace it to drill again if necessary.

## CHOOSING A SCREW

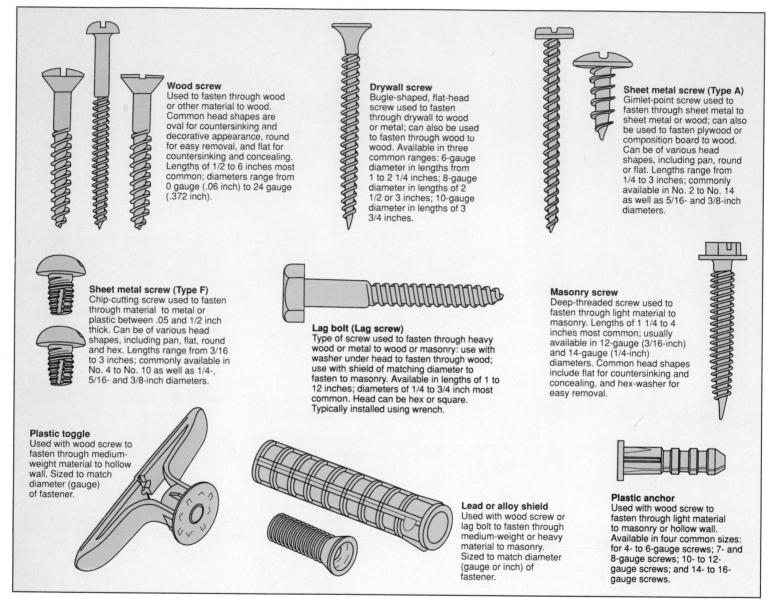

**Wood screw**
Used to fasten through wood or other material to wood. Common head shapes are oval for countersinking and decorative appearance, round for easy removal, and flat for countersinking and concealing. Lengths of 1/2 to 6 inches most common; diameters range from 0 gauge (.06 inch) to 24 gauge (.372 inch).

**Drywall screw**
Bugle-shaped, flat-head screw used to fasten through drywall to wood or metal; can also be used to fasten through wood to wood. Available in three common ranges: 6-gauge diameter in lengths from 1 to 2 1/4 inches; 8-gauge diameter in lengths of 2 1/2 or 3 inches; 10-gauge diameter in lengths of 3 3/4 inches.

**Sheet metal screw (Type A)**
Gimlet-point screw used to fasten through sheet metal to sheet metal or wood; can also be used to fasten plywood or composition board to wood. Can be of various head shapes, including pan, round or flat. Lengths range from 1/4 to 3 inches; commonly available in No. 2 to No. 14 as well as 5/16- and 3/8-inch diameters.

**Sheet metal screw (Type F)**
Chip-cutting screw used to fasten through material to metal or plastic between .05 and 1/2 inch thick. Can be of various head shapes, including pan, flat, round and hex. Lengths range from 3/16 to 3 inches; commonly available in No. 4 to No. 10 as well as 1/4-, 5/16- and 3/8-inch diameters.

**Lag bolt (Lag screw)**
Type of screw used to fasten through heavy wood or metal to wood or masonry: use with washer under head to fasten through wood; use with shield of matching diameter to fasten to masonry. Available in lengths of 1 to 12 inches; diameters of 1/4 to 3/4 inch most common. Head can be hex or square. Typically installed using wrench.

**Masonry screw**
Deep-threaded screw used to fasten through light material to masonry. Lengths of 1 1/4 to 4 inches most common; usually available in 12-gauge (3/16-inch) and 14-gauge (1/4-inch) diameters. Common head shapes include flat for countersinking and concealing, and hex-washer for easy removal.

**Plastic toggle**
Used with wood screw to fasten through medium-weight material to hollow wall. Sized to match diameter (gauge) of fastener.

**Lead or alloy shield**
Used with wood screw or lag bolt to fasten through medium-weight or heavy material to masonry. Sized to match diameter (gauge or inch) of fastener.

**Plastic anchor**
Used with wood screw to fasten through light material to masonry or hollow wall. Available in four common sizes: for 4- to 6-gauge screws; 7- and 8-gauge screws; 10- to 12-gauge screws; and 14- to 16-gauge screws.

**Choosing the right screw for the job.** To help you choose the right screw for the job, refer to the chart *(above)*; shown are typical screws for fastening through and to wood or other materials around the home. For fastening through most materials to wood, a wood screw can do the job; for fastening through heavy wood or metal to wood, use a lag bolt. For fastening through or to material such as masonry, metal or drywall, special screws are available; for fastening to a solid or hollow wall, use the appropriate shield, anchor or toggle. Consult your local hardware store or building supply center for specific recommendations.

After choosing an appropriate type of screw for the materials through and to which you are fastening, determine if any special features are necessary. If the screw is to be installed in a wet or damp location, use a rust-resistant variety: any galvanized-steel type for indoors; hot-dipped galvanized-steel for outdoors; stainless steel for areas subjected to corrosive salt water. For a decorative appearance but less holding power than a steel screw, use a brass or copper-plated screw. If you are fastening through or to metal, ensure the screw is of the same metal to prevent a corrosive reaction.

Use a screw of a suitable length for the dimensions of the materials through and to which you are fastening. For fastening to wood, choose a wood screw, drywall screw, lag bolt or sheet metal screw of a length about 3 times the thickness of the material through which you are

fastening; ensure it is also at least 1/4 inch shorter than the combined thickness of the materials through and to which you are fastening. If you are fastening to wood with a wood screw, the unthreaded portion of its shank should be shorter than the thickness of the material through which you are fastening, its threads extending fully into the wood to which you are fastening. Choose the best diameter (gauge or inch) for the length of screw you are using. In general, choose a small-diameter screw for fastening through light material or to hardwood; choose a large-diameter screw for fastening through heavy material or to softwood or end grain.

For fastening to masonry, choose a screw 1 to 1 1/2 inches longer than the thickness of the material through which you are fastening; use a small-diameter type for fastening through light material, a large-diameter type for fastening through heavy material. If you are not installing a masonry screw, also use an appropriate shield or anchor of a suitable diameter and length. For fastening to a hollow wall, choose a screw slightly longer than the combined thickness of the materials through and to which you are fastening; also use an anchor or a toggle of a matching diameter and length. For fastening together thin sheet metal or plastic materials, choose a gimlet-point sheet metal screw slightly longer than the combined thickness of the materials. For fastening together thick metal or plastic materials, choose a chip-cutting sheet metal screw about 3 times longer than the thickness of the material through which you are fastening.

## CHOOSING AND PREPARING TO USE A HAND SCREWDRIVER

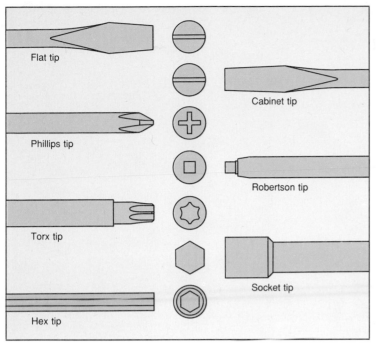

**Choosing and inspecting a screwdriver.** For a large number of screws or large screws that need strong turning force, use a screwdriver bit with an electric drill *(page 106)*. Otherwise, choose a hand screwdriver *(page 96)* suited to the job. For most purposes, a screwdriver with a straight 4- to 6-inch shank is sufficient; for greater turning force, choose a screwdriver with a longer shank and thicker handle. For easiest access in a tight spot, choose a stubby or an offset screwdriver. For fast turning, choose a ratchet screwdriver. Ensure the blade tip of the screwdriver exactly matches the type and size of slot or recess in the head of the screw you are using *(left)*; fit it into the head of the screw to check it. If the blade tip is too small, it may snap or bend the screw head when turning force is applied; if it is too large, it may slip and damage the screw head or the workpiece surface.

Inspect the screwdriver before using it. If the handle is cracked, the shank or blade is bent, or the blade tip is worn or damaged, do not use the screwdriver; replace it. Check also that the screwdriver is clean. If the handle is dirty or greasy, wipe it using a soft cloth dampened with a solution of mild household detergent and water; dry it thoroughly with a clean cloth. To clean gum, pitch or glue off the shank or blade, use a soft cloth dampened with mineral spirits; to remove rust, wear work gloves *(page 25)* and use steel wool. When the screwdriver is in good condition, ensure you know how to use it properly *(steps below)*.

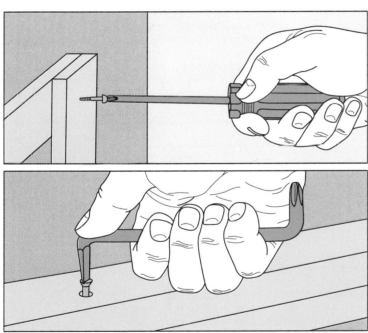

**Using a standard or an offset screwdriver.** To use a standard screwdriver, hold it firmly by the handle in the palm of your hand. Steadying the shank between the thumb and fingers of your other hand, fit the blade tip straight into the screw head. Applying light pressure, turn the handle as far as you can: clockwise to tighten the screw and counterclockwise to loosen it. Still steadying the shank, loosen your grip on the handle, then reposition your hand on it and turn it again. Continue the procedure until the shank does not need steadying, then remove your hand from it and turn the handle the same way *(above, top)*.

To use an offset screwdriver, hold it firmly by the shank in the palm of your hand and fit the blade tip into the screw head. Cradling the shank in your fingers, apply light pressure with your thumb and turn it as far as you can. Lift the blade tip out of the screw head, reposition it and continue the procedure, turning the shank the same way *(above, bottom)*.

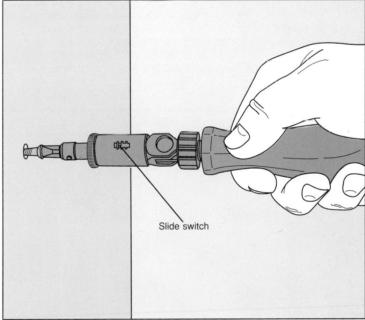

Slide switch

**Using a ratchet screwdriver.** Choose a screwdriver bit with a blade tip that exactly matches the type and size of slot or recess in the head of the screw you are using and install it following the manufacturer's instructions; on the model shown, slide it into the nose and tighten it. Position the slide switch at the desired setting for installing or removing a screw; on most models, there is also a setting for operating as a standard screwdriver. Holding the screwdriver firmly by the handle in the palm of your hand, align the shank with the screw and fit the blade tip into its head; if necessary, steady the shank with your other hand. Applying light pressure, turn the handle as far as you can: clockwise to tighten the screw and counterclockwise to loosen it, Then, turn the handle back in the opposite direction, letting the ratchet mechanism keep the screw steady, and continue the procedure, turning the handle the same way *(above)*.

## CHOOSING AND PREPARING TO USE A SCREWDRIVER BIT

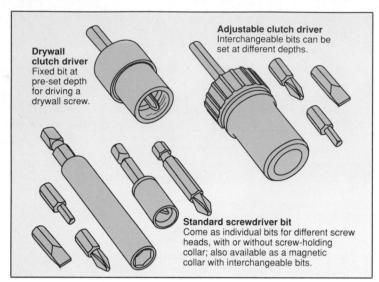

**Drywall clutch driver**
Fixed bit at pre-set depth for driving a drywall screw.

**Adjustable clutch driver**
Interchangeable bits can be set at different depths.

**Standard screwdriver bit**
Come as individual bits for different screw heads, with or without screw-holding collar; also available as a magnetic collar with interchangeable bits.

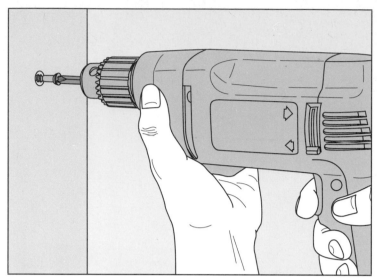

**1** **Choosing a screwdriver bit.** For a small number of screws or small screws that need little turning force, use a hand screwdriver *(page 105)*. Otherwise, use a screwdriver bit with a variable-speed electric drill. Choose a bit *(above)* compatible with your drill that exactly matches the type and size of slot or recess in the head of the screw you are using. For most purposes, a standard bit is sufficient; for fastening at a set depth, use a bit with a clutch driver. Fit the blade tip of the bit into the screw head to check it. If the blade tip is too small, it may snap or bend the screw head when turning force is applied; if it is too large, it may slip and damage the screw head or the workpiece surface. To set an adjustable clutch driver, follow the manufacturer's instructions. Install the bit *(page 101)* and ensure you know how to use it properly *(step 2)*.

**2** **Using the screwdriver bit.** Set the reversing switch to FORWARD for installing screws; REVERSE for removing screws. Wearing safety goggles *(page 25)*, plug in the drill *(page 24)* and fit the blade tip of the bit into the screw head; ensure the power cord is out of the way. Holding the drill steady with both hands, apply light pressure and depress the trigger switch slightly, running the drill at low speed. If you are installing a screw, gradually increase your pressure and the drill speed as the screw takes hold *(above)*, pulling the bit out of its head as soon as it is set flush or the clutch driver stops the bit from turning. If you are removing a screw, gradually decrease your pressure and keep the drill speed constant as it loosens, continuing until it can be turned by hand. If the drill strains or the bit slips, stop; complete the job using a hand screwdriver *(page 105)*.

## FASTENING TO WOOD (SCREWS)

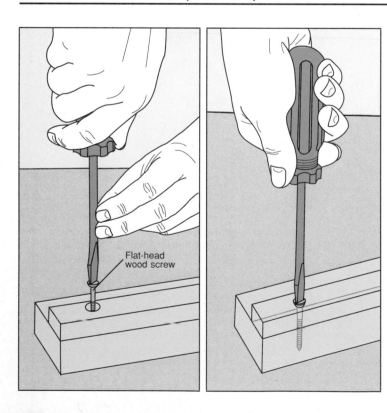

Flat-head wood screw

**Driving a screw into wood.** If necessary, set up on a work surface *(page 17)*; measure and mark *(page 30)* a screw position point. Choose a screw *(page 104)* and prepare to use a hand screwdriver *(page 105)* or a screwdriver bit *(steps above)*; for a lag bolt, fit it with a washer *(page 111)* and plan to use a wrench *(page 109)* or a nutdriver. If you are screwing through a material other than drywall, use a drill *(page 100)* to make a clearance hole and a pilot hole. Make the clearance hole in the wood *(page 102)* or other material *(page 103)* through which you are screwing equal to the diameter of the screw shank. If you are screwing through wood with a flat- or oval-head screw, use a combination bit or a countersink bit *(page 102)* to make a countersink equal in depth to the thickness of the screw head. Make the pilot hole in the wood into which you are screwing about 2/3 the diameter of the screw shank and equal in depth to the screw length to be driven into it if it is hardwood; 1/2 the screw length to be driven into it if it is softwood.

To drive in a screw with a standard screwdriver, as in the instance shown, set the screw into the hole and turn it clockwise one or two times to start it. Gripping the screwdriver firmly by the handle, fit the blade tip into the screw head; if necessary, steady the shank with your other hand. Applying light pressure, turn the handle clockwise, gradually increasing your pressure as you continue *(far left)*. If the screw binds, turn counterclockwise to back it out slightly, then continue driving it in. If the screw still binds, remove it *(page 108)*, then widen and deepen the pilot hole slightly and drive in a new screw. Continue until the screw head is set flush *(near left)*; if you are screwing through drywall, it should dimple the surface slightly. Store your tools and clean up *(page 27)*.

## FASTENING TO MASONRY (SCREWS)

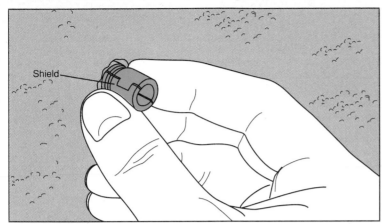

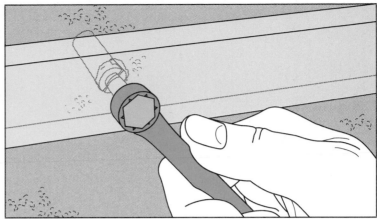

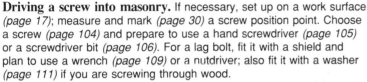

**Driving a screw into masonry.** If necessary, set up on a work surface *(page 17)*; measure and mark *(page 30)* a screw position point. Choose a screw *(page 104)* and prepare to use a hand screwdriver *(page 105)* or a screwdriver bit *(page 106)*. For a lag bolt, fit it with a shield and plan to use a wrench *(page 109)* or a nutdriver; also fit it with a washer *(page 111)* if you are screwing through wood.

Use a drill *(page 100)* to make a clearance hole in the wood *(page 102)* or other material *(page 103)* through which you are screwing equal to the diameter of the screw shank. If you are screwing through wood with a flat- or oval-head screw, use a combination bit or a countersink bit *(page 102)* to make a countersink hole equal in depth to the thickness of the screw head. If you are installing a shield, make a clearance hole in the masonry equal to its diameter and 1/2 inch deeper than its length.

Fit the shield into the hole *(above, left)*, tapping it flush with a ball-peen hammer, if necessary *(page 115)*. If you are installing a masonry screw, use the bit supplied with it to make a pilot hole in the masonry 1/2 inch deeper than the screw length to be driven into it.

To drive in a lag bolt with a box wrench, as in the instance shown, set the bolt into the hole as far as possible by hand. Gripping the wrench firmly by the handle, fit the box onto the bolt head. Applying light pressure, turn the handle clockwise as far as you can, then take the box off the bolt head to reposition the wrench and turn again *(above, right)*, gradually increasing your pressure as you continue. If the lag bolt binds, turn counterclockwise to back it out slightly, then continue driving it in; if it still binds, remove it and drive in a new one. Continue until the bolt head is set flush. Then, store your tools and clean up *(page 27)*.

## FASTENING TO METAL (SCREWS)

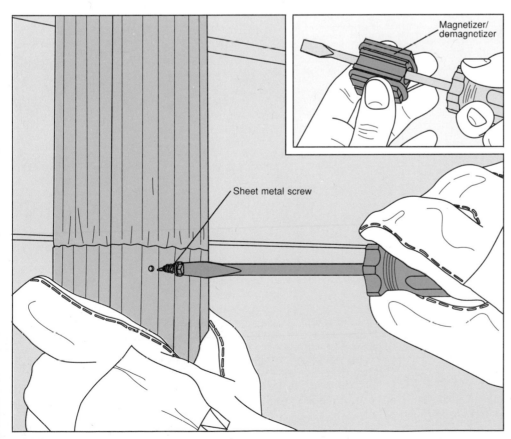

Magnetizer/demagnetizer

Sheet metal screw

**Driving a screw into metal.** If necessary, set up on a work surface *(page 17)*; measure and mark *(page 30)* a screw position point. Choose a screw *(page 104)* and prepare to use a hand screwdriver *(page 105)* or a screwdriver bit *(page 106)*. Then, use a drill *(page 100)* to make a clearance hole and a pilot hole. Make the clearance hole in the metal or other material *(page 103)* through which you are screwing equal to the diameter of the screw shank. Make the pilot hole in the metal into which you are screwing slightly narrower than the diameter of the screw shank: for a gimlet-point screw, drill through the metal; for a chip-cutting screw, drill slightly deeper than the screw length to be driven into it.

To drive in a small seel screw with a standard screwdriver, as in the instance shown, magnetize the shank by inserting it into a magnetizer *(inset)*. Gripping the screwdriver firmly by the handle, fit the blade tip into the screw head, then set the screw tip straight into the hole *(left)*; if necessary, steady the shank with your other hand. Applying light pressure, turn the handle clockwise, continuing until the screw head is set flush; if the screw is loose and can still be turned, remove it and install a larger one. Store your tools and clean up *(page 27)*.

## FASTENING TO HOLLOW WALLS (SCREWS)

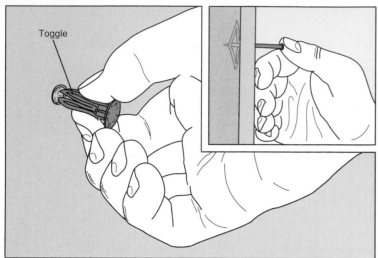
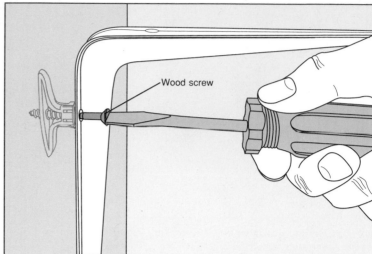

**Driving a screw into a hollow wall.** Measure and mark *(page 30)* a screw position point. Choose a screw *(page 104)* and prepare to use a hand screwdriver *(page 105)* or a screwdriver bit *(page 106)*. For screwing through a medium-weight material, fit the screw with a toggle; for screwing through a light material, fit the screw with an anchor.

Use a drill *(page 100)* to make a clearance hole in the wood *(page 102)* or other material *(page 103)* through which you are screwing equal to the diameter of the screw shank. If you are screwing through wood with a flat- or oval-head screw, use a combination bit or a countersink bit *(page 102)* to make a countersink hole equal in depth to the thickness of the screw head. Then, make a a clearance hole in the wall

equal to the diameter of the toggle, anchor or shield you are using and fit it into the hole *(above, left)*, tapping it flush with a ball-peen hammer, if necessary *(page 115)*. If you are installing a toggle, push a small nail *(page 117)* into it, popping it open against the back of the wall *(inset)*.

To drive in a screw with a standard screwdriver, as in the instance shown, set the screw through the hole of the material you are fastening and into the anchor, then turn it clockwise 1 or 2 times to start it. Gripping the screwdriver firmly by the handle, fit the blade tip into the screw head; if necessary, steady the shank with your other hand. Applying light pressure, turn the handle clockwise, continuing *(above, right)* until the screw head is set flush. Store your tools and clean up *(page 27)*.

## REMOVING SCREWS

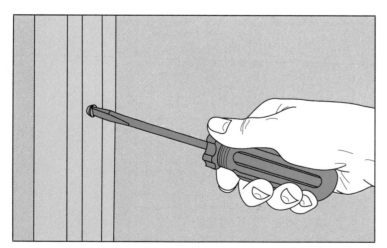
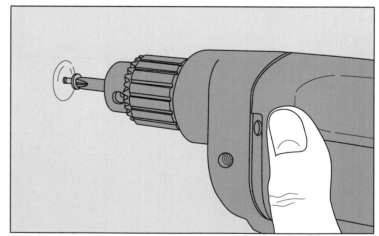

**Using a hand screwdriver.** To remove a large number of screws or large screws that need strong turning force, use a screwdriver bit with an electric drill *(step right)*. To remove a damaged screw, use a screw extractor *(page 109)*. Otherwise, choose an appropriate hand screwdriver *(page 105)*. To use a standard screwdriver, as in the instance shown, hold it firmly by the handle in the palm of your hand and fit the blade tip straight into the screw head; steady the shank with your other hand, if necessary. Applying moderate pressure, turn the handle counterclockwise as far as you can to loosen the screw, then reposition your hand on it and turn it again *(above)*, continuing until the screw can be removed by hand; if the screw loosens but does not rise out of the hole, pry out its head with a utility bar as you turn it. Store your tools and clean up *(page 27)*.

**Using a screwdriver bit.** To remove a small number of screws or small screws that need little turning force, use a hand screwdriver *(step left)*. To remove a damaged screw, use a screw extractor *(page 109)*. Otherwise, prepare to use a screwdriver bit with an electric drill *(page 106)*, setting the drill reversing switch to REVERSE. Wearing safety goggles *(page 25)*, plug in the drill *(page 24)* and fit the blade tip of the bit into the screw head; ensure the power cord is out of the way. Holding the drill steady with both hands, apply moderate pressure and depress the trigger switch slightly, running the drill at low speed. Gradually decrease your pressure and keep the drill speed constant as the screw loosens *(above)*, continuing until it is far enough out to be turned by hand. If the drill strains or the bit slips, stop; complete the job using a hand screwdriver. Store your tools and clean up *(page 27)*.

## REMOVING SCREWS (continued)

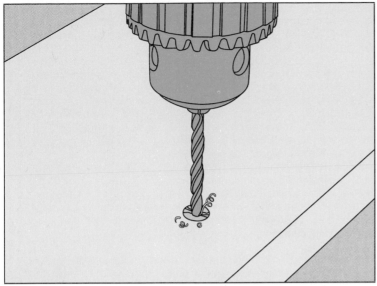

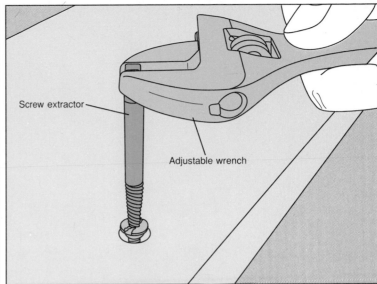

Screw extractor

Adjustable wrench

**Using a screw extractor.** To remove an undamaged screw, use a hand screwdriver or a screwdriver bit *(page 108)*. To remove a damaged screw, use a screw extractor of an appropriate diameter. Prepare to use a drill *(page 100)*, choosing a high-speed twist bit for metal of a size recommended for the extractor. To keep the bit from wandering off the screw head, use a center punch and a ball-peen hammer *(page 115)* to make a starting point at the center of it. Wearing safety goggles *(page 25)*, set the tip of the center punch on the screw head and strike the top of it sharply with the hammer, then set the tip of the bit at the starting point. Holding the drill steady with both hands, apply moderate pressure and depress the trigger switch slightly, running the drill at low speed.

Keeping the bit perpendicular to the surface, maintain your pressure and the drill speed as the bit starts to cut into the screw *(above, left)*, continuing to a depth of about 1/3 the thread length of the extractor—usually about 3/8 inch. Then, fit the tip of the extractor into the hole and turn it counterclockwise once or twice by hand to start it. Fit an adjustable wrench *(page 110)* onto the top of the extractor and tighten its jaws. Holding the wrench handle firmly, apply moderate pressure and turn it counterclockwise, driving the extractor into the hole. Continue until the extractor grips the screw head, loosening the screw and raising it out *(above, right)* enough to be removed by hand. To take the screw off the extractor, hold the wrench handle and use pliers to turn the screw clockwise. Store your tools and clean up *(page 27)*.

## CHOOSING AND PREPARING TO USE A WRENCH

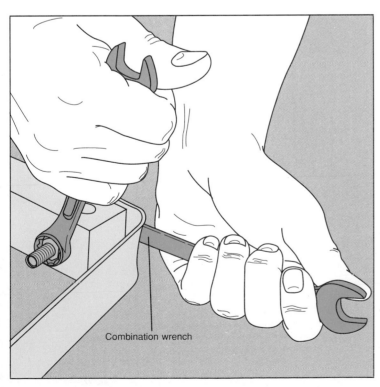

Combination wrench

**Using a box wrench.** Choose the right wrench *(page 96)* for the job. For speed or frontal access with a hex- or square-headed fastener, use a socket wrench; for side access in a tight space, use an open-end wrench *(page 110)*. In general, for strong turning or holding force with a hex-headed fastener, use a box wrench: a 6-point type for strongest turning or holding force; a 12-point type for greatest access. Check that the box wrench exactly matches the standard or metric size of the fastener; it should fit snugly and there should be no slippage.

Inspect the box wrench before using it. If the handle is cracked or bent or the box points are worn or damaged, do not use the box wrench; replace it. Check also that the box wrench is clean. If the handle is dirty or greasy, wipe it using a soft cloth dampened with a solution of mild household detergent and water; dry it thoroughly with a clean cloth. To clean off stubborn grease, use a soft cloth dampened with mineral spirits; to remove rust, wear work gloves *(page 25)* and use steel wool.

Ensure you know how to use the box wrench properly. To tighten or loosen the nut in the instance shown, fit the box wrench onto it and another wrench onto the bolt head. Holding the handle of the wrench on the bolt head steady to keep the bolt from turning, grip the handle of the box wrench and apply moderate to strong pressure to turn it as far as you can: clockwise to tighten the nut *(left)*; counterclockwise to loosen it. Take the box wrench off the nut and reposition it to continue.

## CHOOSING AND PREPARING TO USE A WRENCH (continued)

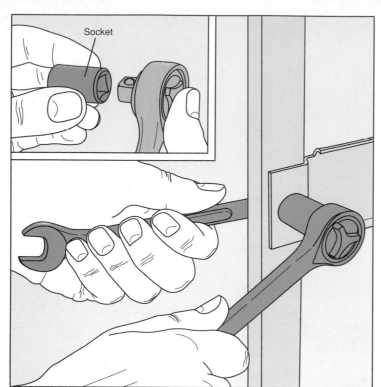

**Using a socket wrench.** Choose the right wrench *(page 96)* for the job. For strong turning or holding force with a hex-headed fastener, use a box wrench *(page 109)*; for side access to a hex- or square-headed fastener in a tight space, use an open-end wrench *(step below)*. In general, for speed or frontal access, use a socket wrench: with a hex-headed fastener, a 6-point type for strongest turning or holding force; a 12-point type for greatest access. With a square-headed fastener, use an 8-point type. Check that the socket exactly matches the standard or metric size of the fastener; it should fit snugly and there should be no slippage. If a nut is threaded too far onto the bolt for a regular socket, try a deep socket or use a box wrench.

Inspect the socket wrench before using it. If the handle is cracked or bent or the socket points are worn or damaged, replace the part. Otherwise, snap the socket onto the handle *(inset)*. Check also that the socket wrench is clean. If the handle is dirty or greasy, wipe it using a soft cloth dampened with a solution of mild household detergent and water; dry it thoroughly with a clean cloth. To clean off stubborn grease, use a soft cloth dampened with mineral spirits; to remove rust, wear work gloves *(page 25)* and use steel wool.

Ensure you know how to use the socket wrench properly. Set the ratchet switch to lock the socket in the direction you are turning when it is positioned: for tightening, clockwise; for loosening, counterclockwise. To tighten or loosen the nut in the instance shown, fit the socket wrench onto it and another wrench onto the bolt head. Holding the handle of the wrench on the bolt head steady to keep the bolt from turning, grip the handle of the socket wrench and apply moderate to strong pressure to turn it as far as you can *(left)*. Reurn the handle back to its starting position without lifting the socket off the nut to continue.

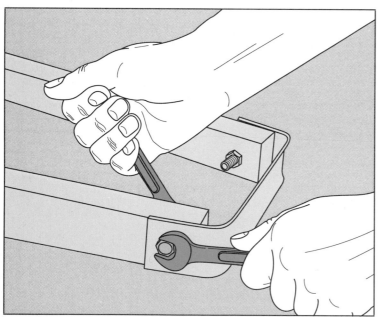

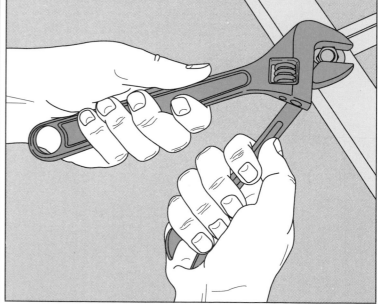

**Using an open-end or adjustable wrench.** Choose the right wrench *(page 96)* for the job. For strong turning or holding force with a hex-headed fastener, use a box wrench *(page 109)*; for speed or frontal access with a hex- or square-headed fastener, use a socket wrench *(step above)*. In general, for side access in a tight space, use an open-end wrench that exactly matches the standard or metric size of the fastener; it should fit snugly and there should be no slippage. Otherwise, use an adjustable wrench; an 8-inch type is usually sufficient.

Inspect the wrench before using it; if it is damaged, replace it. If the handle is dirty or greasy, wipe it using a soft cloth dampened with a solution of mild household detergent and water; dry it thoroughly with a clean cloth. To clean off stubborn grease, use a soft cloth dampened with mineral spirits; to remove rust, wear work gloves *(page 25)* and

use steel wool. To lubricate the worm gear of an adjustable wrench, apply a little light machine oil.

Ensure you know how to use the wrench properly. To tighten or loosen the nut in the instance shown with an open-end wrench, fit it onto the nut and fit another wrench onto the bolt head. Holding the handle of the wrench on the bolt head steady to keep the bolt from turning, grip the handle of the open-end wrench and apply moderate pressure to turn it as far as you can: clockwise to tighten the nut *(above, left)*; counterclockwise to loosen it. Take the wrench off the nut to reposition it and continue. With an adjustable wrench, use the same procedure, positioning the fixed jaw to take the pressure and closing the jaws fully onto the nut, then applying light pressure to turn the handle *(above, right)*. Open the jaws and take the wrench off the nut to reposition it and continue.

## CHOOSING A BOLT, NUT OR WASHER

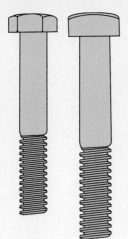

**Machine bolt**
Used to fasten combinations of wood, metal or plastic; can have hex or square head. Coarse-threaded type most common. Typically installed with flat or platform washer behind bolt head and nut as well as with lock washer. Lengths of 1/2 to 24 inches available; up to 8 inches most common. Diameters range from 1/4 to 1 1/4 inches. Shank of large size not fully threaded.

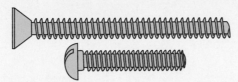

**Stove bolt**
Used to fasten combinations of light wood, metal or plastic; usually has slotted, flat or round head. Coarse-threaded type most common. Typically sold with nut and installed with flat or platform washer behind bolt head and nut as well as with lock washer. Lengths of 3/4 to 4 inches most common; up to 6 inches also available. Diameters from 1/8 to 3/8 inch most common; up to 1/2 inch also available.

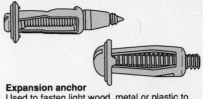

**Expansion anchor**
Used to fasten light wood, metal or plastic to hollow wall; usually has slotted, pan or round head. Types with pointed tip can be driven by a hammer; types without pointed tip require clearance hole equal to anchor diameter. Available in four common sizes to match range of wall thicknesses: XS for up to 1/4 inch; S for 1/8 to 5/8 inch; L for 5/8 to 1 1/4 inches; and XL for 1 1/4 to 1 3/4 inches.

**Carriage bolt**
Used primarily to fasten wood to wood or metal; has round head and square or finned neck. Coarse-threaded type most common; fine-threaded type also available. Typically installed with flat or platform washer behind nut and with lock washer. Can be from 1/2 to 18 inches in length and from 1/4 to 3/4 inch in diameter; range from 3/4 to 6 inches in length and 1/4 to 5/8 inch in diameter most common.

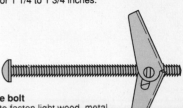

**Toggle bolt**
Used to fasten light wood, metal or plastic to hollow wall; has slotted, round head and is coarse-threaded. Available in lengths from 2 to 6 inches; diameters range from 1/8 to 1/2 inch.

**Flat washer**
Placed behind bolt head or nut to help distribute load. Available in diameters to match bolts.

**Platform washer**
Placed behind bolt head or nut to help distribute load; broad surface distributes load over larger area than flat washer. Available in diameters to match bolts.

**Split lock washer**
Placed behind nut to keep it from loosening; provides greater holding power than friction lock washer. Available in diameters to match bolts.

**Friction lock washer**
Typically placed behind nut; teeth grip nut and material to keep nut from loosening. Available in diameters to match bolts. External-toothed type should be larger than nut with teeth partially visible; concealed teeth of internal-toothed type used for decorative appearance on small bolts.

**Wing nut**
Wing-shaped for tightening or loosening by hand. Typically coarse-threaded and available in No. 6 to 3/4-inch diameters.

**Square nut**
Less common than hex nut; shape provides limited access for tightening or loosening with wrench. Typically coarse-threaded and available in diameters to match bolts.

**T nut**
Points on base embedded into wood for blind fastening—when bolt threads inaccessible after assembly. Typically coarse-threaded and available in No. 6 to 1/4-inch diameters.

**Stop nut**
Nylon insert holds nut tight. Can be coarse- or fine-threaded and available in No. 4 to No. 10 as well as 1/4- to 1-inch diameters. Loses holding power and must be replaced if removed and reinstalled more than 2 or 3 times.

**Hex nut**
Hexagonal shape provides easy access for tightening or loosening with wrench. Can be coarse- or fine-threaded and available in diameters to match bolts. Hot-dipped galvanized-steel bolt may need oversized nut—usually supplied with it.

**Cap nut**
Cap covers sharp edges of bolt and provides decorative appearance; hex nut provides easy access for tightening or loosening with wrench. Typically coarse-threaded and available in No. 6 to 1/2-inch diameters.

**Choosing the right bolt, nut and washer for the job.** To help you choose the right bolt, nut or washer for the job, refer to the chart *(above)*; shown are common types for fastening materials around the home. For fastening heavy, thick wood to wood, a carriage bolt can usually do the job; for fastening metal to wood, use a machine bolt or a stove bolt. For fastening any light material to a hollow wall, use the appropriate expansion anchor or toggle bolt. Consult your local hardware store or building supply center for specific recommendations.

After choosing an appropriate type of bolt for the materials you are fastening, determine if any special features are necessary. If the bolt is to be installed in a wet or damp location, use a rust-resistant variety: any galvanized-steel type for indoors; hot-dipped galvanized-steel for outdoors. A hot-dipped, galvanized-steel bolt may need an oversized nut—usually sold with it. If you are fastening metal, ensure the bolt is of the same metal to prevent a corrosive reaction.

Use a bolt of a suitable length for the dimensions of the materials you are fastening. A carriage bolt, a machine bolt or a stove bolt should be long enough for a nut to be threaded fully onto it; in general, at least 2 or 3 threads of the bolt should protrude from the nut. If you are installing a carriage bolt or a long machine bolt, the unthreaded portion of its shank should be shorter than the combined thickness of the materials you are fastening. If you are installing an expansion anchor, ensure it is the correct size for the thickness of the wall. Choose the best diameter (gauge or inch) for the length of bolt you are installing. In general, use a small-diameter bolt for fastening light, thin materials; a large-diameter bolt for fastening heavy, thick materials.

Ensure a nut is of the same thread type and diameter as the carriage bolt, machine bolt or stove bolt you are installing. Choose washers of an appropriate size for the bolt to help distribute the load of the material you are fastening and to keep the nut from loosening.

## FASTENING WITH CARRIAGE BOLTS

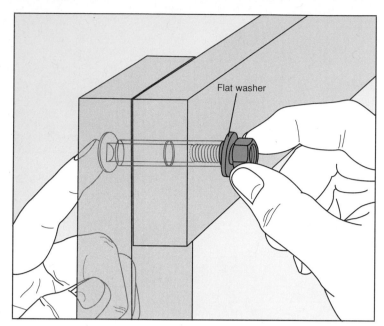

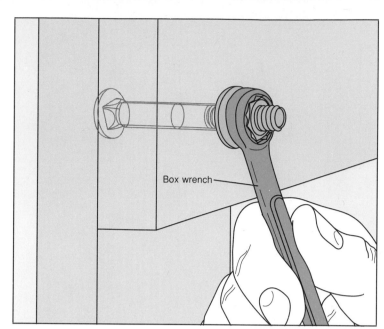

**1** **Installing a carriage bolt.** If necessary, set up on a work surface *(page 17)*. Measure and mark *(page 30)* a position point, then choose an appropriate carriage bolt *(page 111)*. Use a drill *(page 100)* to make a clearance hole in the wood *(page 102)* or other materials *(page 103)* you are fastening equal to the diameter of the bolt shank. Insert the bolt into the hole, pushing it in until its head sits flush; if necessary, tap it in place with a ball-peen hammer *(page 115)*. Fit the bolt with any washer, then thread the nut onto it by hand *(above)*, turning clockwise.

**2** **Tightening the nut onto the bolt.** Turn the nut clockwise onto the bolt as far as you can by hand, then prepare to use a wrench *(page 109)*. To tighten the nut using a box wrench, as in the instance shown, fit the box of the wrench onto it. Grip the handle of the box wrench and apply moderate to strong pressure to turn it clockwise as far as you can *(above)*; if necessary, steady the bolt head with a finger to keep the bolt from turning. Take the box wrench off the nut to reposition it and turn again, continuing until the nut is tightened. Store your tools and clean up *(page 27)*.

## FASTENING WITH MACHINE BOLTS

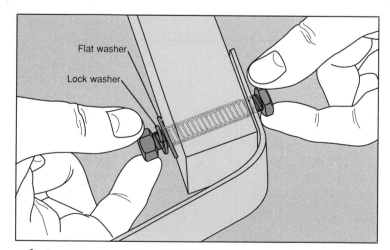

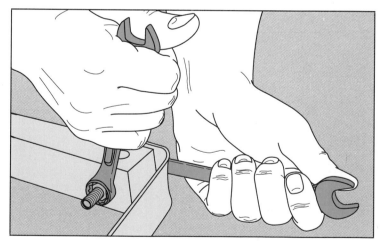

**1** **Installing a machine bolt.** If necessary, set up on a work surface *(page 17)*. Measure and mark *(page 30)* a position point, then choose an appropriate machine bolt *(page 111)*. Use a drill *(page 100)* to make a clearance hole in the wood *(page 102)* or other materials *(page 103)* you are fastening equal to the diameter of the bolt shank. Fit any washer behind the bolt head, then insert the bolt into the hole, pushing it in until its head sits flush; if necessary, tap it in place with a ball-peen hammer *(page 115)*. Fit the bolt with any washer, then thread the nut onto it by hand *(above)*, turning clockwise.

**2** **Tightening the nut onto the bolt.** Turn the nut clockwise onto the bolt as far as you can by hand, then prepare to use a wrench *(page 109)*. To tighten the nut using a box wrench, as in the instance shown, fit the box of the wrench onto it. Fitting another wrench onto the bolt head and holding its handle steady to keep the bolt from turning, grip the handle of the box wrench and apply moderate to strong pressure to turn it clockwise as far as you can *(above)*. Take the box wrench off the nut to reposition it and turn again, continuing until the nut is tightened. Store your tools and clean up *(page 27)*.

## FASTENING WITH STOVE BOLTS

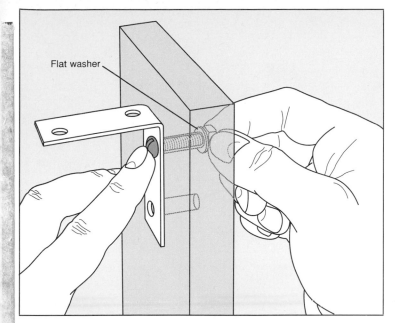

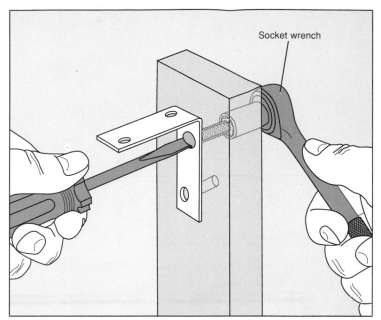

**1** **Installing a stove bolt.** If necessary, set up on a work surface *(page 17)*. Measure and mark *(page 30)* a position point, then choose an appropriate stove bolt *(page 111)*. Use a drill *(page 100)* to make a clearance hole in the wood *(page 102)* or other materials *(page 103)* you are fastening equal to the diameter of the bolt shank. Fit any washer behind the bolt head, then insert the bolt into the hole, pushing it until its head sits flush; if necessary, tap it in place with a ball-peen hammer *(page 115)*. Fit the bolt with any washer, then thread the nut onto it by hand *(above)*, turning clockwise.

**2** **Tightening the nut onto the bolt.** Turn the nut clockwise onto the bolt as far as you can by hand, then prepare to use a wrench *(page 109)* and a hand screwdriver *(page 105)*. To tighten the nut using a socket wrench, as in the instance shown, fit the socket onto it. Fitting the screwdriver into the bolt head and holding its handle steady to keep the bolt from turning, grip the handle of the socket wrench and apply moderate to strong pressure to turn it clockwise as far as you can *(above)*. Reposition the wrench handle to turn again, continuing until the nut is tightened. Store your tools and clean up *(page 27)*.

## FASTENING WITH TOGGLE BOLTS

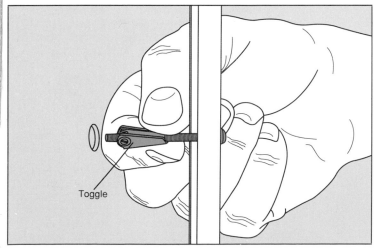

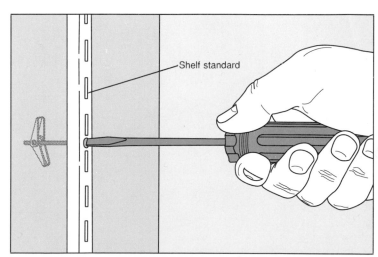

**1** **Installing a toggle bolt.** Measure and mark *(page 30)* a position point, then choose an appropriate toggle bolt *(page 111)*. Use a drill *(page 100)* to make clearance holes: in the wall, equal to the diameter of the closed toggle; in the wood *(page 102)* or other material *(page 103)* you are fastening, equal to the diameter of the bolt shank. Fit any washer behind the bolt head, then insert the bolt through the hole of the material you are fastening and thread the toggle clockwise onto it 2 or 3 turns. Fold the toggle wings closed, then push the bolt through the hole in the wall *(above)*.

**2** **Tightening the bolt.** When the wings spring open behind the wall, turn the bolt clockwise as far as you can by hand; pull gently on it to keep the wings from turning with it. Then, prepare to use a hand screwdriver *(page 105)*. To tighten the bolt using a standard screwdriver, as in the instance shown, fit the blade tip into the bolt head. Gripping the screwdriver by the handle, apply light to moderate pressure to turn it clockwise as far as you can *(above)*. Reposition your hand on the handle to turn again, continuing until the bolt is tightened. Store your tools and clean up *(page 27)*.

## FASTENING WITH EXPANSION ANCHORS

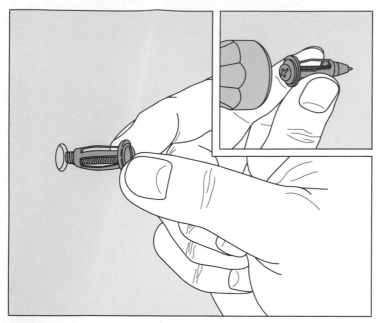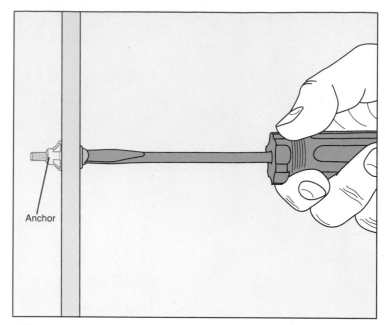

Anchor

**1** **Installing an expansion anchor.** Measure and mark *(page 30)* a position point, then choose an appropriate expansion anchor *(page 111)*; if necessary, use a drill *(page 100)* to make a hole large enough to calculate the wall thickness using a fine wire. To install a flat-tipped bolt, use the drill to make clearance holes: in the wall, equal to the diameter of the anchor; in the wood *(page 102)* or other material *(page 103)* you are fastening, equal to the diameter of the bolt shank. Then, insert the anchor into the hole in the wall *(above)*; if necessary, tap it in place with a ball-peen hammer *(page 115)*. To install a pointed-tipped anchor, drive it into the wall with the hammer *(inset)*.

**2** **Tightening the bolt.** Prepare to use a hand screwdriver *(page 105)*. To tighten the bolt using a standard screwdriver, as in the instance shown, fit the blade tip into the bolt head. Gripping the screwdriver by the handle, apply light to moderate pressure to turn it clockwise as far as you can, tightening the bolt and expanding the anchor leaves behind the wall *(above)*. Reposition your hand on the handle to turn again, continuing until the bolt is tightened. Then, unscrew the bolt, insert it through the hole in the material you are fastening and screw it back tightly into the anchor the same way. Store your tools and clean up *(page 27)*.

## REMOVING CARRIAGE BOLTS, MACHINE BOLTS OR STOVE BOLTS

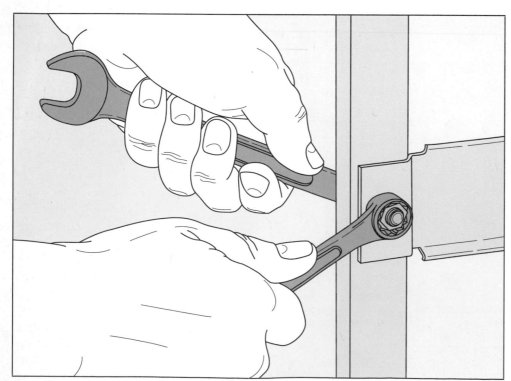

**Using a wrench.** If the nut or bolt head is damaged, use locking pliers or a cold chisel *(page 115)*. Otherwise, prepare to use a wrench *(page 109)*. To loosen the nut using a box wrench, as in the instance shown, fit the box of the wrench onto it. Fitting another wrench onto the bolt head and holding its handle steady to keep the bolt from turning, grip the handle of the box wrench and apply moderate to strong pressure to turn it counterclockwise as far as you can *(left)*. If the nut cannot be loosened, apply penetrating oil on it, then wait 10 to 15 minutes and try again; if it still cannot be loosened, use a cold chisel. Otherwise, take the box wrench off the nut to reposition it and turn again, continuing until the nut is loosened enough to be removed by hand. Take any washer off the end of the bolt, then work the bolt out of the hole; to loosen it, tap the end of it using a ball-peen hammer, if necessary *(page 115)*. Store your tools and clean up *(page 27)*.

## REMOVING CARRIAGE BOLTS, MACHINE BOLTS OR STOVE BOLTS (continued)

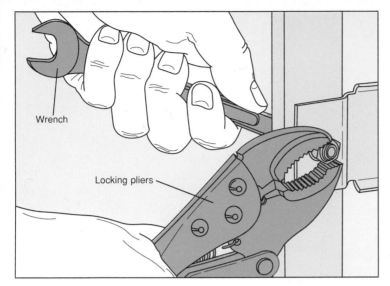

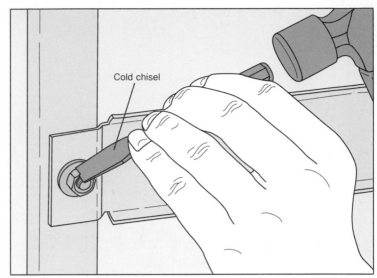

**Using locking pliers.** If the nut and bolt head are not damaged, use a wrench *(page 114)*. Otherwise, use locking pliers to loosen the nut, as in the instance shown. Close the jaws of the pliers onto the nut, positioning the fixed jaw to take the pressure; adjust the handle screw until the jaws grip the nut securely. Then, open the jaws to tighten the screw 1/4 turn and close them again. Fitting a wrench *(page 109)* onto the bolt head and holding its handle steady to keep the bolt from turning, grip the handles of the pliers and apply moderate to strong pressure to turn counterclockwise *(above)*. If the nut cannot be loosened, use a cold chisel *(step right)*. Otherwise, open the jaws to reposition the pliers and turn again, continuing until the nut is loosened enough to be removed by hand. Take any washer off the end of the bolt, then work the bolt out of the hole; tap it using a ball-peen hammer, if necessary *(step below)*. Store your tools and clean up *(page 27)*.

**Using a cold chisel.** If the nut and bolt head are not damaged, use a wrench *(page 114)*. Otherwise, use locking pliers *(step left)* to loosen the nut; if it cannot be loosened, as in the instance shown, use a cold chisel and a ball-peen hammer *(step below)* to strike it in a counterclockwise direction. Wearing safety goggles *(page 25)*, set the blade of the chisel against one side of the nut at about a 90-degree angle across the center of it. Holding the chisel firmly in position, strike the top of it lightly using the hammer until the blade cuts into the nut. When the blade is seated in the nut, lower the angle of the chisel slightly and strike the top of it sharply with the hammer *(above)* until the nut is loosened. If the nut cannot be loosened, cut through the bolt shank using a mini-hacksaw *(page 63)*, then work the bolt out of the hole. Otherwise, finish removing the nut using a wrench or locking pliers. Store your tools and clean up *(page 27)*.

## PREPARING TO USE A CLAW OR BALL-PEEN HAMMER

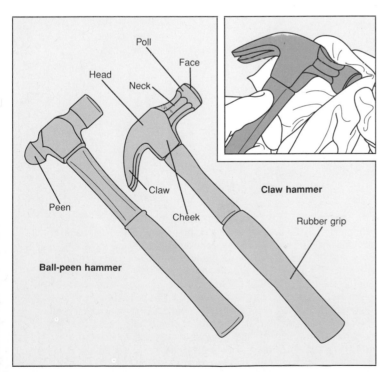

Ball-peen hammer

Claw hammer

**Choosing and inspecting a claw or ball-peen hammer.** Choose the right hammer for the job: a claw hammer for driving most nails and striking a nail set; a ball-peen hammer for driving hardened nails and striking a center punch or a cold chisel. If you are using a claw hammer, ensure it is the correct weight for the nailing to be done: 16 ounces for general purposes; 12 ounces for driving small nails in fine woodwork; 20 ounces for driving nails when sheathing and framing; and 28 ounces for driving spikes 4 inches or more in length.

Inspect the hammer before using it *(left)*. If the handle is bent, cracked or dented, the head is loose, or the poll, neck, face or cheek is cracked, chipped, scored or otherwise damaged, do not use the hammer; replace it. Check also that the hammer is clean. If the handle is dirty or greasy, wipe it using a soft cloth dampened with a solution of mild household detergent and water; dry it thoroughly with a clean cloth. To clean gum, pitch or glue off the face, wear rubber gloves *(page 25)* and use a soft cloth dampened with mineral spirits *(inset)*. To remove rust from the head, wear work gloves *(page 25)* and use steel wool. When the hammer is in good condition, ensure you know how to use it properly *(page 116)*.

## PREPARING TO USE A CLAW OR BALL-PEEN HAMMER (continued)

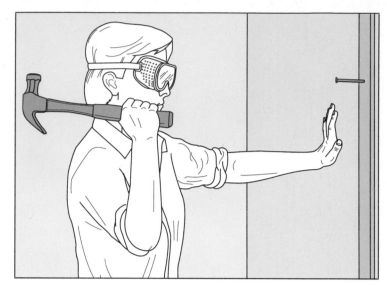

**Hammering with a half swing.** To start a nail, drive or set a small nail or nail in a tight space, hammer with a half swing. Wearing safety goggles *(page 25)*, grip the hammer firmly in your hand at the center of the handle, extending your thumb to help steady it. To start a nail, set the hammer face squarely on the nail head, then pull the hammer straight back to a point in front of you, bending your arm at the elbow and cocking your wrist slightly. Then, swing the hammer forward in a smooth arc, striking the nail head lightly with its face. Repeat the procedure *(above)* until the nail is started. To drive or set a small nail or nail in a tight space, retract your thumb around the handle and continue hammering the same way. Otherwise, hammer with a full swing *(step right)*.

**Hammering with a full swing.** To drive a large nail, hammer with a full swing after hammering with a half swing to start it *(step left)*. Wearing safety goggles *(page 25)*, grip the hammer firmly in your hand near the base of the handle, retracting your thumb around it. Stepping back slightly from your initial position to start the nail, set the hammer face squarely on the nail head, then pull the hammer straight back to a point behind your ear, rolling your shoulder and bending your arm at the elbow *(above)*; avoid cocking your wrist. Then, swing the hammer forward in a smooth arc, striking the nail head sharply with its face. Repeat the procedure until the nail is driven, gradually increasing your momentum as well as the striking force applied by the hammer face.

## PREPARING TO USE A HAND DRILLING HAMMER

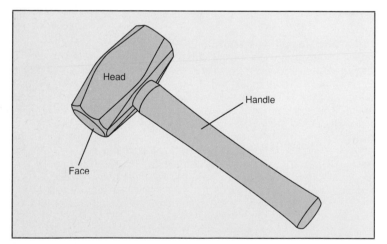

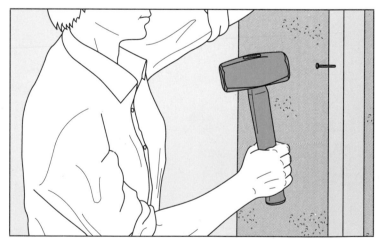

**Choosing and inspecting a hand drilling hammer.** Inspect a hand drilling hammer before using it *(above)*. If the handle is bent, cracked or dented, the head is loose, or a face is cracked, chipped, scored or otherwise damaged, do not use the hammer; replace it. Check also that the hammer is clean. If the handle is dirty or greasy, wipe it using a soft cloth dampened with a solution of mild household detergent and water; dry it thoroughly with a clean cloth. To clean gum, pitch or glue off a face, use a soft cloth dampened with mineral spirits; to remove rust, wear work gloves *(page 25)* and use steel wool. When the hammer is in good condition, ensure you know how to use it properly *(step right)*.

**Hammering with a dead blow.** To drive a masonry nail using a hand drilling hammer, hammer with a dead blow. Wearing safety goggles *(page 25)*, grip the hammer firmly in your hand near the base of the handle, retracting your thumb around it; for greater control, grip it closer to the head. To start the nail, set the hammer face squarely on the nail head, then pull the hammer straight back to a point in front of you, bending your arm at the elbow; avoid cocking your wrist. Swing the hammer forward, throwing its head in a smooth arc and striking the nail head sharply with its face. Repeat the procedure until the nail is started, then continue the same way *(above)* until it is driven.

## CHOOSING A NAIL

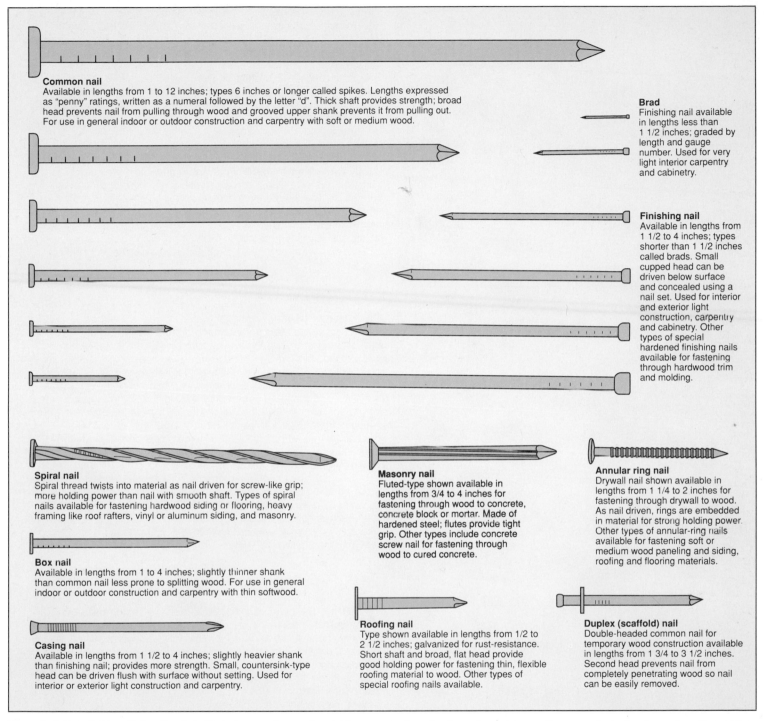

**Common nail**
Available in lengths from 1 to 12 inches; types 6 inches or longer called spikes. Lengths expressed as "penny" ratings, written as a numeral followed by the letter "d". Thick shaft provides strength; broad head prevents nail from pulling through wood and grooved upper shank prevents it from pulling out. For use in general indoor or outdoor construction and carpentry with soft or medium wood.

**Brad**
Finishing nail available in lengths less than 1 1/2 inches; graded by length and gauge number. Used for very light interior carpentry and cabinetry.

**Finishing nail**
Available in lengths from 1 1/2 to 4 inches; types shorter than 1 1/2 inches called brads. Small cupped head can be driven below surface and concealed using a nail set. Used for interior and exterior light construction, carpentry and cabinetry. Other types of special hardened finishing nails available for fastening through hardwood trim and molding.

**Spiral nail**
Spiral thread twists into material as nail driven for screw-like grip; more holding power than nail with smooth shaft. Types of spiral nails available for fastening hardwood siding or flooring, heavy framing like roof rafters, vinyl or aluminum siding, and masonry.

**Box nail**
Available in lengths from 1 to 4 inches; slightly thinner shank than common nail less prone to splitting wood. For use in general indoor or outdoor construction and carpentry with thin softwood.

**Casing nail**
Available in lengths from 1 1/2 to 4 inches; slightly heavier shank than finishing nail; provides more strength. Small, countersink-type head can be driven flush with surface without setting. Used for interior or exterior light construction and carpentry.

**Masonry nail**
Fluted-type shown available in lengths from 3/4 to 4 inches for fastening through wood to concrete, concrete block or mortar. Made of hardened steel; flutes provide tight grip. Other types include concrete screw nail for fastening through wood to cured concrete.

**Roofing nail**
Type shown available in lengths from 1/2 to 2 1/2 inches; galvanized for rust-resistance. Short shaft and broad, flat head provide good holding power for fastening thin, flexible roofing material to wood. Other types of special roofing nails available.

**Annular ring nail**
Drywall nail shown available in lengths from 1 1/4 to 2 inches for fastening through drywall to wood. As nail driven, rings are embedded in material for strong holding power. Other types of annular-ring nails available for fastening soft or medium wood paneling and siding, roofing and flooring materials.

**Duplex (scaffold) nail**
Double-headed common nail for temporary wood construction available in lengths from 1 3/4 to 3 1/2 inches. Second head prevents nail from completely penetrating wood so nail can be easily removed.

**Choosing the right nail for the job.** To help you choose the right nail for the job, refer to the chart *(above)*; shown are typical nails for fastening through and to wood or other materials around the home. For fastening through most materials to wood, a common nail, a box nail, a finishing nail or a casing nail can do the job. For fastening through or to material such as masonry, metal or drywall and fastening through flooring, siding, paneling or roofing material, there are many special types of nails available. Consult your local hardware store or building supply center for specific recommendations.

After choosing a suitable type of nail for the materials through and to which you are fastening, determine if any special features are needed. If the nail is to be installed in a wet or damp location, use a rust-resistant variety: any galvanized-steel type for indoors; hot-dipped galvanized-

steel or aluminum for outdoors. If you are fastening through or to metal, ensure the nail is of the same metal to prevent a corrosive reaction.

Use a nail of a suitable length for the dimensions of the materials through and to which you are fastening. For fastening through wood, plastic or metal to wood, choose a nail of a length about 3 times the thickness of the material through which you are fastening; ensure it is also at least 1/4 inch shorter than the combined thickness of the materials through and to which you are fastening. If you are fastening through plywood or composition board to wood, choose a nail suitable to its thickness: for 1/4-inch panels, a 1-inch nail; for 3/8-inch panels, a 1 1/2-inch nail; for 1/2-inch panels, a 2-inch nail; and for 3/4-inch panels, a 2 1/2-inch nail. For fastening through drywall to wood or through wood to masonry, use a nail 3/4 to 1 inch longer than the drywall or wood thickness.

## FASTENING TO WOOD (NAILS)

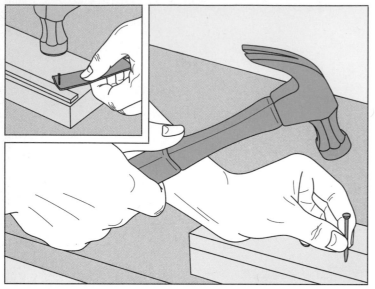

**1 Starting the nail.** If necessary, set up on a work surface *(page 17)*, then measure and mark *(page 30)* a nail position point. Choose a nail *(page 117)* and prepare to use a hammer *(page 115)*. If you are nailing through hardwood or thin softwood, or near the edge of any wood material, use a drill *(page 100)* to make a pilot hole *(page 102)* slightly smaller than the diameter of the nail shank and equal in depth to about 2/3 the nail length; make it at the same angle you plan to drive the nail. If you are nailing through metal or plastic, use a drill to make a clearance hole in it slightly larger than the diameter of the nail shank.

Wearing safety goggles *(page 25)*, set the nail at the marked position point or into the hole; if the nail is too small to hold, push it partway through a thin piece of cardboard, then hold the cardboard to position it *(inset)*. Gripping the hammer firmly in your hand at the center of the handle and extending your thumb to help steady it, hammer with a half swing *(page 116)* to start the nail. Swinging the hammer forward in a smooth arc *(left)*, strike the nail head lightly with its face. Continue hammering with a half swing until the nail is started. Then, lift off any piece of cardboard used to position the nail.

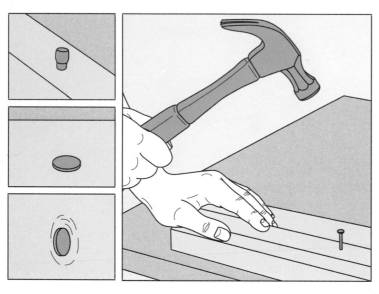

**2 Driving the nail.** If the nail is small or you are nailing in a tight space, retract your thumb around the handle of the hammer and drive the nail by hammering with a half swing as you did to start it *(step 1)*. Otherwise, step back slightly from your initial position to start the nail, moving your free hand well away from the nail. Gripping the hammer firmly in your hand near the base of the handle and retracting your thumb around it, hammer with a full swing *(page 116)* to drive the nail. Swinging the hammer forward in a smooth arc *(left)*, strike the nail head sharply with its face. Continue hammering with a full swing until the nail is driven, gradually increasing your momentum as well as the striking force applied by the hammer face. If the nail bends, remove it *(page 119)*; start again with a new nail. If you are hammering a finishing nail, drive it until its head protrudes about 1/8 inch from the surface *(inset, top)*, then set the nail head *(step 3)*. If you are hammering any other standard nail, drive it until its head is seated flush with the surface *(inset, center)*. If you are hammering a drywall nail, drive it until its head is dimpled about 1/16 inch below the surface *(inset, bottom)*.

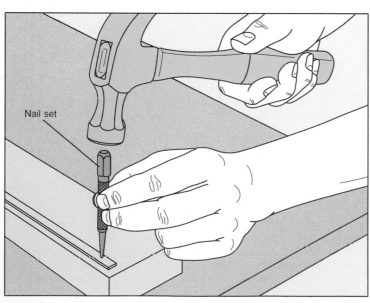

Nail set

**3 Setting the head of a finishing nail.** To set the head of a finishing nail, use a nail set. Choose a nail set with a tip of a diameter equal to or slightly smaller than the nail head; sit the tip of it on the nail head to check it. Holding the nail set between the fingers and thumb of your free hand, align it with the nail and center its tip on the nail head. Gripping the hammer firmly in your hand at the center of the handle and extending your thumb to help steady it, set the hammer face squarely on the nail set; then, pull the hammer straight back to a point in front of you, bending your arm at the elbow and cocking your wrist slightly. Then, swing the hammer forward in a smooth arc, striking the top of the nail set with its face in a short, sharp blow. Repeat the procedure *(left)*, continuing until the nail head is set below the surface to the desired depth: 1/16 inch, if it is to be left exposed; 1/8 to 1/4 inch if it is to be filled over with wood putty. Store your tools and clean up *(page 27)*.

## FASTENING TO MASONRY (NAILS)

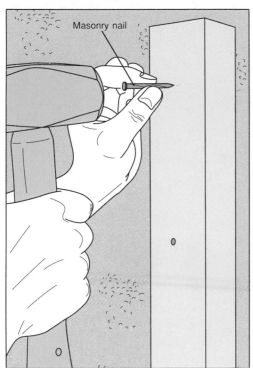

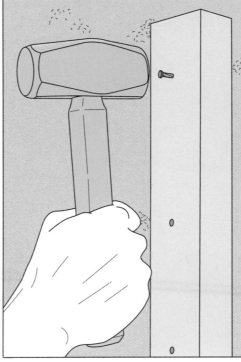

**Starting and driving a nail.** Measure and mark *(page 30)* a nail position point. Choose a nail *(page 117)* and prepare to use a hand drilling hammer *(page 116)*. If you are nailing through a material other than softwood, use a drill *(page 100)* to make a clearance hole in it: in hardwood, slightly smaller than the diameter of the nail shank; in metal or plastic, slightly larger than the diameter of the nail shank.

Wearing safety goggles *(page 25)*, set the nail at the marked position point or into the hole. Gripping the hammer firmly in your hand near the center of the handle and retracting your thumb around it, hammer with a dead blow *(page 116)* to start the nail. Swing the hammer forward *(far left)*, throwing its head in a smooth arc and striking the nail head sharply with its face. Continue hammering the same way until the nail is started, then move your free hand well away from the nail. Grip the hammer firmly near the base of the handle and continue hammering with a dead blow to drive the nail *(near left)*. If the nail bends, remove it *(steps below)*; start again with a new nail. Otherwise, drive the nail until its head is seated flush with the surface. Store your tools and clean up *(page 27)*.

## REMOVING NAILS

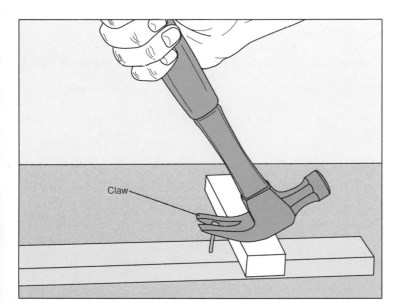

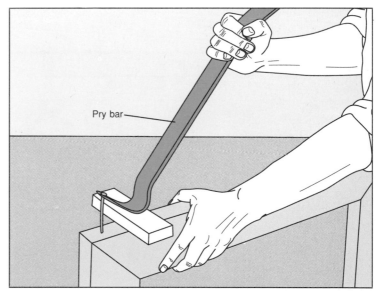

**Using a claw hammer.** If the nail head is damaged, use a nail puller; if it is set below the surface, use a nail set *(page 120)*. Otherwise, prepare to use a claw hammer *(page 115)*. Wearing safety goggles *(page 25)*, fit the claw as far as possible under the nail head, then slip a thin piece of hard scrap material under it; if you cannot fit the claw under the nail head, lift it slightly using a pry bar *(step right)*. Gripping the hammer near the base of the handle, pull back until it is almost perpendicular to the surface. If the nail does not lift out completely, slip a wood block about 1/2 inch thick under the claw and pull the handle back again *(above)*. Continue the procedure using successively thicker wood blocks until the nail lifts out completely; if it bends or strong force is necessary, finish lifting it using a pry bar. Store your tools and clean up *(page 27)*.

**Using a pry bar.** If the nail head is damaged, use a nail puller; if it is set below the surface, use a nail set *(page 120)*. If the nail head is lifted above the surface, use a claw hammer *(step left)*. Otherwise, wear safety goggles *(page 25)* and use a pry bar *(page 96)*. Fit the claw as far as possible under the nail head, then slip a thin piece of hard scrap material under it; if you cannot fit the claw under the nail head, dig the edge or tip under it to lift it slightly. Gripping the pry bar near the base of the handle, pull back until it is almost perpendicular to the surface. If the nail does not lift out completely, slip a wood block about 1/2 inch thick under the claw and pull the handle back again *(above)*. Continue the procedure using successively thicker wood blocks until the nail lifts out completely. Store your tools and clean up *(page 27)*.

## REMOVING NAILS (continued)

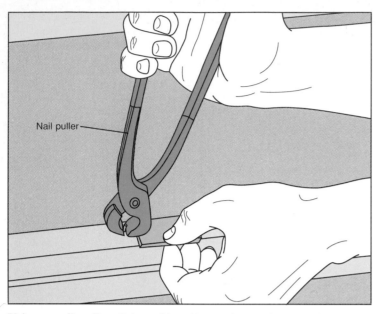

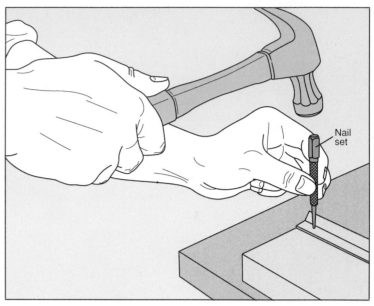

**Using a nail puller.** If the nail head is not damaged, use a claw hammer or a pry bar *(page 119)*; if it is set below the surface, use a nail set *(step right)*. If the nail head is damaged, wear safety goggles *(page 25)* and use a nail puller. Grip the nail shank between the jaws as close to the surface as possible, squeezing the handles enough to bite into it without severing it. Slipping a thin piece of hard scrap material under the jaws, hold the nail puller firmly near the base of the handle and pull back, rocking the jaws onto it *(above)*. If the nail does not lift out completely, grip the nail shank between the jaws again as close to the surface as possible and repeat the procedure, continuing until the nail lifts out completely. Store your tools and clean up *(page 27)*.

**Using a nail set.** If the nail head is not set below the surface, use a claw hammer or a pry bar *(page 119)*; if it is damaged, use a nail puller *(step left)*. Otherwise, prepare to use a claw hammer *(page 115)* and a nail set with a tip of a diameter equal to or slightly smaller than the nail head. Wearing safety goggles *(page 25)*, center the tip of the nail set on the nail head and grip the hammer firmly at the center of the handle, extending your thumb to help steady it. Set the hammer face squarely on the nail set, then pull the hammer straight back to a point in front of you and swing it forward in a smooth arc *(above)*, striking the top of the nail set with its face in a short, sharp blow. Repeat the procedure, continuing until the nail head is driven through the material. Store your tools and clean up *(page 27)*.

## FASTENING WITH POP RIVETS

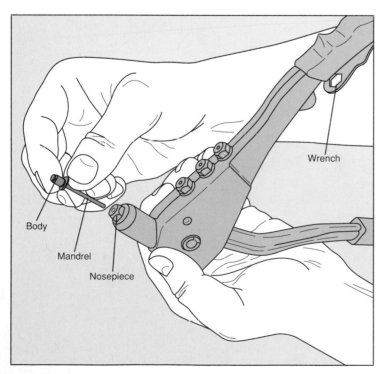

**1 Preparing to use a pop riveter.** Use a pop riveter to fasten together materials of sheet metal or plastic—especially if they are not to be subjected to movement or there is no access behind them. Choose a pop rivet of the same material as the materials you are fastening; with plastic, you can use an aluminum or a plastic type. Ensure the body of the pop rivet is slightly longer than the combined thickness of the materials you are fastening and of a diameter appropriate for the nosepiece of your pop riveter. If you are fastening thin plastic, use a special washer-type pop rivet; or, fit a standard pop rivet with a washer of the same material as it.

If necessary, set up on a work surface *(page 17)*; measure and mark *(page 30)* a position point for a pop rivet. Use a drill *(page 100)* to make a clearance hole through the materials you are fastening equal to the diameter of the pop rivet. Prepare to use a pop riveter; if it is equipped with interchangeable nosepieces, follow the owner's manual instructions to fit it with the one of the correct diameter for the pop rivet—on the model shown, use the wrench supplied with it. Holding the pop riveter with the nosepiece facing upward and the handles opened as far as possible, insert the mandrel of the pop rivet into the nosepiece *(left)*, pushing until the flange rests against it.

## FASTENING WITH POP RIVETS (continued)

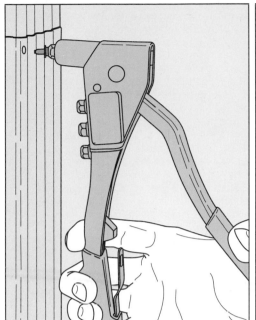
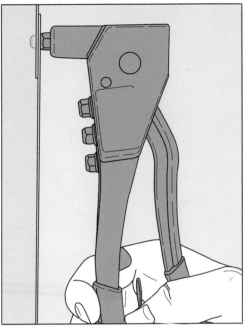
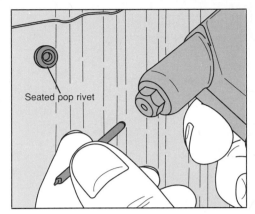

Seated pop rivet

**3 Removing the mandrel.** When the pop rivet is seated in the materials, lift the pop riveter away from the surface. Holding the pop riveter with the nosepiece facing upward, open the handles as far as possible. Then, turn the pop riveter over with the nosepiece facing downward to slide the severed mandrel of the pop rivet out of it *(above)*; discard the severed mandrel. Store your tools and clean up *(page 27)*.

**2 Installing a pop rivet.** Wearing safety goggles *(page 25)*, squeeze the handles of the pop riveter together gently to grip the mandrel; if you are using a standard pop rivet with a washer, fit the washer onto the body, seating it against the flange. Gripping the pop riveter firmly by the handles, push the body of the pop rivet into the hole *(above, left)* until the flange or washer is flush with the surface. Pressing the nosepiece against the surface, squeeze the handles together tightly *(above, right)* to compress the body of the pop rivet and form a head behind the materials; keep squeezing until the mandrel snaps and the pop riveter jumps back from the surface. If the mandrel does not snap, open the handles, then press the nosepiece against the surface and squeeze the handles together tightly again.

## REMOVING POP RIVETS

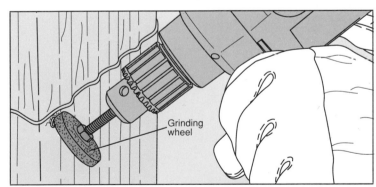

Grinding wheel

**Drilling out a pop rivet.** Prepare to use a drill *(page 100)*, choosing a twist bit suited to the material of the pop rivet and equal to the diameter of its body—about 1/2 the diameter of the exposed flange. Wearing safety goggles *(page 25)*, set any drill speed switch to FAST and reversing switch to FORWARD, then plug in the drill *(page 24)* using an extension cord, if necessary *(page 23)*. Gripping the drill firmly, hold it perpendicular to the surface and push the bit against the center of the flange. Ensuring the power cord is clear of the bit, depress and hold the trigger switch to run the drill at high speed. Apply even pressure to drill through the pop rivet *(above)*. If the pop rivet turns with the bit, stop; complete the job by grinding it off *(step right)*. Store your tools and clean up *(page 27)*.

**Grinding off a pop rivet.** Prepare to use a drill *(page 100)*, installing a grinding wheel attachment as you would another bit *(page 101)*. Wearing safety goggles and work gloves *(page 25)*, set any drill speed switch to FAST and reversing switch to FORWARD, then plug in the drill *(page 24)* using an extension cord, if necessary *(page 23)*. Gripping the drill firmly, hold an edge of the grinding wheel against the flange of the pop rivet. Ensuring the power cord is clear of the grinding wheel, depress and hold the trigger switch to run the drill at high speed. Apply even pressure to grind off the flange *(above)*, leaving the body of the pop rivet exposed. Then, set a center punch on the body and strike the top of it sharply with a ball-peen hammer *(page 115)*, driving the pop rivet through the materials. Store your tools and clean up *(page 27)*.

## PREPARING TO GLUE

| Glue | Characteristics |
|---|---|
| White glue | Polyvinyl-acetate type for general use indoors with wood or other porous materials; not toxic or flammable. Allows for working time of 15 to 20 minutes, sets in about 2 hours and cures in 24 hours; dries clear but does not sand well. Apply at room temperature in dry conditions; clamp materials until glue sets and clean up excess with water before setting time elapses. |
| Yellow glue | Made of aliphatic resin for general use indoors with wood or other porous materials; not toxic or flammable. Allows for working time of 3 to 5 minutes, sets in about 1/2 hour and cures in 24 hours; does not dry clear but sands well. Apply at room temperature in dry conditions; clamp materials until glue sets and clean up excess with water before setting time elapses. |
| Contact cement | Solvent-based types for use indoors primarily with wood or plastic—for example, veneers or laminates; toxic and some types flammable. Sets in 10 to 30 minutes and bonds on contact almost instantly; allows for no working time once materials contact. Apply in well-ventilated area; materials require only momentary, uniform hand pressure. Clean up excess with appropriate solvent immediately after materials contact. |
| Epoxy | Typically two-part resin and hardener mixed together for bonding almost any material; may be toxic, not flammable. Allows for working time up to setting time: from 5 minutes to 2 hours depending on type; most types cure in 24 hours. Apply wearing rubber gloves and safety goggles (page 25) in well-ventilated area; materials require contact until epoxy sets. Clean up excess by cutting it away after setting time elapses. |
| Instant glue | Made of cyanoacrylate and sold under various brand names for bonding almost any material; not toxic or flammable. Allows for working time up to setting time: from 10 to 60 seconds, depending on type; typically cures fully in 24 hours. Apply wearing rubber gloves and safety goggles (page 25) in well-ventilated area; materials require intimate contact until glue bonds. Clean up excess with acetone immediately after materials bond. |

**Choosing the right glue for the job.** To help you choose the right glue for the job, refer to the chart (left); it provides information on common glues for fastening most materials around the home. Use a glue suited to the materials that sets, or hardens, and cures, or reaches maximum strength, at an appropriate rate: a slow-setting type if you need time to position the materials; a fast-setting type if you cannot clamp the materials; a fast-curing type if you need to use the materials quickly. Consult your local hardware store or building supply center for specific recommendations.

Before using a glue, read the manufacturer's product information and instructions; glues of the same category can vary in formulation. Check the label for a list of materials with which the glue can bond and any bonding conditions—also for the toxicity and potential hazards of the glue as well as any solvent recommended for cleaning up a spill. After using a glue, close its container securely and store it well out of reach (page 27) or dispose of it safely according to the environmental regulations of your community.

## FASTENING WITH WHITE OR YELLOW GLUE

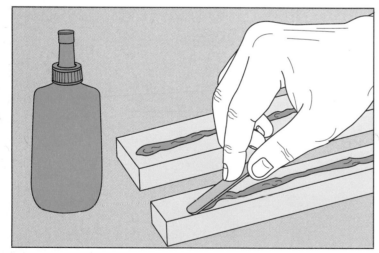

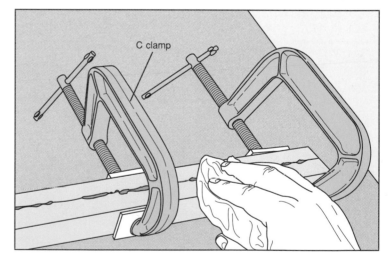

C clamp

**1 Applying the glue.** If necessary, set up on a work surface (page 17); measure and mark (page 30) position points on the materials. Choose a white or yellow glue (step above) and a type of clamp (page 96). Position the materials to check that they fit together closely; if necessary, trim or smooth any surface (page 78). Prepare the surfaces for bonding and apply the glue following the manufacturer's instructions; to clean an oily wood surface, use a cloth dampened with mineral spirits. In the instance shown, squeeze a narrow bead of glue along the length of each surface to be bonded, then use a disposable stick to spread it into a thin, uniform layer over each entire surface area to be bonded (above). To spread the glue over a large surface area, use a putty knife; to spread it into small cracks or crevices, use a toothpick.

**2 Fastening the materials.** Position the materials as soon as the glue is spread, making adjustments within the working time specified by the manufacturer. To press the materials together and hold them in place, use C clamps, pipe clamps (page 123) or web clamps (page 124). In the instance shown, install a C clamp every 6 to 8 inches along the length of the materials. If a thin, even line of glue does not squeeze out along each joint, remove the clamps and separate the materials to apply more glue (step 1). Otherwise, use a cloth dampened with water to wipe off the excess glue before it sets (above); or, use a putty knife to scrape it off. Clean glue off your tools the same way. Keep the materials clamped until the glue sets; do not use them until it cures. Store your tools and clean up (page 27).

## FASTENING WITH CONTACT CEMENT

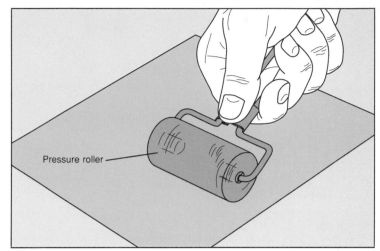

Pressure roller

**1** **Applying the contact cement.** If necessary, set up on a work surface *(page 17)*; measure and mark *(page 30)* position points on the materials. Choose a type of contact cement *(page 122)*. Position the materials to check that they fit together closely; if necessary, trim or smooth any surface *(page 78)*. Prepare the surfaces for bonding and apply the contact cement following the manufacturer's instructions; to clean an oily wood surface, use a cloth dampened with mineral spirits. In the instance shown, use a paintbrush to apply a thin, uniform coat of the contact cement over each entire surface area to be bonded, spreading it in one direction without working it back and forth *(above)*; if it is absorbed by the material, apply a second coat. To apply the contact cement over a large surface area, pour it into a foil-lined paint tray and use a short-nap paint roller. Clean off excess contact cement before it sets with the solvent recommended.

**2** **Fastening the materials.** Let the contact cement set on the materials until it is no longer tacky; a time of 10 to 30 minutes is usually specified by the manufacturer. Then, position the materials exactly; with contact cement, there is no working time for making adjustments. In the instance shown, use a slipsheet of kraft paper or waxed paper large enough to cover the entire coated surface area of one material; if the materials are awkward to handle, work with a helper. Setting the slipsheet on the coated surface area of one material, position a corner of the other material, then pull the slipsheet slightly away from the corner and press the coated surface areas together; apply uniform pressure with your hand. Continue positioning the materials the same way, then smooth and apply pressure using a pressure roller, working from the center in turn toward each edge *(above)*. Store your tools and clean up *(page 27)*.

## FASTENING WITH EPOXY

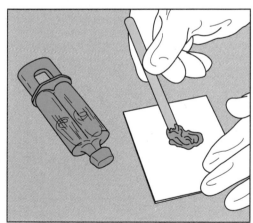

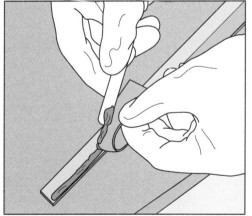

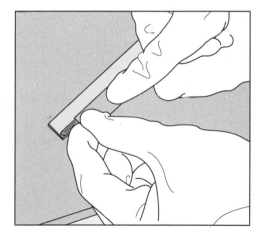

**1** **Mixing and applying the epoxy.** If necessary, set up on a work surface *(page 17)*; measure and mark *(page 30)* position points on the materials. Choose a type of epoxy *(page 122)*. Position the materials to check that they fit together closely; if necessary, trim or smooth any surface *(page 78)*—small gaps usually can be filled with the epoxy. Prepare the surfaces for bonding and apply the epoxy following the manufacturer's instructions; to clean an oily wood surface, use a cloth dampened with mineral spirits. In the instance shown, wear rubber gloves and safety goggles *(page 25)* to mix a small amount of epoxy resin and hardener on a piece of scrap material with a disposable stick until they are blended together thoroughly *(above, left)*. Then, use the stick to apply a thin, uniform layer of the epoxy over each entire surface area to be bonded *(above, right)*. To apply the epoxy over a large surface area, use a putty knife; to work it into small cracks or crevices, use a toothpick.

**2** **Fastening the materials.** Position the materials as soon as epoxy is applied, making adjustments within the working time specified by the manufacturer. Keep the materials in contact with each other until the epoxy sets, holding them together uniformly with your hands *(above)* or pressing them together evenly using weights; do not use the materials until the epoxy cures. Cut off excess epoxy before it cures with a utility knife. Store your tools and clean up *(page 27)*.

## USING C CLAMPS

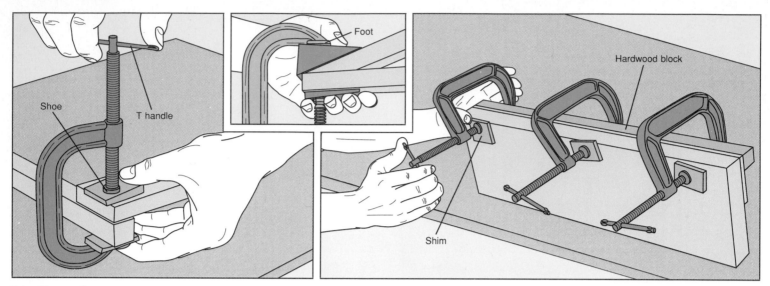

**Installing a C clamp.** For pressure or holding power over a span of more than 12 inches, use pipe clamps *(steps below)*; over a non-linear span, use web clamps *(page 125)*. For pressure or holding power over a span of up to 12 inches, use C clamps. C clamps are available in different sizes with reaches from 1 to 12 inches; a 6-inch type is usually sufficient. For extended clamping reach away from the edge of materials, use deep-throated C clamps. Plan to install a C clamp across the materials you are joining every 6 to 8 inches along the joint.

To install a C clamp, turn the T handle of the screw enough to position the jaws loosely across the materials you are joining. If one material is less than 1 inch thick, use a thick, flat block of hardwood equal in length to the joint to distribute the pressure of the C clamp evenly along it. Otherwise, use a thin, flat block of wood as a shim to keep the shoe or the foot of the C clamp from marking the materials.

For example, set one shim under the foot and hold the C clamp in position. Setting another shim under the shoe, turn the T handle of the screw by hand to tighten the shoe against it *(above, left)*; do not use a tool to apply turning force. If necessary, use a wedge-shaped wood block to provide parallel clamping surfaces for the foot and the shoe *(inset)*. Install a C clamp across the materials every 6 to 8 inches along the joint the same way, tightening each shoe in turn a little at a time *(above, right)*.

## USING PIPE CLAMPS

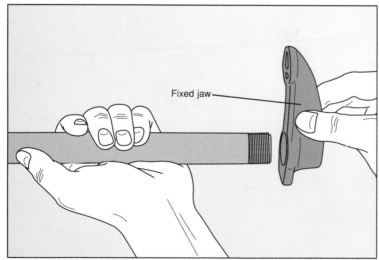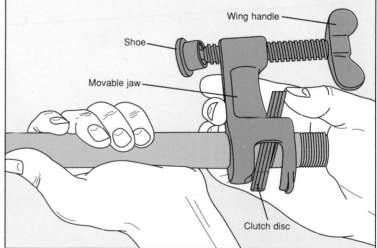

**1 Setting up a pipe clamp.** For pressure or holding power over a span of up to 12 inches, use C clamps *(step above)*; over a non-linear span, use web clamps *(page 125)*. For pressure or holding power over a span of more than 12 inches, use pipe clamps. A pipe clamp consists of a two-piece set of jaws connected to a length of black, end-threaded pipe. A 3/4-inch pipe 3 to 4 feet in length is usually sufficient; to ensure a fit, buy sets of jaws and lengths of pipe together. Plan to install a pipe clamp across the materials you are joining every 6 to 8 inches along the joint.

To set up the type of pipe clamp shown, thread the fixed jaw onto one end of the pipe *(above, left)* and turn it clockwise to tighten it securely. Turn the wing handle of the screw to set the shoe near the hub, then align the clutch discs and slide the movable jaw onto the other end of the pipe *(above, right)*; orient it so the shoe is aligned with the foot of the fixed jaw. To set up other types of pipe clamps, use the same procedure; with some types, the fixed jaw may be fitted with the screw and clutch discs. Slide the movable jaw far enough for the pipe clamp to fit loosely across the materials you are joining.

## USING PIPE CLAMPS (continued)

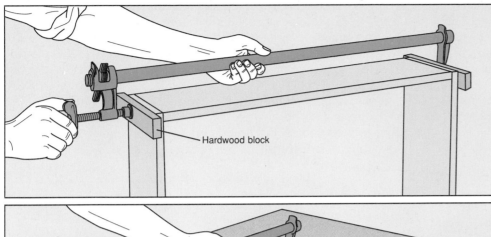

Hardwood block

Shim

**2 Installing a pipe clamp.** To install a pipe clamp, position it loosely across the materials you are joining. If one material is less than 1 inch thick, use a thick, flat block of hardwood equal in length to the joint to distribute the pressure of the pipe clamp evenly along it. Otherwise, use a thin, flat block of wood as a shim to keep the shoe or the foot of the pipe clamp from marking the materials.

For example, set one block along the joint under the foot of the fixed jaw, then hold the pipe clamp in position. Setting another block along the joint under the shoe of the movable jaw, turn the wing handle of the screw by hand to tighten the shoe against it *(left, top)*; do not use a tool to apply turning force.

Install a pipe clamp across the materials every 6 to 8 inches along the joint the same way, tightening each shoe in turn a little at a time. If you are using more than two pipe clamps, raise the materials onto wood blocks, then install a pipe clamp alternately across the top and the bottom of them to help keep them from bowing or warping *(left, bottom)*.

## USING WEB CLAMPS

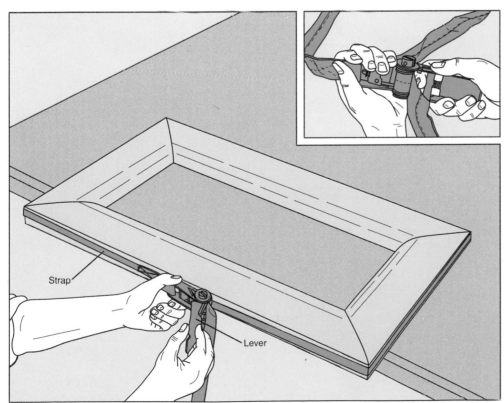

Strap

Lever

**Installing a web clamp.** For pressure or holding power over a span of up to 12 inches, use C clamps; over a span of more than 12 inches, use pipe clamps *(page 124)*. For pressure or holding power over a non-linear span, use web clamps. A typical web clamp has a strap 15 feet long for use with round, irregular-shaped or multi-jointed materials.

To install a web clamp in the instance shown, follow the manufacturer's instructions. With the type of web clamp shown, depress the spring lock on the ratchet mechanism and snap the lever back as far as possible *(inset)*, releasing the tension of the strap. Pull the strap to unroll it from the ratchet mechanism until it forms a loop large enough to fit around the materials; if necessary, unroll it completely from the ratchet mechanism.

Wrap the strap around the materials; feed the end of it back through the ratchet mechanism if you unrolled it completely. Then, crank the lever back and forth to tighten the strap around the materials; if necessary, fit small pieces of cardboard under the strap to keep it from marking the materials. Continue cranking the lever *(left)* until the strap is tight.

# FINISHING

Applying a finish to a surface may be the only repair needed to restore a workpiece to like-new appearance or the final step of a repair project. While the basic tools used to remove and apply finishes are familiar to most, their improper use can easily mean an unsuccessful job. Unsightly roller marks on a painted surface or air bubbles in a coat of clear finish are problems that can be avoided by handling tools properly. This chapter covers the basic tools and techniques used for any finishing job, large or small, whether to remove damaged finish or apply a coat of paint, stain or varnish.

To choose the finishing tool best suited to your task, consult the Troubleshooting Guide *(page 128)* and the inventory presented below. Since finishing jobs on many large objects and surfaces may require the use of a number of tools, refer to the specific repair acts in the chapter to help decide which group of tools is best for your situation. Consult the act on preparing to apply a finish *(page 132)*, which provides basic information on how to read the labels of finishing products both to choose the best finish for a job and to prepare the surfaces and finish for application.

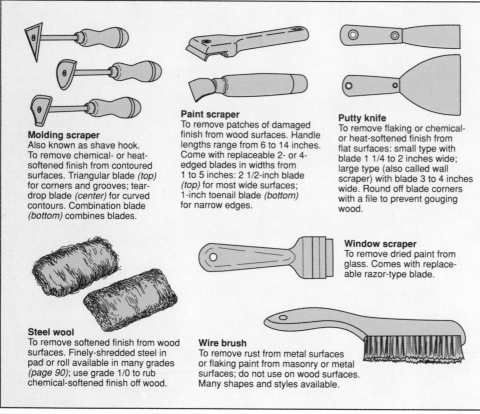

**Molding scraper**
Also known as shave hook. To remove chemical- or heat-softened finish from contoured surfaces. Triangular blade *(top)* for corners and grooves; teardrop blade *(center)* for curved contours. Combination blade *(bottom)* combines blades.

**Paint scraper**
To remove patches of damaged finish from wood surfaces. Handle lengths range from 6 to 14 inches. Come with replaceable 2- or 4-edged blades in widths from 1 to 5 inches: 2 1/2-inch blade *(top)* for most wide surfaces; 1-inch toenail blade *(bottom)* for narrow edges.

**Putty knife**
To remove flaking or chemical- or heat-softened finish from flat surfaces: small type with blade 1 1/4 to 2 inches wide; large type (also called wall scraper) with blade 3 to 4 inches wide. Round off blade corners with a file to prevent gouging wood.

**Steel wool**
To remove softened finish from wood surfaces. Finely-shredded steel in pad or roll available in many grades *(page 90)*; use grade 1/0 to rub chemical-softened finish off wood.

**Window scraper**
To remove dried paint from glass. Comes with replaceable razor-type blade.

**Wire brush**
To remove rust from metal surfaces or flaking paint from masonry or metal surfaces; do not use on wood surfaces. Many shapes and styles available.

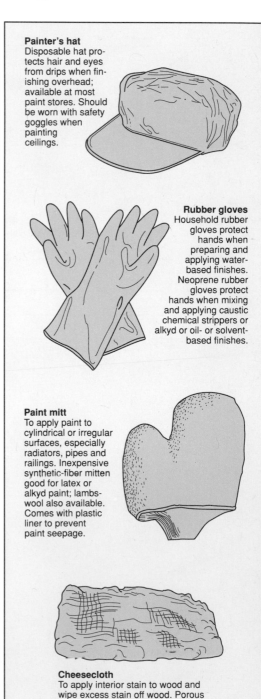

**Painter's hat**
Disposable hat protects hair and eyes from drips when finishing overhead; available at most paint stores. Should be worn with safety goggles when painting ceilings.

**Rubber gloves**
Household rubber gloves protect hands when preparing and applying water-based finishes. Neoprene rubber gloves protect hands when mixing and applying caustic chemical strippers or alkyd or oil- or solvent-based finishes.

**Paint mitt**
To apply paint to cylindrical or irregular surfaces, especially radiators, pipes and railings. Inexpensive synthetic-fiber mitten good for latex or alkyd paint; lambswool also available. Comes with plastic liner to prevent paint seepage.

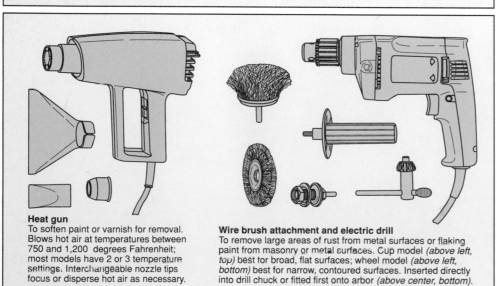

**Heat gun**
To soften paint or varnish for removal. Blows hot air at temperatures between 750 and 1,200 degrees Fahrenheit; most models have 2 or 3 temperature settings. Interchangeable nozzle tips focus or disperse hot air as necessary.

**Wire brush attachment and electric drill**
To remove large areas of rust from metal surfaces or flaking paint from masonry or metal surfaces. Cup model *(above left, top)* best for broad, flat surfaces; wheel model *(above left, bottom)* best for narrow, contoured surfaces. Inserted directly into drill chuck or fitted first onto arbor *(above center, bottom)*.

**Cheesecloth**
To apply interior stain to wood and wipe excess stain off wood. Porous cloth should be clean and lint-free.

Many finishes, strippers and solvents contain hazardous chemicals; read their labels carefully and follow all safety instructions, wearing any hand, eye and respiratory protection recommended. Have the tools necessary for a job at hand before starting. Protect adjacent surfaces and objects to avoid dripping a finish or stripper where it is not wanted. Test your finish and technique on a piece of scrap material or an inconspicuous surface. Work slowly, watching the progress of your work carefully. Use good lighting so it is easy to spot and correct flaws. Keep cloths and solvents handy to clean up.

Proper care of your finishing tools will improve their performance and increase their life. If you take a break during a finishing job, seal containers and wrap your tools in airtight plastic or aluminum foil until you are ready to start again. Always clean your tools immediately after a job is finished and store them properly. Seal leftover finishes, refuse and empty cans in tightly-covered containers in a cool, dry place; call your local department of environmental protection or public health for recommended procedures on disposing of hazardous materials safely.

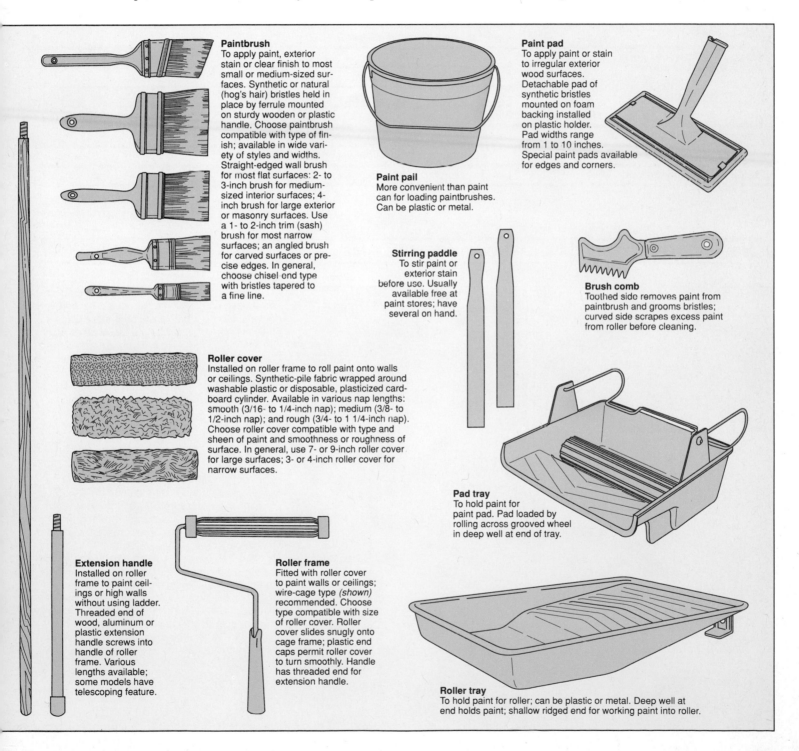

**Paintbrush**
To apply paint, exterior stain or clear finish to most small or medium-sized surfaces. Synthetic or natural (hog's hair) bristles held in place by ferrule mounted on sturdy wooden or plastic handle. Choose paintbrush compatible with type of finish; available in wide variety of styles and widths. Straight-edged wall brush for most flat surfaces: 2- to 3-inch brush for medium-sized interior surfaces; 4-inch brush for large exterior or masonry surfaces. Use a 1- to 2-inch trim (sash) brush for most narrow surfaces; an angled brush for carved surfaces or precise edges. In general, choose chisel end type with bristles tapered to a fine line.

**Paint pail**
More convenient than paint can for loading paintbrushes. Can be plastic or metal.

**Paint pad**
To apply paint or stain to irregular exterior wood surfaces. Detachable pad of synthetic bristles mounted on foam backing installed on plastic holder. Pad widths range from 1 to 10 inches. Special paint pads available for edges and corners.

**Stirring paddle**
To stir paint or exterior stain before use. Usually available free at paint stores; have several on hand.

**Brush comb**
Toothed side removes paint from paintbrush and grooms bristles; curved side scrapes excess paint from roller before cleaning.

**Roller cover**
Installed on roller frame to roll paint onto walls or ceilings. Synthetic-pile fabric wrapped around washable plastic or disposable, plasticized cardboard cylinder. Available in various nap lengths: smooth (3/16- to 1/4-inch nap); medium (3/8- to 1/2-inch nap); and rough (3/4- to 1 1/4-inch nap). Choose roller cover compatible with type and sheen of paint and smoothness or roughness of surface. In general, use 7- or 9-inch roller cover for large surfaces; 3- or 4-inch roller cover for narrow surfaces.

**Pad tray**
To hold paint for paint pad. Pad loaded by rolling across grooved wheel in deep well at end of tray.

**Extension handle**
Installed on roller frame to paint ceilings or high walls without using ladder. Threaded end of wood, aluminum or plastic extension handle screws into handle of roller frame. Various lengths available; some models have telescoping feature.

**Roller frame**
Fitted with roller cover to paint walls or ceilings; wire-cage type (shown) recommended. Choose type compatible with size of roller cover. Roller cover slides snugly onto cage frame; plastic end caps permit roller cover to turn smoothly. Handle has threaded end for extension handle.

**Roller tray**
To hold paint for roller; can be plastic or metal. Deep well at end holds paint; shallow ridged end for working paint into roller.

## TROUBLESHOOTING GUIDE

| PROBLEM | PROCEDURE |
| --- | --- |
| **Removing paint from wood** | For preparing a surface to apply paint, use a paint scraper *(step below)*, a putty knife *(p. 129)*, a chemical stripper *(p. 130)* or a heat gun *(p. 131)* |
| | For preparing a surface to apply clear finish, use a chemical stripper *(p. 130)* or a heat gun *(p. 131)* |
| **Removing clear finish from wood** | For preparing a surface to apply paint or clear finish, use a paint scraper *(step below)*, a putty knife *(p. 129)*, a chemical stripper *(p. 130)* or a heat gun *(p. 131)* |
| **Removing paint from metal** | Use a wire brush, a wire brush attachment with an electric drill *(p. 129)*, a chemical stripper *(p. 130)* or a heat gun *(p. 131)* |
| **Removing paint from masonry** | Use a wire brush or a wire brush attachment with an electric drill *(p. 129)* |
| **Removing paint from drywall or plaster** | Use a putty knife *(p. 129)* |
| **Removing paint from glass** | If paint still wet, use a clean lint-free cloth |
| | If paint dry, use a window scraper *(p. 129)* |
| **Applying paint to wood, metal, masonry, drywall or plaster** | For a small, flat surface, use a paintbrush *(p. 133)* |
| | For a large, flat surface, use a roller *(p. 137)* |
| | For a small, irregular surface, use a paint mitt *(p. 140)* |
| | For a large, irregular surface, use a paint pad *(p. 140)* |
| **Applying clear finish to wood** | Use a paintbrush *(p. 135)* |
| **Applying exterior stain to wood** | Use a paintbrush *(p. 136)* or a paint pad *(p. 140)* |
| **Applying interior stain to wood** | Use cheesecloth *(p. 136)* |

## USING A SCRAPING OR BRUSHING TOOL TO REMOVE FINISH

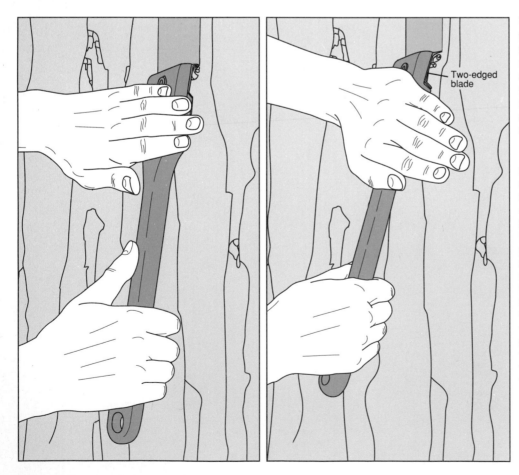

Two-edged blade

**Using a paint scraper.** Use a paint scraper to remove damaged finish from a flat wood surface, checking it before starting. If the blade is dull, change it. With the two-edged blade type shown, press the scraper firmly against a surface, then unscrew the blade and take it off. If the back edge of the blade is still sharp, orient the blade with the sharp edge forward and reinstall it; otherwise, install a new blade.

To use the scraper, wear safety goggles *(page 25)* and respiratory protection *(page 26)*, making pull strokes parallel to the wood grain; on a vertical surface, start at the top. Gripping the scraper firmly by the handle, rest the blade against the surface. Keeping the handle at a low angle, use the fingers of your other hand to apply light pressure against the blade, then pull the scraper firmly and slowly along the surface *(far left)*; adjust your pressure against the blade to keep it flat as you pull. If the finish is difficult to remove, raise the handle to a higher angle and press down firmly against the blade with the palm of your other hand, then pull the scraper along the surface the same way *(near left)*. If the scraper gouges the surface, decrease your pressure against the blade. When you are finished, store your tools and clean up *(page 27)*.

## USING A SCRAPING OR BRUSHING TOOL TO REMOVE FINISH (continued)

**Using a putty knife.** To remove loose finish from a wood, drywall or plaster surface, use a putty knife; wear safety goggles *(page 25)* and respiratory protection *(page 26)*. Work making push strokes; on wood, parallel to the grain. On a vertical surface, start at the bottom. Gripping the putty knife firmly by the handle, rest the blade against the surface. Keeping the handle at a low angle, push lightly and quickly along the surface, driving the blade under the loose finish *(above)*. If the putty knife gouges the surface, lower the angle and apply less pressure. When you are finished, store your tools and clean up *(page 27)*.

**Using a wire brush.** To remove loose paint from a metal or masonry surface, use a wire brush; wear work gloves, safety goggles *(page 25)* and respiratory protection *(page 26)*. On a vertical surface, work from the top to the bottom of it. Holding the brush firmly by the handle, rest the bristles against the surface. Applying light pressure, sweep quickly back and forth in short strokes, dislodging the loose paint *(above)*. To clean accumulated particles from the bristles of the brush, tap the back of the handle against a sturdy surface. When you are finished, store your tools and clean up *(page 27)*.

**Using a window scraper.** To remove dried paint from glass, use a window scraper. On the model shown, set the blade for scraping, wearing work gloves *(page 25)* to slide it from its stored position sideways out of the tip; if the cutting edge is dull, replace the blade. To install a blade, orient its cutting edge forward and slide it sideways into the tip. To use the scraper, wear safety goggles *(page 25)* and make push strokes. Holding the scraper by the handle with the blade against the surface, push firmly to drive the blade under the paint *(above)*. When you are finished, store your tools and clean up *(page 27)*.

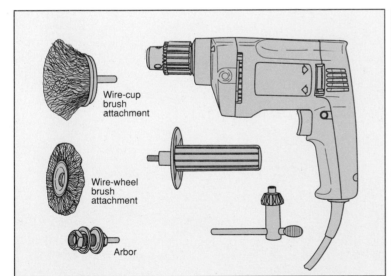

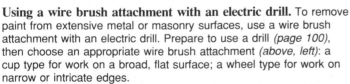

**Using a wire brush attachment with an electric drill.** To remove paint from extensive metal or masonry surfaces, use a wire brush attachment with an electric drill. Prepare to use a drill *(page 100)*, then choose an appropriate wire brush attachment *(above, left)*: a cup type for work on a broad, flat surface; a wheel type for work on narrow or intricate edges.

Wearing work gloves *(page 25)*, follow the owner's manual instructions to install the wire brush attachment on the drill. For the wheel brush attachment shown, bolt it with a washer on each side of it onto an arbor, then insert the arbor into the drill chuck; for the cup brush attachment shown, insert it directly into the drill chuck. Tighten the wire brush attachment in the drill chuck as you would any bit *(page 101)*.

Wearing safety goggles *(page 25)* and respiratory protection *(page 26)*, set any drill speed switch to FAST and any reversing switch to FORWARD, then plug in the drill *(page 24)* using an extension cord, if necessary *(page 23)*. Gripping the drill firmly with both hands, ensure the power cord is clear of the wire brush attachment. If you are using a wheel brush attachment, position the tips of its bristles against the surface, then depress and hold the trigger switch to run the drill at high speed; applying firm, even pressure, move the wheel brush attachment along the surface in the direction opposite to its rotation to dislodge the paint *(above, right)*. If you are using a cup brush attachment, use the same procedure, keeping the drill perpendicular to the surface *(inset)*. When you are finished, store your tools and clean up *(page 27)*.

## USING A CHEMICAL STRIPPER TO STRIP OFF FINISH

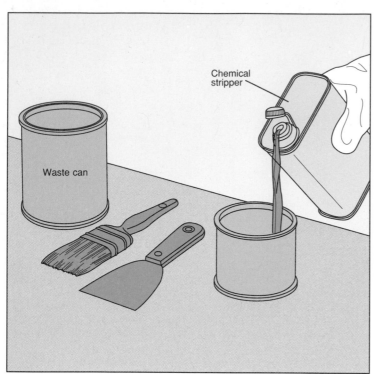

**1** **Preparing to use a chemical stripper.** Choose a chemical stripper for the type of finish and surface you are stripping. Use a paste stripper for horizontal or vertical application, especially if the old finish is thick; use a liquid stripper only for horizontal application, especially if the surface is grooved or carved. If you are working on wood, avoid using a stripper that requires a water wash to remove the residue.

Most strippers contain methylene chloride—which emits toxic fumes that can be deadly. Work outdoors away from direct sunlight. If you must work indoors, set up in an extremely well-ventilated area away from heat and ignition sources; open windows and exterior doors and set up a fan to direct vapors outdoors. Keep people and pets away. Set up to work on a work surface *(page 17)*; position the workpiece horizontally, if possible. Protect surfaces not to be stripped with drop cloths. Remove any hardware and movable parts to strip them separately. Scrape off any loose finish *(page 128)*.

Assemble supplies for the job: an old natural-bristle paintbrush; a putty knife for work on flat surfaces; molding scrapers or steel wool for work on contoured surfaces; clean metal or glass containers with tight lids for waste; and clean cloths. Wear rubber gloves, safety goggles *(page 25)* and a respirator *(page 26)*; also wear a long-sleeved shirt and long pants. Prepare the stripper for use following the manufacturer's instructions; then, pour a small amount into a wide-mouthed container *(left)* and reseal the original container.

**2** **Applying the chemical stripper.** Strip flat surfaces first, then strip moldings and carvings. On a large flat surface, work in 3-by-3 foot sections, from end to end and from side to side; on a vertical surface, start at the top. Dip the brush into the stripper, coating half the bristle length. Use short, light strokes in one direction to apply a thick, even coat of stripper *(above)*; avoid overbrushing. The finish should begin to wrinkle and bubble; if not, wait a few minutes, then apply more stripper. Let the stripper react for the time specified by the manufacturer—usually 15 minutes; do not wait longer or the stripper may dry, making removal difficult. Then, test the penetration of the stripper, pressing the tip of a putty knife into the softened finish. If the putty knife does not penetrate to the surface beneath, repeat the procedure; otherwise, remove the finish from the flat *(step 3)* or carved *(step 4)* surface.

**3** **Stripping a flat surface.** To remove softened finish from a flat surface, use a putty knife. Work making push strokes; on wood, parallel to the grain. Holding the putty knife firmly by the handle, position the blade at the edge of the softened section of finish. Keeping the handle at a slight angle to the surface, lightly and steadily push the blade into the softened finish and along the surface, lifting off the finish in a continuous strip *(above)*. If the putty knife gouges the surface, lower the angle of the handle and apply less pressure. As softened finish accumulates on the blade, stop and deposit it in a waste can; then, reposition the putty knife and continue, lifting and disposing of the softened finish until the surface is stripped. To strip other sections of a large surface or remove unstripped finish that remains, apply more stripper *(step 2)*, then use the same procedure to remove the softened finish. When the entire surface is stripped, clean it *(step 5)*.

## USING A CHEMICAL STRIPPER TO STRIP OFF FINISH (continued)

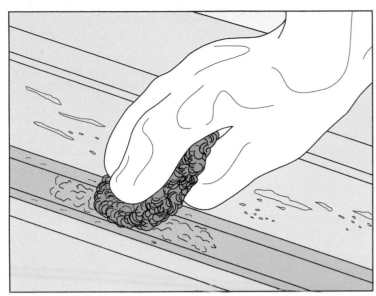

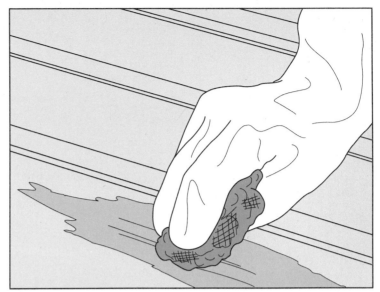

**4** **Stripping a contoured surface.** To remove softened finish from a carved surface, use a molding scraper as you would a putty knife on a flat surface *(step 3)* or a pad of grade 1/0 steel wool; on wood, work parallel to the grain. Holding the pad of steel wool at an edge of the softened finish, use brisk, back-and-forth scrubbing strokes to dislodge the softened finish and lift it off the surface *(above)*. When the steel wool is saturated with softened finish, change to a fresh pad. Continue the procedure until the surface is stripped. To strip other sections or remove unstripped finish that remains, apply more stripper *(step 2)*, then use the same procedure to remove the softened finish. When the entire surface is stripped, clean it *(step 5)*.

**5** **Cleaning the stripped surface.** Clean stripper residue from the surface to ensure proper adhesion of any new finish. Use the solvent recommended by the stripper manufacturer, following the instructions on the solvent label. Pour a small amount of solvent into a metal or glass container and reseal the original container. Dip a clean cloth into the solvent, dampening but not soaking it. On a large surface, work in successive sections; on wood, parallel to the grain. Holding the cloth at one edge of the surface, use a long, smooth stroke in one direction to rub on the solvent *(above)*; on wood, do not saturate the surface or wet glue joints. Continue until the surface is clean, changing to a clean cloth as necessary. Store your tools and clean up *(page 27)*.

## USING A HEAT GUN TO STRIP OFF FINISH

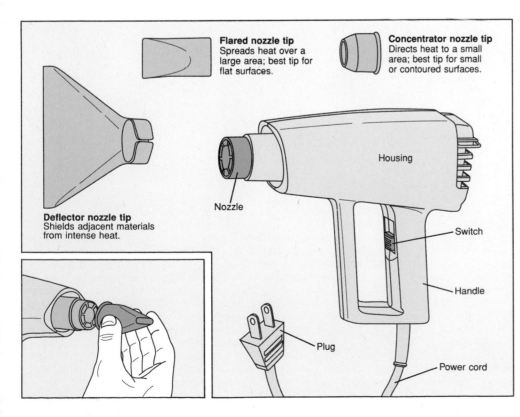

**Flared nozzle tip**
Spreads heat over a large area; best tip for flat surfaces.

**Concentrator nozzle tip**
Directs heat to a small area; best tip for small or contoured surfaces.

**Deflector nozzle tip**
Shields adjacent materials from intense heat.

Nozzle

Housing

Switch

Handle

Plug

Power cord

**1** **Preparing to use a heat gun.** With the heat gun unplugged and cool, inspect its parts *(left)*, consulting your owner's manual. If the power cord or plug is loose or frayed or the nozzle, handle, switch or housing is cracked, do not use the heat gun until it is repaired. Brush off any dust; for vents or other recessed areas, wear safety goggles *(page 25)* and use compressed air. Clean the handle using a soft cloth dampened with a solution of mild household detergent and water; do not wet any internal parts. Use steel wool to clean paint off any nozzle tip.

Choose an appropriate nozzle tip for the stripping to be done; types for the heat gun shown are illustrated at left. To install a nozzle tip on the heat gun, ensure it is unplugged and cool, then push on the nozzle tip *(inset)*; pull on the nozzle tip to remove it. Work outdoors with the heat gun; if you must work indoors, set up in a well-ventilated area with a fan to direct vapors outdoors. Set up to work on a work surface *(page 17)*, using canvas drop cloths to protect surfaces not to be stripped. Never use a heat gun on flammable surfaces such as drywall or plastic, on hollow walls that could conceal flammable material, on cracked walls, or on chemical stripper.

## USING A HEAT GUN TO STRIP OFF FINISH (continued)

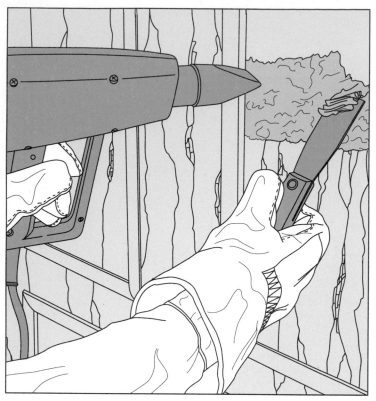

**2 Removing finish with the heat gun.** Scrape off any loose finish *(page 128),* then assemble the putty knives, paint scrapers and molding scrapers necessary to lift off finish softened by the heat gun. Keep a fire extinguisher rated ABC on hand *(page 11)* and wear safety goggles, work gloves *(page 25)* and respiratory protection *(page 26).* Make sure the heat gun is set to OFF, then plug it in *(page 24)* using an extension cord, if necessary *(page 23).*

To start, consult your owner's manual; for the model shown, use the lowest heat setting. Holding the nozzle tip about 2 inches away from the surface, sweep the gun back and forth over a small section at a time, constantly moving it to prevent burning the finish or the surface beneath; if you are stripping wood, work with the grain. Never touch the nozzle tip; do not allow it to touch anything or point at anything other than the surface you are stripping. If the finish does not begin to blister and soften, switch the heat gun to a higher heat setting.

When the finish softens, lift it off using a putty knife, a paint scraper or a molding scraper; on wood, work with the grain. Use light, steady push strokes with a putty knife *(left)*; pull strokes with a paint scraper or a molding scraper. Keep the heat gun far enough ahead to prevent the flow of hot air from burning your hand. Continue the same way until the finish is stripped. For stubborn areas, use a concentrator nozzle tip; unplug the heat gun and allow it to cool first. When you are finished, turn off and unplug the heat gun, let it cool, then remove the nozzle tip and clean it. Remove any remaining finish with chemical stripper, if necessary *(page 130).* Store your tools and clean up *(page 27).*

## PREPARING TO APPLY A FINISH

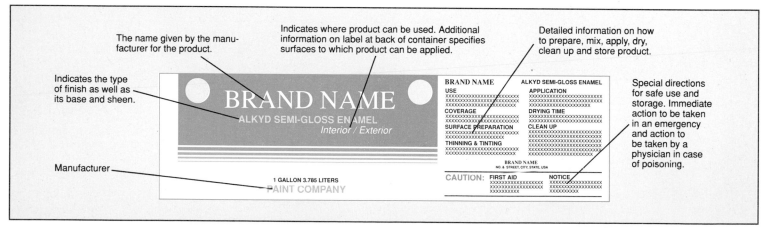

**Choosing a finish.** When buying a finish, read the label carefully *(above),* choosing the type that can provide the appearance you want. To hide a surface behind a finish, choose a paint; for wood, an opaque stain can also be used. To show a wood surface through a finish, choose a clear finish or a transparent stain. If you are choosing a paint, ensure its sheen is suitable; while high- or semi-gloss paint is more durable than flat paint, it also makes surface and application flaws more visible. And while alkyd or oil-based types are easier to clean when dry than latex types, they have stronger odors, are messier to apply and take longer to dry.

Choose a finish suitable for the type of surface; for an exterior surface, ensure the finish is marked for exterior use—choose a mildew-resistant type. Check the surface coverage of a container of the finish and buy enough for the job; if buying more than one container, choose containers with the same lot number to ensure that colors

match. Also check the clean-up information on the label; buy enough of the finish solvent to clean your tools and any accidental spills.

Before applying a finishing product, follow the manufacturer's instructions for surface preparation; to remove old finish, use a scraping or brushing tool *(page 128),* a chemical stripper *(page 130)* or a heat gun *(page 131).* Then, smooth the surface *(page 78)* and seal, prime or fill it, ensuring it is clean, dust-free and dry. To apply the finish, follow all safety precautions on the label. In general, wear work gloves *(page 25)* and a long-sleeved shirt; for overhead work, wear safety goggles *(page 25)* and a painter's hat. If the label contains POISON vapor warnings, wear respiratory protection *(page 26)* and ensure the work area is properly ventilated; indoors, open windows and exterior doors, setting up a fan to direct vapors outdoors. Protect surfaces not to be finished with newspapers or drop cloths. Follow the manufacturer's instructions for preparing the finish, applying additional coats and cleaning up.

## PREPARING TO USE A PAINTBRUSH

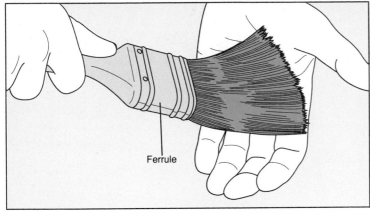

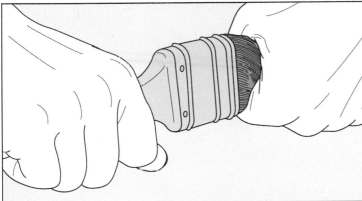

**Choosing a paintbrush.** Use a paintbrush to apply a finish to a small or irregular surface, when good control is necessary—especially on wood. For a very large finishing job, you may also need a roller *(page 137)*, a paint pad or a paint mitt *(page 140)*. To choose the best paintbrush for the job, refer to page 127 for information. In general, use a synthetic-bristled paintbrush; to apply an alkyd or oil-based paint or a clear finish, you can also use a natural-bristled paintbrush. For efficiency, choose a paintbrush slightly narrower than the width of the surface you are finishing. Use a paintbrush with a straight-cut edge to apply a finish to a large, flat surface; a paintbrush with an angled edge to apply a finish in a precise line along the edge of a surface or to a carved surface. If you are applying a clear finish or a stain, use a type of paintbrush specifically for its application.

Inspect a paintbrush before using it. If there is dried finish on the bristles, clean the paintbrush *(page 141)*. If the bristles are splayed apart or matted together in clumps, use another paintbrush. To check that the bristles are in good condition, hold the paintbrush by the handle with one hand and press the bristles firmly against the palm of the other hand *(left, top)*; the bristles should feel springy and fan out evenly without clumping. Then, release the bristles; they should spring back to their original shape. Check also that the paintbrush is sturdy, gripping the handle firmly with one hand and twisting the bristles with the other hand *(left, bottom)*; there should be no movement of the ferrule. If the paintbrush fails any test, use another paintbrush.

## USING A PAINTBRUSH TO APPLY PAINT

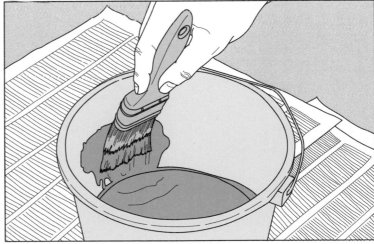

**Loading a paintbrush.** Prepare to paint *(page 132)*, then choose an appropriate paintbrush *(step above)*. If you are applying less than a full container of paint, pour a sufficient amount into a wide-mouthed paint pail and seal the original container. If you are using a new paintbrush, prepare it for the type of paint you are applying. For work with a latex paint, dip the bristles into water; for work with an alkyd or oil-based paint, dip the bristles into mineral spirits. Press the excess out of the bristles into a clean, dry cloth. Then, dip the paintbrush into the paint, coating half the bristle length, and work the paintbrush back and forth on newspaper for several strokes. To load the paintbrush for painting, dip the bristles into the paint, coating one-third their length for precise work; half their length otherwise. Lift the paintbrush *(above, left)* and remove any excess by gently tapping the tips of the bristles against the inside of the paint pail *(above, right)*.

## USING A PAINTBRUSH TO APPLY PAINT (continued)

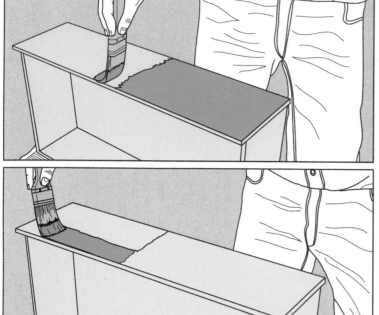

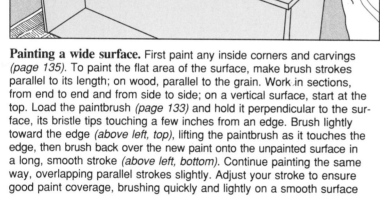

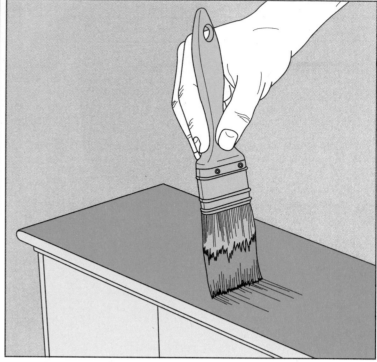

**Painting a wide surface.** First paint any inside corners and carvings *(page 135)*. To paint the flat area of the surface, make brush strokes parallel to its length; on wood, parallel to the grain. Work in sections, from end to end and from side to side; on a vertical surface, start at the top. Load the paintbrush *(page 133)* and hold it perpendicular to the surface, its bristle tips touching a few inches from an edge. Brush lightly toward the edge *(above left, top)*, lifting the paintbrush as it touches the edge, then brush back over the new paint onto the unpainted surface in a long, smooth stroke *(above left, bottom)*. Continue painting the same way, overlapping parallel strokes slightly. Adjust your stroke to ensure good paint coverage, brushing quickly and lightly on a smooth surface such as metal; more slowly and firmly on a porous surface such as masonry. When the paint coverage thins, reverse your strokes to brush back lightly over the painted section, smoothing drips and bubbles, and filling in missed spots. Then, hold the paintbrush perpendicular to the surface and lightly draw the bristle tips in one direction along it *(above, right)*, smoothing brush marks in a series of parallel, overlapping strokes. Reload the paintbrush and continue, stopping periodically to inspect your work. When you are finished, clean the paintbrush *(page 141)* and allow the paint to dry following the manufacturer's instructions; if necessary, smooth the surface *(page 78)* and apply another coat. Store your tools and clean up *(page 27)*.

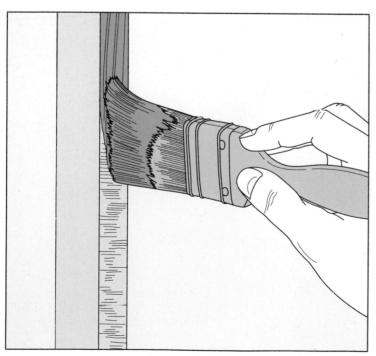

**Painting a narrow surface.** First paint any inside corners and carvings *(page 135)*. To paint the flat area of the surface, work from one end to the other end and from side to side; on a vertical surface, start at the top. Load the paintbrush *(page 133)* and hold it parallel to the surface, its bristle tips touching an edge. Using a light stroke, brush in one direction across the surface to the other edge, lifting the paintbrush as it touches the edge. Continue painting the same way, overlapping parallel strokes slightly. When the paint coverage thins, reverse your stroke to brush back lightly over the painted section, smoothing drips and bubbles, and filling in missed spots. Then, hold the paintbrush almost perpendicular to the surface with the width parallel to the surface length and lightly draw the bristle tips in one direction along it *(left)*, smoothing brush marks in one long stroke. Reload the paintbrush and continue, stopping periodically to inspect your work. When you are finished, clean the paintbrush *(page 141)* and allow the paint to dry following the manufacturer's instructions; if necessary, smooth the surface *(page 78)* and apply another coat. Store your tools and clean up *(page 27)*.

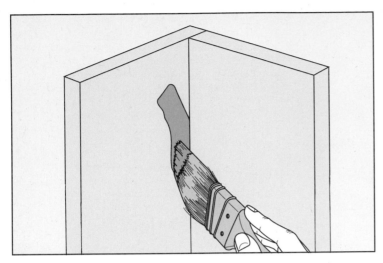

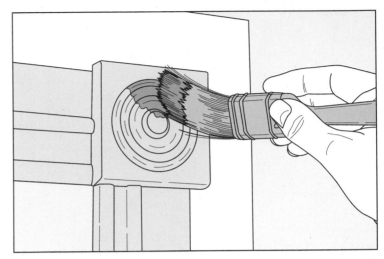

**Painting an inside corner.** Before painting a flat surface, cut in or paint any edge of it at an inside corner; to avoid painting onto the adjacent surface, use a technique called beading. Start at one end of the edge; on a vertical surface, start at the top. Load the paintbrush *(page 133)* and hold it at a slight angle away from the corner with its width parallel to the edge and its bristle tips touching slightly away from the edge. Then, press the paintbrush against the surface to spread the bristle tips to within 1/16 inch of the edge and gently draw it along the surface *(above)*, forcing a thin bead of paint into the corner. When the paint coverage thins, reload the paint brush and continue. After painting each edge at an inside corner, paint the flat area of the surface *(page 134)*.

**Painting a carving.** Before painting a flat surface, paint any carving on it. Load the paintbrush *(page 133)*, then hold it perpendicular to the surface and use the bristle tips to dab paint into the recesses of the carving *(above)*. Use short back-and-forth strokes to brush paint onto the raised surfaces of the carving; on wood, parallel to the grain. When the paint coverage thins, reload the paintbrush and continue. When the carving is covered, work with an almost dry paintbrush. First, draw pooled paint out the recesses using the bristle tips. Then, hold the paintbrush perpendicular to the surface and lightly draw the bristle tips in one direction across the raised surfaces, smoothing the paint with parallel overlapping strokes; on wood, parallel to the grain. After painting each carving, paint the flat area of the surface *(page 134)*.

## USING A PAINTBRUSH TO APPLY CLEAR FINISH

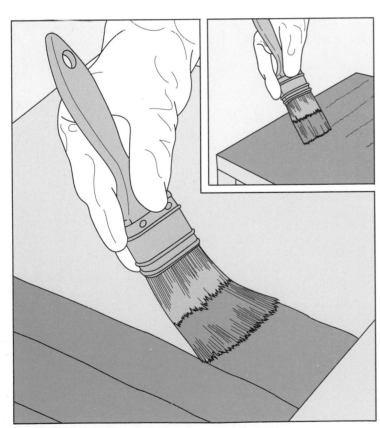

**Applying clear finish.** Prepare to apply a clear finish *(page 132)*, setting up in a dust-free area. Then, choose an appropriate paintbrush *(page 133)*. Pour as much finish as needed into a wide-mouthed jar or can and seal the original container. Wait until the finish is bubble-free, then make brush strokes parallel to the wood grain. Work in sections from end to end and from side to side; on a vertical surface, start at the top.

To load the paintbrush, dip the bristles into the finish, coating one-third their length; then, lift the paintbrush and remove any excess by gently tapping the bristle tips against the inside of the container. Hold the paintbrush at about a 45-degree angle to the surface with its bristle tips touching an edge. Using a slow, smooth stroke, brush lightly in one direction along the surface to the other edge or until the finish coverage becomes uneven. Lift the paintbrush at the end of the stroke, then reload it. Continue applying the finish the same way, overlapping parallel strokes slightly *(left)*.

When the surface is covered, cross-brush it, making brush strokes perpendicular to the wood grain. Loading the paintbrush as often as necessary, use the same procedure to brush lightly in one direction on top of and perpendicular to the first strokes. Stop periodically to check your work; if necessary, use the bristle tips to smooth missed spots.

Then, use an almost dry paintbrush to tip off the surface. Holding the paintbrush almost perpendicular to the surface with its bristle tips barely touching the surface, use light, long, smooth strokes in one direction along the grain *(inset)* to soften brush marks and smooth out bubbles. When you are finished, clean the paintbrush *(page 141)* and allow the finish to dry following the manufacturer's instructions; if necessary, smooth the surface *(page 78)* and apply another coat. Store your tools and clean up *(page 27)*.

## USING A PAINTBRUSH TO APPLY EXTERIOR STAIN

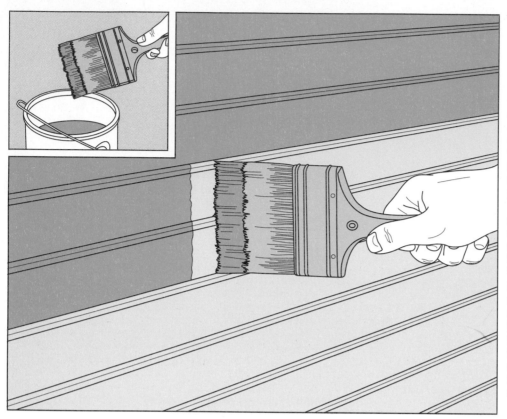

**Applying stain.** Prepare to apply a stain *(page 132)*, working out of direct sunlight on a calm, dry day. Choose an appropriate paintbrush *(page 133)*. If you are applying less than a full container of stain, pour a sufficient amount into a wide-mouthed jar or can and seal the original container. To apply the stain, make brush strokes parallel to the wood grain. Work in sections from end to end and from side to side; on a vertical surface, start at the top. To load the paintbrush, dip one-third its bristle length into the stain, then lift it out and let excess stain drip off *(inset)*; with a scooping motion, turn the paintbrush with its bristles facing up.

Hold the paintbrush at about a 45-degree angle to the surface, its bristle tips touching a few inches from an edge *(left)*. Using short, steady back-and-forth strokes, brush toward the edge, then back along the unstained surface. When the stain coverage becomes uneven, reload the paintbrush. Continue applying the stain the same way, overlapping parallel strokes slightly. Examine the surface as you work; if the stain drips or pools, use the bristle tips of the paintbrush to smooth it out. When you are finished, clean the paintbrush *(page 141)* and allow the stain to dry following the manufacturer's instructions; if necessary, apply another coat. Store your tools and clean up *(page 27)*.

## USING CHEESECLOTH TO APPLY INTERIOR STAIN

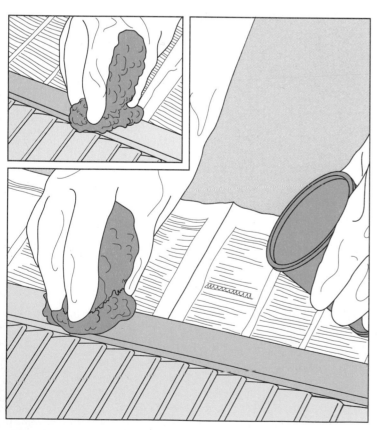

**Applying stain.** Prepare to apply a stain *(page 132)*, then assemble a number of pieces of clean lint-free cheesecloth and fold each piece into a pad. If you are applying less than a full container of stain, pour a sufficient amount into a wide-mouthed jar or can and seal the original container. To stain the surface, make wiping strokes parallel to the wood grain. Work in sections from end to end and from side to side, on a vertical surface, start at the top.

Wearing rubber gloves, dip the corner of a cheesecloth pad into the stain, dampening but not soaking it. Beginning at an edge of the surface, use a quick, steady stroke to wipe one generous, continuous strip of stain onto the surface *(left)*; continue to the other edge or until the stain coverage becomes uneven. Then, refold the cheesecloth and load a dry part of it. To continue the same strip, press the pad onto the wet edge and wipe the same way. Repeat the procedure to continue applying the stain, overlapping parallel strokes slightly; change to a new pad when the cheesecloth becomes saturated.

Let the stain stand until it dulls slightly and approximates the final color desired. Then, use a dry pad to wipe excess stain off the surface *(inset)*; as the cheesecloth becomes saturated, refold it and continue. If the color is too dark, rub harder to lighten it; if it is too light, apply more stain. Allow the stain to dry following the manufacturer's instructions. If necessary, apply another coat of stain; a water-based type raises the wood grain and requires light smoothing *(page 78)* before another coat. Follow the manufacturer's instructions to apply a clear finish *(page 135)*, if desired. Store your tools and clean up *(page 27)*.

## PREPARING TO USE A ROLLER

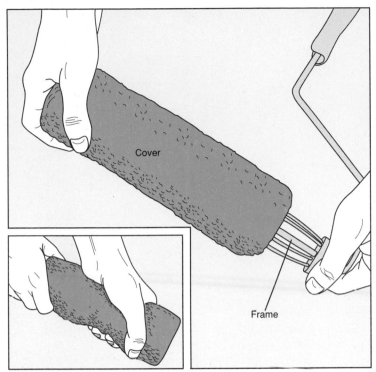

**Choosing and assembling a roller.** Use a roller to apply paint to a large surface such as a wall or ceiling. For a very large finishing job, you may also need a paintbrush *(page 133)*, a paint pad or paint mitt *(page 140)*. To choose the best roller cover for the job refer to page 127 for information; also choose a sturdy roller frame. If you are working overhead, use an extension handle. Follow the recommendations of the paint manufacturer to choose the appropriate roller cover material for the type of paint and its sheen, with the correct length of nap for the surface. In general, use a synthetic roller cover with a short nap for smooth surfaces; a long nap for rough surfaces.

Inspect a roller cover before using it. If there is dried finish on the nap, use another roller cover. If you are using a new roller cover, prepare it for the type of paint you are applying. For work with a latex paint, dampen the roller cover with water, then squeeze it tightly, running your hands along it to remove any loose fibers *(inset)*. For work with an alkyd or oil-based paint, wear rubber gloves *(page 25)* to dampen the roller cover with mineral spirits, then use the same procedure to remove any loose fibers. Shake off any excess liquid and let the roller cover dry. To assemble the roller, push the roller cover onto the frame *(left)*; to work with an extension handle, screw it into the end of the frame handle.

## USING A ROLLER TO APPLY PAINT

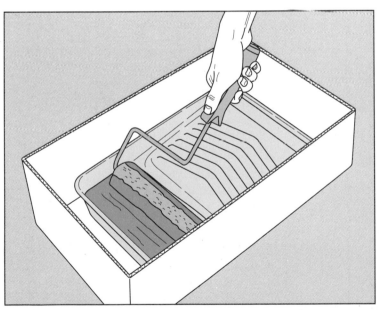
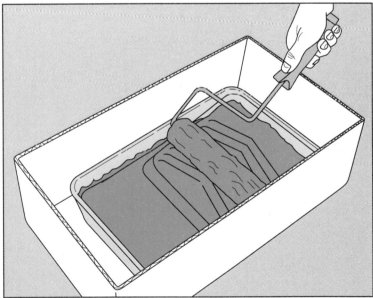

**Loading a roller.** Prepare to paint *(page 132)*, then choose an appropriate roller cover and assemble a roller *(step above)*. Place a roller tray in a cardboard box to contain splashing and facilitate moving it, then fill the well of the roller tray about halfway with paint; seal the original container. To load the roller, dip it into the paint, rolling it to coat the roller cover completely and evenly *(above, left)*; then, roll it up the ridges of the tray. If the roller slides and does not turn, it may be unevenly loaded; wearing rubber gloves *(page 25)*, turn it by hand until it is uniformly full of paint. To remove excess paint, roll the roller repeatedly over the ridges, starting at the top and going down toward but not into the well *(above right)*; to squeeze out excess along an edge of the roller cover, tilt the roller and wipe off the edge on the ridges. Continue until the roller is evenly loaded; the nap of the roller cover should be full of paint without dripping. Work the roller back and forth on newspaper for several strokes, then reload it the same way for painting. To avoid drips when moving the roller to the surface to be painted, hold the frame with the roller cover pointing up.

## USING A ROLLER TO APPLY PAINT (continued)

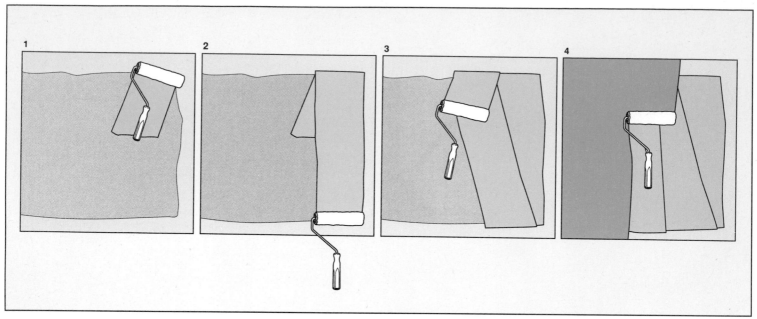

**Basic rolling pattern.** If you are painting wood, make strokes in the direction of the grain; otherwise, work up and down on a vertical surface, along the shortest dimension on a ceiling and along the longest dimension on a horizontal surface. Load the roller *(page 137)* and position it on the surface with the open end of the roller cover toward and a few inches from an edge. If you are working on a vertical surface, first make an angled upstroke toward the edge *(above, 1)*. Keeping the roller on the surface, then make a long, straight downstroke, slightly overlapping any wet edge *(above, 2)*. Follow with a continuous series of long, angled upstrokes and downstrokes *(above, 3)*. When

the roller begins to run dry and apply paint spottily, roll back over the painted surface the same way at slightly less of an angle *(above, 4)*, smoothing any lap marks and filling any missed spots. If the paint coverage is still uneven, make a series of parallel, slightly overlapping strokes that barely touch the surface; roll up or down in the direction that gives the smoothest appearance, lifting the roller at the end of each stroke. If you are painting a smooth, uneven surface, roll at a 90-degree angle to the direction of the other strokes to fill in any missed spots. Follow the same basic rolling pattern to work on a ceiling or a horizontal surface.

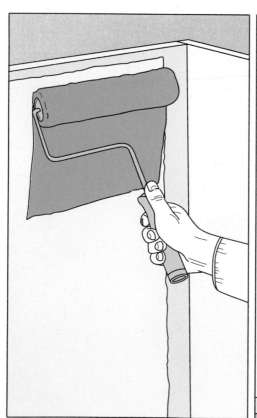

**Using a paint roller on a low surface.** First, use a paintbrush to apply a 2-inch strip of paint along any edge at an inside corner *(page 135)* or obstruction. If you are painting a large, flat surface such as a ceiling or a wall that cannot be reached without stretching or bending, use a paint roller with an extension handle *(page 139)*. Otherwise, follow the basic rolling pattern *(step above)* to apply paint with the roller, loading it as necessary *(page 137)*.

Gripping the roller by the handle of the frame, move it slowly and lightly along the surface *(far left)*, letting its weight spread the paint evenly. If the roller starts to skid, lighten your pressure; if the paint spatters, slow down. When working near the bottom of a vertical surface *(near left)*, avoid lifting the roller off it. Continue painting the same way, repeating the basic rolling pattern as necessary. When you are finished, clean the roller *(page 141)* and allow the paint to dry following the manufacturer's instructions; if necessary, smooth the surface *(page 78)* and apply another coat. Store your tools and clean up *(page 27)*.

Extension handle

**Using a paint roller with an extension handle on a ceiling.**
First, use a paintbrush to apply a 2-inch strip of paint along any edge at an inside corner *(page 135)* or obstruction. If you are painting a flat surface that can be reached without stretching or bending, use the paint roller on the low surface *(page 138)*. Otherwise, use the roller with an extension handle of an appropriate length; with your arms up and out in front of you, it should be able to reach at least 3 feet ahead. Wearing safety goggles *(page 25)* and a painter's hat, follow the basic rolling pattern *(page 138)* to apply paint with the roller, loading it as necessary *(page 137)*.

Gripping the roller at the end and the center of the extension handle, make smooth strokes about 5 feet long; keep your arms out in front of you and avoid using the roller directly overhead. Use the lower hand on the extension handle to move the roller back and forth, pressing it lightly against the surface; keep your other hand around the extension handle to steady and guide the roller, allowing the extension handle to slide up and down through it *(left)*.

Move the roller slowly along the surface, applying enough pressure against it to spread the paint evenly. If the roller starts to skid, decrease your pressure; if the paint spatters, slow down. Bring your arms up as you move the roller away from you to keep it pressed against the ceiling. Continue painting the same way, repeating the basic rolling pattern as necessary. When you are finished, clean the roller *(page 141)* and allow the paint to dry following the manufacturer's instructions; if necessary, smooth the surface *(page 78)* and apply another coat. Store your tools and clean up *(page 27)*.

**Using a paint roller with an extension handle on a wall.** First, use a paintbrush to apply a 2-inch strip of paint along any edge at an inside corner *(page 135)* or obstruction. If you are painting a flat surface that can be reached without stretching or bending, use the paint roller on the low surface *(page 138)*. Otherwise, use the roller with an extension handle of an appropriate length; standing a few feet away from the wall, the roller should be able to reach the entire length of the surface with your arms extended comfortably. Wearing a painter's hat, follow the basic rolling pattern *(page 138)* to apply paint with the roller, loading it as necessary *(page 137)*.

Gripping the roller at the end and the center of the extension handle, stand a few feet away from the surface at a slight angle to it and make smooth strokes up and down along it. Maintain a constant distance from the wall, stepping sideways when necessary. Use the lower hand on the extension handle to move the roller up and control it on the downstroke; keep your other hand around the extension handle to support and guide the roller, allowing the extension handle to slide through it.

Move the roller slowly and lightly along the surface *(left)*, letting its weight spread the paint evenly. If the roller starts to skid, decrease your pressure; if the paint spatters, slow down. When working toward the bottom of the surface, increase your pressure against the roller slightly. When starting an upstroke from the bottom of the surface, lift with the hand at the center of the extension handle. Continue painting the same way, repeating the basic rolling pattern as necessary. When you are finished, clean the roller *(page 141)* and allow the paint to dry following the manufacturer's instructions; if necessary, smooth the surface *(page 78)* and apply another coat. Store your tools and clean up *(page 27)*.

## USING A PAINT PAD TO APPLY PAINT OR EXTERIOR STAIN

Pad tray

**Setting up and loading the pad.** Prepare to apply a finish *(page 132)*, using a pad for an irregular surface such as lapped board siding. For a large finishing job, you may also need a paintbrush *(page 133)*; if you are applying paint, also a roller *(page 137)* or a paint mitt *(step below)*. Inspect a paint pad before using it. If the bristles are flattened or separated from the foam backing or the foam backing is crusted with dried finish, replace the pad; on the model shown, bend up the tabs and slide the pad out of the holder, then install a new pad and fold the tabs down. To apply finish using the paint pad, make light, smooth, long strokes; on wood, parallel to the grain. Work in sections from end to end and from side to side; on a vertical surface start at the top. Fill the well of a pad tray about halfway with finish and seal the original container.

To load the pad, pull it over the roller of the pad tray *(above, left)* wetting only the bristles. Continue until the bristles are evenly covered but not dripping; to remove excess, wipe the pad on the ridges of the pan. Positioning the toe of the pad on the surface at an edge, draw it lightly and slowly in one direction along the surface, lowering it until the bristles are flat *(above, right)*. When the pad starts to apply finish spottily, lift it slowly and gently off the surface to avoid creating air bubbles. Reload the pad and continue the same way, overlapping parallel strokes slightly and smoothing out any unevenness immediately. When you are finished, clean the pad *(page 141)* and allow the finish to dry following the manufacturer's instructions; if necessary, smooth the surface *(page 78)* and apply another coat. Store your tools and clean up *(page 27)*.

## USING A PAINT MITT TO APPLY PAINT

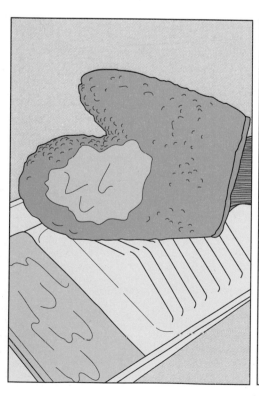

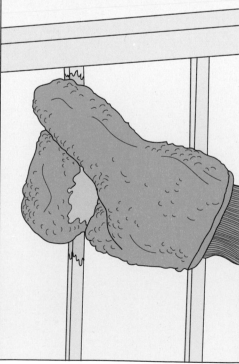

**Using a paint mitt.** Prepare to paint *(page 132)*, using a paint mitt for round or irregular surfaces—on railings or pipes, for example. Inspect a paint mitt before using it; if its fibers detach easily or are crusted with dried paint, replace it. To apply paint using the paint mitt, pour some paint into a roller tray, then put on the paint mitt; if desired, put on a rubber glove first *(page 25)* for extra protection. To load the paint mitt, dip it into the paint, coating only as much of it as you need for the surface: usually the palm *(far left)*; avoid coating the back. The paint mitt should be soaked but not dripping; remove any excess by wiping it on the ridges of the roller tray.

To paint a number of small surfaces at one time—for example, on a baluster—wrap the paint mitt around it and rub up and down *(near left)*. To paint a large surface—for example, a radiator—place the paint mitt flat on the surface and rub back and forth. For a crevice, work in the paint with the tip of the paint mitt. Reload the paint mitt and continue the same way. When you are finished, clean the paint mitt *(page 141)* and allow the paint to dry following the manufacturer's instructions; if necessary, smooth the surface *(page 78)* and apply another coat. Store your tools and clean up *(page 27)*.

## CLEANING FINISH APPLICATORS

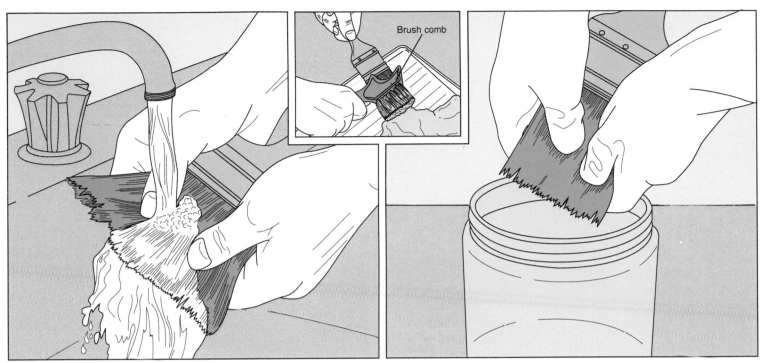

Brush comb

**Cleaning paintbrushes.** Before cleaning any paintbrush, draw the teeth of a brush comb through the bristles to remove excess finish *(inset)*. To clean off latex paint or a water-based finish, wash the paintbrush under warm running water, adding a few drops of liquid household detergent. Separate the bristles between your thumbs to let the water penetrate *(above left)*. Continue until the water runs clear, then use the brush comb to remove any finish close to the ferrule and repeat the procedure. To clean off an alkyd or oil-based finish, pour the solvent recommended by the manufacturer or mineral spirits into a wide-mouthed glass or metal container. Wearing rubber gloves *(page 25)* agitate

the brush in the solvent, then lift it out to work in the solvent with your hands *(above right)*. If the solvent becomes extremely cloudy, use a fresh batch, repeating the procedure as necessary. If the paintbrush does not come clean, suspend it overnight in the solvent, threading a stiff wire through the hole in the handle and hooking its ends onto the container. Otherwise, rinse the paintbrush with water. Shake any excess liquid off the paintbrush, then separate the bristles with a brush comb and hang up the paintbrush to dry. When the paintbrush is dry, store it in its original plastic sleeve; or, wrap it in kraft paper and fasten the paper around the ferrule with an elastic band. Store your tools and clean up *(page 27)*.

**Cleaning rollers, paint pads or paint mitts.** Consider discarding any roller cover, pad or paint mitt used to apply an alkyd or oil-based finish; otherwise, clean them using a solvent as you would a paintbrush *(step above)*. To clean off latex paint or a water-based finish, use warm water. Before cleaning a roller cover, remove excess paint by drawing the rounded edge of a brush comb along it *(inset)*.

Then, push the roller cover off the frame using the brush comb and wash it under warm running water; add a few drops of liquid household detergent. Work the paint out of the roller cover with your fingers *(left)*, continuing until the water runs clear. Shake any excess water off the roller cover, then raise the nap using your fingers and stand the roller cover on end to dry. When the roller cover is dry, wrap it in kraft paper and store it upright.

To clean off a paint pad or a paint mitt, wash it under water the same way. Place a paint pad with its bristles facing up to dry it and store it. Store a paint mitt when it is dry in a perforated plastic bag. To clean off a roller tray or a pad tray, pour any usable finish back into the original container and seal it tightly. Wash off any remaining latex paint or water-based finish with warm water; wear rubber gloves *(page 25)* and use a cloth dampened with mineral spirits to wipe off any remaining alkyd or oil-based finish. Store your tools and clean up *(page 27)*.

# INDEX

Page references in *italics* indicate an illustration of the subject mentioned. Page references in **bold** indicate a Troubleshooting Guide for the subject mentioned.

## ACKNOWLEDGMENTS

**The editors wish to thank the following:**
Adjustable Clamp Co., Chicago, Ill.; Arkon Safety Equipment Inc., Montreal, Que.; Isaac Ary, Ary Paint, Montreal, Que.; Atlas Screw & Specialty Co., Elizabeth, N.J.; Angela Babin, Art Hazards Information Center, New York, N.Y.; Wayne Bergman, Olympic HomeCare Products Co., Bellevue, Wash.; Fred Burns, EZ Paintr Corp., Milwaukee, Wis.; Barry Coates, Westmount Fire Department, Westmount, Que.; Sharon Dalton, Underwriter's Laboratories, Northbrook, Ill.; Garrett Wade Co., New York, N.Y.; Halbert Gober, Organbuilder, St-Basil-le-Grand, Que.; Michael J. Gottsacker, Mona, Meyer & McGrath, Bloomington, Minn.; Lee Valley Tools Ltd., Ottawa, Ont.; Lufkin, Division CooperTools, Raleigh, N.C.; Peter Martin, Competitive Student Services, Montreal, Que.; Miklos Matay, Qualitas Painting & Decorating Reg'd, Montreal, Que.; Maze Nails, Peru, Ill.; Robert S. Miller, Franklin International, Columbus, Ohio; Giles Miller-Mead, Aviron Technical Institute, Montreal, Que.; Millers Falls Tool Co., Alpha, N.J.; William Mills, Montreal, Que.; Milwaukee Electric Tool (Canada) Ltd., Scarborough, Ont.; Milwaukee Electric Tool Corp., Brookfield, Wis.; Minwax Co., Inc., Montvale, N.J.; Chris Moynan Painter-Decorator Reg'd, Montreal, Que.; Nicholas Harrison Munro, Montreal, Que.; Clifford Neumann, Montreal, Que.; Terence Newcomen, Jr., St. Lazare, Que.; Nicholson, Division CooperTools, Raleigh, N.C.; Norton Co., Worcester, Mass.; Padco Inc., Minneapolis, Minn.; Tony Picard, Competitive Student Services, Montreal, Que.; Lee Plein, Footprint Tools Ltd., New Canaan, Conn.; Porter Cable Corp., Jackson, Tenn.; Power Tool Institute, Inc., Yachats, Oreg.; Rubberset Co. (Canada), Dorval, Que.; Ryobi America Corp., Itasca, Ill.; Sandvik Saws and Tools Co., Scranton, Pa.; George Sivy, ITW/Devcon, Danvers, Mass.; Skil, Division of Emerson Electric Canada Ltd., Markham, Ont.; John Tardif, Madawaska, Maine; 3M, St. Paul, Minn.; Usher-Jones Industries Inc., Montreal, Que.; Vermont American Tool Company, Lincolnton, N.C.; Wagner Spray Tech Corp., Minneapolis, Minn.; Henry Walthert, Canadian Institute of Treated Wood, Ottawa, Ont.; Wood-Kote Inc., Portland, Oreg.

The following persons also assisted in the preparation of this book:
Daniel Bazinet, Linda Jarosiewicz, Julie Leger, Jennifer Meltzer, Kelly Mulcair, Solange Pelland.